STRANGE FUTURE

Strange Future

MIN HYOUNG SONG

PESSIMISM AND THE

1992 LOS ANGELES RIOTS

DUKE UNIVERSITY PRESS

DURHAM AND LONDON 2005

Contents

Preface

Strange Future was written with two beliefs in mind. First, academic criticism is too important to be deprecated in the name of a thoughtless populism. One of my colleagues gave substance to this belief when she said to me one day, after a visiting speaker said something about not liking to read critical essays, that she did not appreciate this comment because the critical essay is the most elegant form of expression she knows. Perhaps long after my colleague has forgotten ever saying this, the last part of this statement has stuck with me. It signals a preference for a kind of writing that is habitually put down as too elitist, too removed from what really matters to people, and so on. In private conversations, I too have found myself engaged in this kind of populism, trying to demonstrate to the person I happened to be talking to that I am not these things, that I am not *that* kind of academic, that I should somehow be exempt from the scorn reserved exclusively for people who spend their days thinking. My colleague's comment stopped me dead. Why do such denunciations so easily roll off my tongue, and why is it that such denunciations are so often greeted by people who should know better with a conspiratorial smile or a silence that suggests complicity?

This is surely a problem, especially given the demonstrable fact that it matters what academics write. We address some of the most important and pressing concerns of our times; we have the power, and the leisure, to start conversations that will otherwise never begin; we have the freedom to explore and develop ideas that are often, in many other circumstances, risky to state too openly. If we do not, therefore, defend a taste for what we do for a living, we have already partially conceded the serious nature of our work and, in the process, made it that much more difficult to defend our right to speak difficult, complicated, occasionally inchoate, and often unpopular thoughts. Against those who wish to strip this right from us, and there is a rising chorus to this effect, we must be able to respond that it matters what we do, even if we (much less frequently than is asserted) make factual errors, say something offensive, put out an idea that isn't fully thought through, express ourselves in a manner that is not easily comprehended, concern ourselves with topics that seem overly rarified. Indeed, we should be able to say that what we academics do for a living is not a right but a necessary social imperative. Not how dare a professor say something that sounds anti-American, thus abusing a privilege that can be taken away, but how admirable that he or she is willing to be so courageous at a time when fear and reaction demand conformity of thought like a vise squeezing all of us from top to bottom, side to side. How liberating, we should say, to come across someone willing to struggle with obdurate concepts in a way that doesn't speak down to the reader.

Second, *Strange Future* was written with the belief that focusing on the specific—whether it be a single historical event, a single geographical local, or the struggles of a single ethnic or racial group—is one of the best ways to ground discussion about issues of far-ranging significance. The very development of my research into a book supports this belief. This research began as a study on Korean American literature, which I undertook largely because I am of Korean descent and I was interested in thinking about how others like myself had carved out a place in the world of creative expression. As I began work on this study by reading recent novels by young Korean American authors, I discovered that I needed to learn more about the 1992 Los Angeles riots. It was a pivotal event for many Korean Americans, and much of the scholarship about Korean Americans kept returning to this event. Finally, as I researched the riots, trying to understand why it was so significant for my ethnic group, I began to understand that (1) I couldn't focus just on my group if I wanted to write about the riots and (2) the issues raised by everything I was reading addressed some far-reaching questions about the changing meaning of race, economic relations, national identity, and mass mobility within and across national borders.

Thus, *Strange Future* developed from the specific to the much more general, while remaining insistent on a firm commitment to the specificity that sparked its creation in the first place. It is for this reason that I call this book a work of Asian American studies. The focus on a single racial group, and even the focus on a single ethnicity within a particular racial group, enabled me to write about issues that potentially affect everyone who reads this book. Of course, it has become common sense that, as Anne Cheng puts it, "race studies holds much intellectual capital in academic research today" (2001, 169). But I fear that this observation is only superficially true. The mention of race outside academia is greeted with a great deal of hostility, so much so that it often feels as if an actual thought police exists to bully people away from talking about race in public except in the most dismissive way possible. If there is intellectual cachet in studying race within academia, this cachet does not translate well into what happens beyond its walls. Even within academia, as well, there is an undeniable suspicion that we are paying too much attention to race and that race ought not to matter quite so much as some assert, because it gets in the way of thinking about more important matters, such as the classics, humanity, and universal experiences. Such criticisms are almost always stated as if a concern with race automatically militates against concerning ourselves with these other matters.

And finally, underlying the suspicion that we pay too much attention to race in academic criticism is the assumption that attention to the specific—it hardly matters what the specific is—can only interest those who are being specified, so that Asian American literature is only interesting to Asian American readers, feminist studies only interesting to women, queer theory only interesting to gays and lesbians, and so forth. Obviously, I believe this assumption is wrong. Although there are no guarantees, attending to the specific, and especially to the specific that is frequently overlooked, has the capacity to draw us outside of ourselves and into deep contact with others whose living concerns overlap our own. This is so partially because none of us are defined by any one thing and because none of us can remain isolated for very long. A lack of attention to the specific, on the other hand, only encourages a view from afar, like trying to find out how people live in their homes by observing their movements from a satellite in geosynchronous orbit.

IT SHOULD GO without saying that I received an extraordinary amount of help. Several chapters were written from scratch while I enjoyed a postdoctoral fellowship sponsored by the Asian American Studies Program at the University of Illinois, Urbana-Champaign. Susan Moynihan, a visiting scholar at the time, proved herself to be an indispensable and fiercely intellectual friend. The following people at Illinois also deserve rich thanks for their support of my research and for so warmly including me in their lives: Sharon Lee, Mary Ellerbe, Esther Kim, Martin Manalansan, Moon-kie Jung, Clark Cunningham, and Nancy Abelmann. I thank George Yu, the acting director of the program, for all of his encouragement. Although Kent Ono was made director of the program the year after I left, it has been my privilege to have made his acquaintance. Don Nakanishi, director of the Asian American Studies Center at UCLA, gave me access to his school's libraries during my too-brief stay in Southern California during the summer of my postdoctoral year. I have not been able to thank him properly for making it possible for me to continue my work there.

This book would not have been possible without the generosity of my home institution. Boston College provided me with a Research Expense Grant, a Research Incentive Grant, a year's leave to go to Illinois, and a significant subvention to pay for the incidental costs of publishing this book, all of which provided me with the resources and the time to write. Brendan Rapple at the O'Neill Library provided research support with cheery alacrity, and the Media Technology Services office provided me important assistance in preparing some of the images for this book. In addition, I wish to name all of the members of my department individually for all their help; since I can't, I will force myself to foreground a few who read parts of my manuscript in various stages of development and gave me important feedback: Christopher Wilson, Frances Restuccia (who was the colleague I mentioned at the start of the preface), Carlo Rotella, Robin Lydenberg, Kalpana Seshadri-Crook, Rosemarie Bodenheimer, Robert Chibka, Andrew Sofer, and Rhonda Frederick. Ramsay Liem, though not in my department, has nevertheless been a wonderful ally at BC and an all-around inspiration. At Tufts, where I earned my graduate degrees, Elizabeth Ammons, Jean Wu, Yuko Matsukawa, and Modhumita Roy were my much beloved mentors.

My cohorts outside of these institutions have borne a great deal of my neuroses in the writing of this book, and they deserve my most heartfelt appreciation. Emma Jinhua Teng's constant friendship has sustained me through challenging years of graduate training and junior professorship.

James Kyung-Jin Lee read the *entire* manuscript in draft form and was kind enough to overlook its many flaws, which gave me a great boost when I needed it most. Viet Nguyen commented on one of the chapters, and didn't take offense at the way I nitpick at his work. Victor Jew accompanied me one long afternoon for an informative drive down Vermont Avenue, which runs along the places hardest hit by the riots. Susette Min allowed me the use of her and her partner's beautiful apartment while I conducted research in Los Angeles, during which time Jane Iwamura, Lili Kim, and Sandy Oh, alongside some of the others whom I have already named, helped keep my summer evenings hopping socially and intellectually. Marie Lo was by far the toughest critic of my writing, and it is better as a result. Rajini Srikanth has been, and continues to be, a valued friend, collaborator, and advisor. At various stages of this book's development, the following individuals listened to me talk endlessly about my ideas, stayed up with me late into the night during periods of grave doubt, and generally made my life rich with their company (I list them alphabetically): Sylvanie Bramaud, Yoonmee Chang, Patricia E. Chu, Caryn Crosthwait, Jane Elizabeth Dougherty, Montye Fuse, Kimberly Hébert, Greg Howard, Amelia Katanski, Daniel Kim, Stacy Klein, Eric Lai, Bessie Lee, Sunyoung Lee, Shauna Lo, Sandra Park, Eric Reyes, Christian and Ali Sheridan, Jewel Shim, Chris Tang, James Wu, and Annie Yamamoto. I apologize to the many others whom I could not mention here. Sadly, Sonya Lee passed away as I was just beginning work on the manuscript. The world has suffered by her absence.

Before starting this book in earnest, I went on KEEP (Korean Exposure and Education Program); this is an intensive and grueling three-week tour of South Korea sponsored by grassroots organizations that are dedicated to fostering relations between Korean American and Korean activists. Through the hard work of the all-volunteer members who generously donate their precious time and passion to the ideals of democratic participation, KEEP continues to be simply transformative for those lucky enough to go. I thank Helen Kim and Eunhy Kim especially, who cocoordinated the trip my year. Dai Sil Kim-Gibson generously provided me with images to accompany my discussion of her documentary *Sa-I-Gu: From Korean Women's Perspective* and spared quite a bit of time to discuss her opinions of the documentary with me. The images were taken by Kuling Choy Siegel. I also thank Elaine Kim for taking the time to talk to me about her involvement in producing this documentary, and about her thoughts on the riots and Korean Americans more broadly. Photofest in New York provided the images from the film *Strange Days* and the play *Twilight: Los Angeles, 1992*. An earlier version of chapter 5, "A Diasporic Future? Historical Trauma and *Native Speaker*," appeared in *LIT: Literature, Interpretation, Theory*.

Finally, I thank the people directly responsible for converting a rough manuscript into a book. Ken Wissoker and his staff, especially Courtney Berger and Kate Lothman, and Sonya Manes were characteristically amazing, and I cannot say enough good things about the experience I have had with them in the publication of this book. I also thank the two anonymous readers for all their constructive remarks; these have improved the quality of my argument visibly. Needless to say, the responsibility for any mistakes made in the book belongs to me exclusively.

I dedicate *Strange Future* to my mother Hye Kyoung and father Tae Kyoung, my sister Min and brother-in-law Nate, and of course Grace.

Introduction

When the Strange Erupts in Culture

At the start of the 1990s, or thereabout, the future became a place of national decline. Rarely in popular political discourses, works of creative expression, or academic criticism produced during the early years of this decade in the United States was there a vision of the future that was upbeat. Instead, there was talk from across the political spectrum of places we as a country should not want to go, of legislation designed to punish rather than reward, and of desires predicated on the reactive protection of what we already have. "For two centuries," the liberal-turned-conservative historian Arthur Schlesinger Jr. wrote in *The Disuniting of America* (1992), the enormously influential polemic that set the pace for mainstream responses to this pessimism, "Americans had been confident that life would be better for their children than it was for them. . . . Amid forebodings of national decline, Americans now began to look forward less and backward more. The rising cult of ethnicity was a symptom of decreasing confidence in the American future" (41). As in this quotation, about the only optimistic thing we might have heard from similarly minded pundits in the past decade was a yearning to maintain a former glory, a recapturing of a conviction in our greatness that we had somehow—through inattention, the calumny of foreigners and other nonconformists, or the collusion of malicious-minded cabals—let slip through our fingers, even as others were quick to point out how less than glorious this same past was.[1] The alternative to nostalgic greatness, the assertion that we will remain great because we have always been great, was the cleansing figuration of disaster, a terrible cataclysmic event or a slow ebbing of living standards that would alter the way we think, that would reshape social relations, and that would compel us to begin anew. While none of this (the dark future, the search to restore a largely fictive past, the almost erotic desire for a redemptive disaster) is unprecedented in American culture, the pervasiveness of this pessimism throughout the last decade of the twentieth century seems at the very least noteworthy.

Where did this pessimism come from? How did this pessimism shape the turn toward cultural politics that became so pronounced in the 1990s? Can this pessimism be a source of inspiration for the imagination of more attractive futures than the ones currently available to us? *Strange Future* seeks to address these questions by focusing on the 1992 Los Angeles riots. This historical event, perhaps more than any other event marking out passage through the dark years of the 1990s and beyond, has been exemplary in its ability to spark imaginative and critical works of profound pessimism. In literature, Paula Woods, Héctor Tobar, Paul Beatty, and Gary Phillips have all written novels (*Inner City Blues* [1999], *The Tattooed Soldier* [1998], *White Boy Shuffle* [1996], and *Violent Spring* [1994], respectively) that directly incorporate the riots as key elements of the stories of racism, violence, and corruption they have to tell, while in the immediate wake of civil unrest Walter Mosley, Karen Tei Yamashita, Cynthia Kadohata, Neal Stephenson, and Octavia Butler have scrupulously tracked the region's descent into economic polarization, social disarray, and ham-fisted reaction.[2] In film, the response to the violence represented by the riots has been less thoughtful, but no less voluminous. *Falling Down* (1993), *Independence Day* (1996), *Volcano* (1997), and a host of other disaster films have reveled in the detailed destruction of Los Angeles (sometimes in addition to other American cities), almost as if willing dystopia, while valiantly struggling to recuperate heroic—and largely heteronormative—figures of American might. In comparison, slightly less mainstream films such as *Menace II Society* (1993), *Strange Days* (1995), *Safe* (1995), and more recently *Dark Blue* (2002) seem more probing in their exploration of class inequalities and fears of racial lawlessness. In urban studies, a recognizable "Los Angeles school" came to maturity during this decade, fostered by the work of scholars such as Mike Davis, Edward Soja, Allan Scott, William Fulton, and Norman Klein. Their combined output—characterized as it has been by a keen attention to the city's deep social, racial, and economic inequalities; historic disregard for the environment; hunger for constant land development; and the many other concerns brought to the foreground by the riots—has been, as David Halle puts it mildly, "uneasy about much of what it finds" (2003, 10).[3] The growing popularity of neoconservative thought during this same decade (as crystallized in foundational books by Arthur Schlesinger Jr., Allan Bloom, and Charles Murray) seems, as well, to have been fueled by the riots and the dissatisfaction with the social order it has kindled.[4] Finally, and perhaps most noteworthily, a rapidly maturing generation of Korean American cultural producers have incorporated the riots into their work. In documentaries such as *Sa-I-Gu: From Korean Women's Perspective* (1993), *Another America* (1996), and *Wet Sand: Voices from L.A. Ten Years Later* (2003); in the compilation entitled *East to America: Korean American Life Stories* (Kim and Yu 1996); in the novel *Native Speaker* (C. Lee 1995); and, perhaps most important, in the proliferating scholarship by academics such as Edward Chang, Claire Jean Kim, Elaine Kim, Kwang Chung Kim, Jennifer Lee, Pyong Gap Min, Edward Park, Kyeyoung Park, and Eui-Young Yu, the year 1992 is never far from mind as a measure of what social lows are possible in this country.

Taken together, the enormity and variety of this archive suggest that the Los Angeles riots have become more than a historical event, something that occurred in the past with discernible causal links with other events that preceded and postdated it. The Los Angeles riots have also become a cultural-literary event, an important source of tropes for imagining the seemingly endemic social problems plaguing the United States and the country's possible futures. Thus, when we follow the combined turn of these tropes, they lead us to a particular vision of the future that is replete with uncontrollable change, social disorder, and wholesale violence. In large part, this happens because our future has become populated by foreigners, nonconformists, and racial others. These others bear with them the material traces of a history that exists in contradiction to the state's own self-serving stories. In a climate of reaction, the presence of the *strange*—as I will be calling the bearers of a materiality that demands narrative invention—discourages thinking about collective solutions to widely shared problems. As a result, the presence of the strange speeds a retreat into atomistic individualism, a celebration of unregulated wealth accumulation, and a fearful support for authoritarian rule. In short, the state has responded to pervasive uncertainty about national identity at a time of mass mobility and wildly fluctuating economic fortunes with predictable coercion, even as the supporters of this response have found themselves increasingly more isolated and less likely to socialize even with those like themselves.[5] The rising tide of neoconservative beliefs that has characterized the post–Cold War political climate in the United States sought to make unhampered economic opportunism, state coercion, and an accompanying diminishment of social services appear a remedy to national decline, when in fact these are symptomatic of, if not also a major contributor to, a polarization of social experiences and a heightened mood of misgiving about the future.

The 1992 Los Angeles riots were a sharp rebuke of these beliefs, an apparently spontaneous outburst of public violence that demanded relief from too much policing, too little social interaction, and an individualism that rewards greed without concern for consequences. As cultural producers drawn to the riots as a source of aesthetic challenge have repeatedly concluded, the substantial gains of the few at the expense and repression of the many, even with the help of powerful ideological interventions, cannot continue without the accumulation of powerful emotions that will find expression one way or another. Often this expression turns against the state, seeing in specters of byzantine bureaucracies and unfeeling functionaries a cause for disenfranchisement, powerlessness, and discontent. This expression also, just as often, turns against those who are most nearby, who are not afforded the full protection of the state, and who may be seething with their own barely suppressed anger. The most inventive of these cultural producers, in acknowledging how destructive expression can become, have found themselves experimenting with other possible forms that such expression might take, and with how such expression might help convene a public with a less predictable relationship to the strange than the one afforded by brute reaction.

Strange Future seeks to focus attention on these aesthetic experiments. It does so in the hope that such attention will yield renewed appreciation of the 1992 Los Angeles riots as more than an isolated incident. The intervening years since the riots, while doing little to heal, have nevertheless provided space for reflection on an event that was too difficult to dwell on in its immediate aftermath. These years have allowed us time to connect this event to larger trends, endemic ways of seeing, and mistakes that continue to be made. These years have also afforded us some luxury in paying attention to viewpoints that were largely inchoate, ignored, or simply caricatured in the first heat of urban rioting. Finally, these years have compelled us to place the role of Korean Americans in shaping our understanding of this event more at the center. It is now obvious, in a way it perhaps would not have been in the early 1990s, that for Korean Americans the riots loom large as an important historical event, one to which many Korean American activists, artists, creative writers, and scholars have returned, and will return, in their works again and again—in addition to whatever else might arrest their imagination. Because of this interest, Korean Americans have been disproportionately responsible for influencing how we continue to remember the riots and, thus, disproportionately responsible for insuring that the memory of the riots continues to shape, after all these turbulent and depressing years, a greater understanding of the world we share.

⋯ SALIENT CAUSES OF PESSIMISM

Over a five-day period, ending when Mayor Thomas Bradley lifted the dusk-to-dawn curfew, fifty-four people died as a direct result of the riots, more than 2,000 people were injured, more than 800 buildings were burned to the ground, and the region suffered nearly $1 billion in property damage (Cannon 1999, 347). About half of the over 12,000 people arrested during the riots were Latinos (Davis 1992a, 1). Of these, almost 80 percent were recent immigrants, many from Guatemala and El Salvador, and only a third were employed, usually as casual laborers (Valle and Torres 2000, 47). In addition, 30 percent of those who died were also Latinos, and 40 percent of the damaged businesses were Latino owned (Chang and Diaz-Veizades 1999, 26). Another 10 percent of those arrested were white (Davis 1998, 371). Although Korean American casualties were low—one death—Korean American–owned businesses were the hardest hit. Nearly half of all property damage was suffered by ethnic Korean merchants, many of whom were uninsured; ten months after the riots, a mere quarter of these merchants had reopened their businesses (Kim and Kim 1999, 26). Everyone in the region was affected when a county twice the size of Delaware was brought to a virtual standstill for a whole week as nightly curfews were imposed, streets and highways blockaded, and airports grounded. Related disturbances also affected numerous cities across the country, including San Francisco, Las Vegas, New York, Denver, Buffalo, Peoria, Toledo, Bridgeport, Providence, and Atlanta (Cannon 1999, 249).[6]

These numbing statistics attest to the riots' significant place in American history as a moment of national crisis. A number of large historical forces seem to have converged in these days of protests, beatings, shootings, looting, and burning to call attention to how our country had changed in recent years in a way that cannot simply be called progress. The riots thus seemed to articulate in a concentrated moment of violence a widespread feeling of discontent with the social order. If this is so, what were the names of these historical forces that caused so many to feel discontented? I wish to argue that these forces might be grouped under three specific headings. Each of these headings at once names actual historical changes and the fears that such changes easily generate: the economic losses of a capaciously defined white middle class, the daily misery of poor blacks abandoned in urban islands of poverty, and the influx of nonwhite immigrants. Together, the changes represented by these headings disrupted old political alliances while awakening new racial anxieties, fueling in the process the simultaneous popularity of cutbacks to government services and increases in punitive legislation. These changes also frustrated attempts to pin down with classic sociological models, which were either fixated on black-and-white racial conflict or on the desirability of an ill-defined assimilation, the coordinates upon which the processes of political interaction were being formed. What the 1992 Los Angeles riots definitively demonstrated in their racial complexity, and what continues at a minimum to make the riots important for us to study, is the need to abandon such sociological models.

To turn, then, to the first of these changes: if many in this country were feeling pessimistic about the nation's future after the end of the riots, this pessimism became more pronounced in contrast with what had once been expected. The state, guided by liberal ideas about how capitalist economies should be managed, enabled many blue-collar whites in the immediate wake of the Second World War to enter an expanded definition of the middle class in the United States. This move was facilitated by programs such as the Serviceman's Readjustment Act (more commonly known as the G.I. Bill of Rights), interstate highway construction, and Federal Housing Administration–guaranteed mortgages. All of these programs, largely paid for by taxes on corporations with fixed capital investments—in terms of factories and lifetime employees with generous pensions—and by a commitment to maintaining a military budget that continued to increase after Japan's surrender in 1945, allowed an unprecedented period of suburban development. Single-family home ownership along recently constructed residential streets, paid for by long-term and reliable employment at fixed sites of work, increasingly became an expectation with the help of government intervention, even as these same programs, which were notorious for discriminating against communities of color, had the long-term effect of widening social inequities, bankrupting urban cores, and tolerating destructive reinvestments of capital. The sense of well-being fostered by these state-sponsored programs may have contributed to a delayed realization, especially in St. Louis, Detroit, Buffalo, and Pittsburgh, for example—places hit earliest and hardest by these long-term effects—of how vulnerable such white working-class gains were proving themselves to be.[7]

By the end of the war in Viet Nam, just as laws reforming institutionalized discrimination in housing, hiring, education, immigration, and so forth were being passed, this state-led form of capital-white worker compromise, also known loosely as Keynesianism, began to break down. Corporations faced with flat profits sought to decrease expenses by moving production to places with fewer environmental regulations, fewer taxes, and cheaper labor. As manufacturing jobs moved south into the Sunbelt, often, accelerating a process that had begun as early as the mid-1940s, workers everywhere in the United States—but especially in the traditional urban cores near rusting industrial sites—were compelled to accept less (Sugrue 1996, 125–152). Increases in executive pay, which were extremely substantial during the past thirty years, came at the expense of their workers, both white and blue collar, whose incomes virtually stayed the same or went down (Mishel, Bernstein, and Schmitt 2001, 1). Even during a period of intense productivity growth, as seems to have been the case in the late 1990s, profits were shared disproportionately, facilitating—rather than decreasing—income inequalities.[8] Those near the bottom of the economic pyramid who could do so followed increasingly mobile jobs. Those who could not were abandoned in neighborhoods with fewer and fewer sources of income, as well as fewer restaurants, grocery stores, safe housing options, adequately equipped schools, and engaging social possibilities.[9] The abandoned were demonized as innately shiftless, violent, and self-destructive; they were consistently shunned as neighbors and coworkers; and, to add insult to injury, they found themselves the objects of popular entertainment, as their numerous problems were exploited as ever more exaggerated sources of titillation in countless crime dramas, investigative exposés, and policy documents (Sugrue 1996, 231–258; Wilson 1996, 111–146; Johnson, Farrell, and Stoloff 2000). Many of the abandoned were also black, which further punctuated the difference between those left behind and those lucky enough to go after the unequal returns of perpetual economic restructuring. Unsurprisingly, the difficult lives of the many black people stranded in isolated urban neighborhoods of burned-out lots and empty streets, dramatized for us on celluloid and in print, greatly encouraged the belief that national decline was well under way by the early 1990s.[10]

The riots also drew imperfectly interpellated subjects to question their attachment to cherished ideologies of individual uplift through assimilation and capitalist self-interest even as it brought these same subjects into what novelist Chang-rae Lee in *Native Speaker* (1995) might call "scabrous" conflict with long economically disenfranchised African American groups.[11] In popular memory, the main victims of the riots' violence were Korean American, or *kyopo*, merchants.[12] According to one's perspective, these merchants either deserved what they got for their rude behavior—that is, racist disdain for their black customers and participation in a political economy that facilitated capital extraction from the impoverished neighborhoods in which they worked but did not reside—or were sacrificial lambs at the alter of racial scapegoating who were forced by circumstance to absorb the brunt of black resentment against a white-dominated economic elite. Both of these explanations were favorites of the mainstream media, which went out of its way to depict the violence of the riots as a racial conflict between blacks and Koreans while simultaneously downplaying the role of Latinos and Latinas (K. Kim 1999, 2; also see K. Park 1997, Min 1996, Chang and Diaz-Veizades 1999, C. Kim 2000, and E. Park 2001a). The prominence that these explanations thus received placed Korean American merchants at the interstitial joint between white holders of power and a black underclass (the middleman theory), in effect operating to uphold in the popular imagination a black-white racial order that mirrors an extremely reductive class bifurcation.

At the same time, the sudden cultural visibility of Korean Americans can also be said to presage—the thinnest beginning of a much thicker wedge in ingrained perception—a more complicated urban racial geography for the many observers of the riots accustomed to thinking about race in more time-honored ways. As the figures found at the start of this section suggest, the ethnic and racial diversity of those involved in the riots belied easy racial dichotomization. Many Latinos were involved in the violence both as looters and vandals, and they were operators of small businesses that were looted and vandalized. There were also whites who joined in substantial numbers the black and brown bodies taking to the streets in protest. Unsurprisingly, the confusing diversity of those involved in the violence, perhaps most loudly heralded by the sudden visibility of kyopo merchants, has led many close observers to distance this event from its most obvious predecessor, the Watts Uprising of 1965, because 1965 was also the year that President Lyndon Johnson signed the Hart-Celler Immigration and Nationality Act into law. This piece of legislation is largely seen as enabling people of many different backgrounds to come together in the same geographical location, supposedly reaffirming the nation's commitment to a history of welcoming immigrants after a mere decades-long lapse, and in the process it helped make Los Angeles one of the most racially and ethnically diverse places on Earth. As Marilyn Halter notes, conveying received wisdom, "Here was legislation that . . . has led to kaleidoscopic demographic change and to so complete a shake-up of the country's racial and ethnic composition that by 2050, when today's preschoolers will have reached middle age, there will be no white majority; every American will belong to a minority group" (2000, 3–4).[13] Years of dramatic rates of immigration had altered the racial face of the city of Los Angeles, representing for many what will soon follow in the rest of the nation, and they have seemingly aggravated the days of violence and protest that could no longer be filtered through the lens of black-and-white racial conflict.

The riots thus foregrounded many anxieties that accelerated during the 1980s surrounding the influx of new, and racially diverse, immigrants.

In this context, it seems significant to note that "more immigrants arrived during" this decade "than in any since the early twentieth century,"
80 percent of these immigrants coming from Latin America and Asia
(Rogin 1998, 41). Suddenly, it seemed, in already racially diverse places
such as Los Angeles, which received the major brunt of this influx (which
suggests as well how unsatisfying the black-and-white discourse about
race has always been in many parts of the United States), settled and
emergent middle-class Mexican American, Japanese American, Chinese
American, African American, and Jewish residents, alongside the once
numerically dominant Midwestern Anglo transplants, found themselves
facing added competition for jobs, government services, and electoral
power. Their competitors were new arrivals from Central America, who
were willing to work for very little, and new arrivals from all over the
Pacific Rim, who apparently had access to mysterious sources of capital.
Alliances had to be redrawn while old ones were revised, and suppressed
hostilities were inevitably reincarnated, sometimes in surprising opposi-
tions (Valle and Torres 2000). The resulting configurations of social relations, especially the exodus of whites from the region, were then sold to
the rest of the country as a cautionary image of what might happen soon
if immigration trends continued unchecked (Rieff 1991). It is not too difficult to imagine that the orchestrated hostility against government-
sponsored programs—such as bilingual education; Aid to Families with
Dependent Children (AFDC); federal mandates requiring the consider-
ation of minority, women, and Vietnam War–veteran candidates for jobs
and admission to postsecondary education; government enforcement of
workplace safety requirements; and so forth—had been abetted by what
appeared to be, in this cautionary image, an alien invasion of unintel-
ligible languages, oddly aromatic foods, and unfamiliar faces. In the waning years of the twentieth century, this alien invasion became, as much as
the diminished expectations of a capaciously defined white middle class
and the daily misery of poor urban blacks, a privileged sign of ongoing
national decline.[14]

It is thus worth reiterating that these—alien invasion, the misery of
poor urban blacks, the declining fortunes of a white middle class—comprised, at the start of the 1990s, the triptych sign of the societal changes
causing the nation to experience a decline. If this is true, then no group

during the days of the Los Angeles riots occupied the social position demarcated by the threat of alien invasion more than Korean Americans. They were uniformly seen as small business owners who operated liquor stores in predominantly black neighborhoods, who hid behind the thick bullet-proof glass surrounding their cash registers, who hired only their own kind, who worked long hours mechanically as if they were little more than unfeeling machines, who preyed on black customers by eyeing them suspiciously and quickly telling them to leave once they had spent their money, and who spoke a broken guttural English when they weren't shooting words at each other in a language that no one else could understand. Korean Americans cared only about themselves, looked down on their black customers, and wanted almost nothing to do with their white neighbors. As Nancy Abelmann and John Lie observe, reiterating an assessment that has been widely shared by many critics of the way Korean Americans were represented,

> In the media barrage during and after the riots, Korean Americans came to occupy a particular place in the American ideological landscape. They were often invoked to support one point or another about the L.A. riots. Imagined variously as quintessential or exceptional immigrants, as culturally legible or inscrutable, as racist or oppressed, Korean Americans emerged at the crossroads of conflicting social reflections on the L.A. riots. Through the Korean American story, observers decried the "death of the immigrant dream," underscored intra-minority racism, and again and again offered formulaic cultural contrasts between Korean Americans and African Americans. (1995, 1)

Violently thrust into the national spotlight after years of obscurity, Korean Americans appeared as shadowy figures armed with automatic weapons protecting their stores against menacing black and brown bodies while, at the same time, maintaining an intense anger at whites who they said dominated the country's centers of power. They were, in short, a spectacle without precedent. This allowed others, as Abelman and Lie observe, to slot Korean Americans into already available explanations about the national meaning of the riots, rendering them flexible signifiers for a wide variety of already entrenched and competing perspectives. The diversity of meanings heaped upon them suggests, however, the ways in which Korean Americans evaded such easy categorization. They could not be securely interpreted as the latest representatives of the immigrant dream or of its death, scapegoat or capital extractor, victim or victimizer. For a brief moment, Korean Americans registered in the national media as the synecdoche of the cumulative fears generated by widespread non-white immigration. By not fitting snugly into a single narrative about American nationhood, either as a site of struggle for the promotion of "social egalitarianism" or for the protection of "individual liberty" (Brown 1995, 67), they simply seemed to figure the breakdown of any notion of a common national identity altogether.[15] It did not take long for people with these fears to target other groups in Southern California, such as Mexican immigrants during the debate around Proposition 187, but for a brief and devastating instant Korean Americans found themselves bearing the primary brunt of such fears alone.[16] The latter chapters (4 and 5)of this book focus specifically on this group, then, because of the unwanted prominence that the independent merchants, who make up a rough third of the Korean American population (Jennifer Lee 2002, 46), experienced during the riots. How did this unwanted prominence, I will ask, prompt new attempts at self-understanding and how did it affect an emerging generation's sense of what is politically desirable?

· · · OVERDETERMINATION, RIOTING, AND CULTURE

If, as I have been arguing, the 1992 Los Angeles riots are indeed a window through which we can make out the contours of an emergent "strange future" suggested by our recent history of a dwindling white middle class, the daily misery of poor urban blacks, and the influx of immigrants from all over the world, it is not necessarily a very transparent window. The riots' terrible destructiveness was a social wounding that created an opening in the body politic of the nation. It laid bare the many contradictions and pathologies quivering beneath America's skin-deep claims to civil society. Like any serious wound, the result was messy and hard to contain. Dean Gilmour, a lieutenant in the Los Angeles County Coroner's office interviewed by Anna Deavere Smith for her stage production of *Twilight: Los Angeles, 1992* (1994), suggests the difficulty involved in defining such a historically overdetermined event:

Are all gang shootings during this time riot-related?
I mean, we have gang shootings every day
of the year.
What would set these apart from being riot-related? (191)

By calling this event overdetermined, I am thinking of Louis Althusser's theoretical insistence that any historical event is the product of causes that exceed what we can discern. The present is always a confluence of chains of historical causation that overlaps the sum of any single historical narrative. Therefore, we should not be surprised at the way Gilmour foregrounds the difficulties of defining a discrete event called the Los Angeles riots. What appears as a definable event in time reveals itself, upon closer inspection, to be implicated fully in continuities of trends and preoccupations, such as daily gang shootings, that precede and endure past such an event. We cannot, in other words, claim to isolate such an event from the larger plexus of concerns that cradles its historical contextualization. Does this mean, as Althusser feared, that we have to give up the hope of isolating a "historical event" that is separable "from the infinity of things which *happen* to men day and night, things which are as anonymous as they are unique" (1977, 126)?

In the pursuit of keeping such hope alive, we might argue that the major reason why so many politically minded cultural critics shy away from referring to what happened in Los Angeles at the end of April 1992 as "rioting" is because this is an implicit acceptance of the inadequacy of historical thinking. To refer to Los Angeles riots per se suggests exactly a moment of overdetermination: a dizzying array of historical causations and unrelated sensory perceptions that do not add up to anything coherent, a meta-event that can only be talked about in terms of our inability to comprehend what has happened, a throwing up of arms in exasperation that such scenes of violence could have been motivated by any kind of logic at all. It might as well have been forged by the will of God, for all we know. Certainly, the term *riots* suggests multiplicity, fragmentation, competing points of view. It gestures toward an absence that has to stand in for what could not be captured as a whole. Ruminating on the riots, Norman Klein remarks, "Many reporters were close enough to see a rock crash through their windshield, or to interview looters on the spot. However, in an event as massive as this, to be present at one street corner does not make you a reliable source. Nor does it give you enough background to discuss long-term causes, the subtleties of a particular street, its normalcies, its survival" (1997, 224). To take the view of a fictive reporter on the street, who sees only part of a "massive" event unfolding in unfamiliar terrain and involving people with whom he or she does not regularly converse, is to give into something Althusser calls "bad infinity" (1977, 126). If we accept such a view, we might as well not even call the Los Angeles riots an event, much less a historical event.

For those invested in guarding the relative, and for a shrinking few incredibly sizable privileges, afforded by the status quo, such a point of view is just as acceptable as the arguments we might have heard after the violence that rocked Watts in 1965, when the root causes of that violence were traced back to hot weather, the full moon affecting the tides, and a possible meteorite shower (Horne 1997, 54). If we believe there are as many causes as there were participants and witnesses to such an event, we are also accepting the view that the riots were chaotic, baseless, irrational or prerational, or simply so beyond our ability to comprehend that it finally gets all of us off the hook. If we cannot know why it happened, we cannot have been complicit in its destructiveness, nor can we be responsible for the conditions that might have led to such an outburst of rage. We—those who did not participate directly in the looting, the burning, the shootings, the beatings, and so forth—were simply bystanders shocked to see the news footage unrolling on our television sets. We might simply conclude that such senseless violence is rooted in the essential perdition of humanity and resolve to cordon off those without self-control from those who have maintained at least a semblance of rationality, as we have been implicitly doing in the past two decades as longer and longer prison sentences become the preferred response to crime, drug use, and other acts of social disruption. For those involved more directly, however, they may find the reasons they gave violent expression to the temporary and spontaneous reclamation of public spaces that are usually regulated against them obfuscated by such a stance, or worse, explained away as the product of something that cannot be articulated with any measure of coherence.

Why, then, do I insist on using the term *riots* and not the less dismissive terms that other critics have adopted? First, *rebellion* or *uprising* or *insurrection* or even *revolution* seem to me to go too much in the opposite direction. They glamorize what was in fact deadly and symptomatic of deeply underlying problems in our society. Much of what happened in South Los Angeles (the new name given to South Central after the riots), to judge from the accounts I have come across, suggests that the event was spontaneous, not premeditated, and therefore indicative of visceral reactions to circumstances as they unfolded. There was no discernible tradition of established oppositional political organization at work, no fully expressible leadership rooted in the needs of the multitudes, and no thought-out way for channeling the rage at an unjust judicial and economic system toward productive social protest. This is not to say, however, that those involved in the riots were somehow driven by a lack of reason, burning and beating and shooting in a fit of uncontrolled rage, for this would be to suggest that rage and its corollary grief do not in themselves operate by their own sets of logic. If we wish to emphasize this aspect of the violence that engulfed Los Angeles in 1992, then certainly it would make sense to push the rhetorical marker further to one side and to use terms that may seem inflated given the circumstances; but this is dependent completely on rhetorical contingency, which for the purposes of this book is secondary to why I continue to use *riots*.

Second, terms such as *unrest* or *disturbance*, in their guise of neutrality, sidestep the issues raised by the problem of naming itself. If we accept the premise that it matters what we call what happened in South Los Angeles in 1992, we cannot then pretend scholarly distance from these events by coining a term that we feel will not offend anyone. While there may be, again, occasion when it would be appropriate to maintain this distance, in such occasions we need to be explicit about why we feel this aptness. Otherwise, such a practice generally fails to get at what is most productive about this debate.

Third, one especially inventive alternative to *riots* is the Korean term *sa-i-gu*, which literally means 4-2-9, the date (29 April) the riots began. To call it this, as I will explore at some length in chapter 4, is to center a perspective that is quite different from that of the reporter on the street or even the angry bodies carrying out the violence. This is, undoubtedly, an important perspective to consider, and can do much to enrich our understanding of a complexity that most mainstream commentators usually restrict in the name of familiarity. At the same time, this perspective is still only part of a larger story, and it should not be allowed untroubled to represent a whole.

Since there seems to be no unproblematic term by which we can refer to this historical event, I continue to use the derogatory term *riots*. By insisting on the pessimism generated by this event and by insisting further that this pessimism finds its most meaningful expression in works of cultural production, I want to suggest as well that the overdetermination of rioting aptly names a still-forming articulation of dissatisfaction with the current social order. Because there is no movement, as such, to give shape to this dissatisfaction and because there are so few outlets for this dissatisfaction to find concrete redress, it is only in culture, as Lisa Lowe argues, that this dissatisfaction can make itself known. Lowe writes, "This is not to argue that cultural struggle can ever be the exclusive site for practice; it is rather to argue that if the state suppresses dissent by governing subjects through rights, citizenship, and political representation, it is only through culture that we conceive and enact new subjects and practices in antagonism to the regulatory *locus* of the citizen-subject, by way of culture that we can question these modes of government" (1996, 22). Cut off from other avenues of influence in the shaping of the structures of power that govern and restrict how we might live our lives, we turn to the terrain defined by culture to experiment, conceive, and put into practice what has been denied other opportunities for expression. The strange "erupts in culture" (Lowe 1996, 22), then, when our needs cannot find accommodation in established channels of governance. This cultural turn is a retreat to a political place of last resort.

· · · **THE AESTHETIC CHALLENGE**

If a cultural turn is indeed a retreat, what would it take to prevent this retreat from becoming a rout? Can a retreat also be a regathering of forces and energies that can prepare us for what lies ahead? Can cultural politics be thought of as the necessary preparation for a comprehensive, assertive, and coordinated movement to resuscitate and redefine a dying public sphere? In short, how can we make the strange politically meaningful when it erupts in culture? These questions point to an aesthetic challenge. Numbers and facts alone, as important as they are to debate, cannot—as the word *overdetermination* suggests—penetrate the thicket of social relations and received habits of thought that condition our understanding of the 1992 Los Angeles riots. Narrative conventions, the manipulation of language and the visual, the borrowing and refashioning of familiar tropes, the experimentation with perspective, and, most important, the popular circulation of certain special metaphors deserve our utmost attention. These are, or have become, in an age of migratory populations and proliferating multimedia outlets, an essential part of how we use art to interpret life (Appadurai 1996, 53–64). Without critical attention to these component parts of our culture's rich figurative vernacular, we are stuck with crude stories that repeat what has already been told. The latter contain a richer complexity in clichés about innate racial differences, primordial conflicts, and the ignorance of masses (Herrnstein and Murray 1994; Huntington 1996; Bloom 1987). Against the story that adheres to the familiar, then, intellectual work that is attentive to form, language, genre, medium, and narrative—in addition to race, class, and gender— immerses itself in the hard to follow, the not entirely understood, the evanescent reality that despite its fogginess can nevertheless be partially comprehended.

Unfortunately, the aesthetic project of postmodernism, which gave voice in the 1970s and 1980s to a sense of having arrived at some "late" era in history and in doing so was an attempt to tackle the aesthetic challenge I am writing about here, feels quaint and therefore incapable of capturing a cultural moment that became, and is becoming, more foreboding with each passing year.[17] We as a society have, it seems, emerged from the twentieth century battered, bruised, and prone to be skeptical about what the next decade, much less the next century, has in store for us—this despite the fact that the United States has also emerged from the previous century as what Michael Hardt and Antonio Negri suggestively call "the central figure in the newly unified world order" (2000, 182). Paul Smith usefully characterizes this "central figure" as an entity in the mid-1990s "lurching toward the millennium insanely anguished about its future and at the same time wracked by memories of its childhood" (1997, 189). Unsurprisingly, when we as intellectuals look back at the past decade, what we seem to find is a history filled, like so many decades before it, with struggles that have become co-opted for ends opposite to each other, a ceaseless ingenuity in the search for novel ways to inflict harm on one another, and perhaps a numbing of our senses that needs to be repeatedly reawakened, like trying to walk on a foot that has fallen asleep. For many critics, it seems, this understanding of history is a self-evident truth. It is something so obvious that we need to wonder why we cannot accept it as such. "So we have ceased to believe in many of the constitutive premises undergirding modern personhood, statehood, and constitutions," Wendy Brown writes, "yet we continue to operate politically as if these premises still held, and as if the political-cultural narrative based on them were intact" (2001, 4). Seen from this perspective, the 1990s inaugurated by the violence of the Los Angeles riots were especially disheartening for intellectuals both because there was no enduring sense of collective progress to be found anywhere and because no compensatory narrative presented itself as a replacement for cherished notions of progress.

In the absence of an enduring sense of collective progress or other compensatory narrative, the violence, the iconography, and the emotions produced by the 1992 Los Angeles riots can appear in retrospect as yet more proof of Walter Benjamin's familiar image of history: "one single catastrophe which keeps piling wreckage upon wreckage" (1969, 257). Or, for a more updated version of this image, we might turn to J. G. Ballard. In the cult novel *Crash* (1973), Ballard revels in the erotic puckering of flesh as it retains its violent meeting with modernity and the dazed look of strangers brought into sudden intimacy after an automobile accident: "We looked at each other through the fractured windshields, neither able to move. Her husband's hand, no more than a few inches from me, lay palm upwards beside the windshield wiper. His hand had struck some rigid object as he was hurled from his seat, and the pattern of a sign formed itself as I sat there, pumped up by his dying circulation into a huge blood-blister—the triton signature of my radiator's emblem" (20). Notions of progress have stalled at this moment, in the meeting of body, machinery, and commodity logo. The immobile gaze of strangers locked over a violated figure captures the social predicaments enunciated by pain, trauma, wounding, injury, and haunting. These metaphors have gained critical *and* cultural currency because they provide a way to speak about a deep-seated frustration about progress in graphic detail while, at the same time, paying respect to the materiality that aggravates such frustration. To put it another way, these metaphors have helped us to confront our own deeply held resistance to believing that social conditions have stagnated, or in some cases worsened, for many in this country since the 1960s.

Thus, the heightened circulation of pain, trauma, wounding, injury, and haunting as metaphors about a social body in trouble remind us that, while civic boosters have succeeded in at least partially drawing attention away from a mounting sense that the United States has embarked upon a long road of decline, as Reagan did at an earlier moment and as Clinton accomplished at the height of his administration, historical events such as the 1992 Los Angeles riots nevertheless have a materiality that cannot be ignored for too long. And while neoconservatives have tried to direct the frustration created by this sense of decline, when it could not be denied, against crime-prone blacks and sneaky nonwhite immigrants, against sexual permissiveness and the corruption of the nuclear family, against the laziness of the American labor force and the unfair trade practices of our neighbors across the Pacific, cultural producers who have turned to the materiality of the riots as a source of creative inspiration have had other stories to tell about the decline of the nation. It is, perhaps, because such a materiality refuses to remain interred that so many cultural critics have turned away from invocations of postmodernism, which suggests the preeminence of the sign over the world (and for which reason now feels so dated), in favor of metaphors that signify through the figure of the body an inescapable worldliness. Often, critics use these metaphors as if they are interchangeable even if the cultural phenomena to which these metaphors attach meaning are often quite, but not discretely, separable. In what follows, I wish to trace briefly the differentiation in meaning between these metaphors that critics have implicitly suggested. I am, therefore, endeavoring to refine a vocabulary that is already in use, in the hopes that this will allow us to speak more precisely about where the cultural turn of the 1990s might eventually lead us:

1. The metaphor of *pain* as it is currently understood in a critical sense probably found its first distillation in *The Body in Pain: The Making and Unmaking of the World* (1985), where Elaine Scarry insists, "Physical pain

has no voice" (3). From this simple assertion, she outlines the ethical and political necessity of finding a way to make pain expressible through language, an aesthetic project, because when pain has no voice it is too easy to inflict pain on others. Pain thus became an object of inquiry commensurate with the real, that which is beyond language but which exerts an organizing pull. Pain is everywhere and nowhere. It speaks but without a voice. It is felt as what is most irreducible about physical existence but also the most suspect because intangible. The investigation and making audible pain's cry have become almost a religious exercise in many critical circles, a form of Christology where belief in the transformative powers of bearing witness to suffering endures as a test of faith, forgiveness, and redemption. To render pain into expression is to enable a political awakening without which, it seems, we feel incapable of eliciting movement toward a lofty goal.

2. The metaphor of *trauma* provides a language for giving expression to a present caught in the gaze of a past full of newly discovered horrors. Thus transfixed, the present is incapable of articulating a future that might bring relief to these horrors. The concept of history, even as it has undergone severe critique, bears down upon us, saturates our very beings, and acts at times almost as if it were a weight tied to the top of our heads that prevents us from looking up toward a desirable future. Trauma discovers pain at its most concentrated and violently inflicted manifestation, a flashing instant that cannot be forgotten even as it is, like pain, inarticulate. As with survivors of the Holocaust, child sexual abuse, and veterans of the Vietnam War, for whom post-traumatic stress disorder, or PTSD, became a political cause as well as a diagnosable mental disorder, trauma as metaphor retains the notion of sudden violence pressing on the linings of the brain. In the suddenness and harshness of this violence, trauma imprints a groove that leaves one reliving the violence as if in a waking ceaseless dream. If the metaphor of pain is about the body's dislocation, its lack of a physical place in space, then the metaphor of trauma is about the body's removal from the flow of causes and effects, the body's lacking awareness of temporality.

3. The metaphor of *wounding*, in its insistence on a rupture of private and public, of inside and out, of person and sociality, articulates a disjuncture of interpersonal experiences, a disparity among perspectives

accountable by group formations, a structural inequality lived as individual isolation and personal suffering that cannot be communicated across subjective gulfs no matter how technologically sophisticated we become. Cut off from thinking positively about the future, we are also cut off from each other. Wounding renders the notion of the social itself diseased. The social is pain inducing. The social becomes possible only in spectacles of bodily suffering. Wounding calls attention to the site of pain, the rendering of trauma's print on human flesh, the separation of skin and tissue becoming representative of an evisceration of a social body that has little possibility of mending.

4. The metaphor of *injury* is a double-edged response to a making visible of identities that once could be assumed, a power that had been asserted more powerfully because deployed without possibility of comment, and as a reassertion, in more naked and coercive a manner, of the centrality of such identities as a norm desperately seeking to maintain itself as such. Injury points to what has been lost and is often accompanied by a sense of grievance at the loss. Who is at fault? Where does the responsibility lie? How can one be compensated? Claims to making pain more visible can be seen, then, as an overvaluation of victimization and dismissed as such without the actual harm itself being brought to light. In this way, we are again divorced from thinking about the future because the present social order, stripped of its powers of consensus forging and compelled to protect itself through more obviously coercive means, grips desperately to an idealization of a past. Aggressive apologists for such a social order cannot afford to tolerate articulations of past injuries that might necessarily debunk such idealization, even as they themselves desire to claim their own sense of injury.

Unlike the metaphor of wounding, then, which focuses on the pain of social encounters (a spatial orientation), the metaphor of injury looks to the past (a temporal orientation). We might, therefore, think of wounding and injury as the opposites, respectively, of pain and trauma. The latter two metaphors figure a lack that defies representation in space and in time, respectively, while the former two metaphors figure an attempt, in representation, to reify lack as something that can be situated in space and time. The figure on page 23 illustrates the complementary differences between these four metaphors. These differences are presented in a circular diagram to suggest that the boundaries around these metaphors are not discrete. Rather, their meanings flow into each other, mutually reinforcing a foreboding that the social order is in trouble while simultaneously grounding this foreboding in the intimate materiality of human bodies.

5. If figure 1 allows us to "see" the complementary differences between pain, trauma, wounding, and injury, *haunting* evades such illustration. Haunting metaphorizes lack as a ghostly presence in both time and space. It points to a being that can be represented and that defies representation simultaneously. It is the repeated—and inevitable?—failure of discourse to give pain a voice that has led to this paradox in haunting, which in turn aligns haunting with a form of melancholia. Haunting is an apparition of the weak, the disempowered, the forgotten, the excluded, the murdered, and so forth that intrudes upon a present too willing to sweep disturbing plaints of injustice into a dustbin. Pain unspoken and unheeded finds its own, albeit insubstantial, form, and becomes more insistent the more we try to turn away and refuse its spectral being-in-the-world. All the bodies that have been violated, shunned, and buried in mass graves (actual or figurative) return without any material means to demand rectification of past and continuing wrongs but, nonetheless, with a persistence that will not leave the powerful alone. We might think of recent critical interest in Marx and his specter of Communism, the American Indian religious figure Wovoka and his ghost dance, the Mexican story of *la llorona* ("the crying woman" who mourns for her dead children even after her own death), Maxine Hong Kingston and her childhood among ghosts (1989 [1975]), and M. Night Shyamalan's cinematic reinvention of the ghost story in *The Sixth Sense* (1999), among other superabundant examples, to consider the ways haunting has been used to question what triumphant narratives of progress leave out.

Together, pain, trauma, wounding, injury, and haunting help us to visualize in a figurative language grounded in the materiality of the body the struggle to make meaning out of the strange. These metaphors hold us firm in the belief that to say that something is complex is not to say that something cannot be understood. The kind of intellectual labor that these metaphors perform acknowledges, as Avery Gordon puts it, that "the power relations that characterize any historically embedded society are never as transparently clear as the names we give them imply," while

Pain

DEFIES SPATIAL
REPRESENTATION

Trauma

DEFIES TEMPORAL
REPRESENTATION

Wounding

ENCOURAGES SPATIAL
REPRESENTATION

Injury

ENCOURAGES TEMPORAL
REPRESENTATION

assuming that "the stories people tell about themselves, about their troubles, about their social worlds, and about their society's problems are entangled and weave between what is immediately available as a story and what their imaginations are reaching toward" (1997, 3, 4). This kind of intellectual labor cannot make the future brighter for us; nor is intellectual labor necessarily something that should do this. This kind of intellectual labor can, however, confront us with our own worst fears by refusing to ignore what cannot, in any case, be ignored in the long run: the estrangement at the heart of contemporary life.

Such a confrontation with fear, then, is one important political implication these metaphors of the body's violation have conjured up for the many critics who have tried to explain their cultural magnetism, and that I will elaborate on in the rest of this book. For now, I merely wish to note that all of these metaphors might be classed under a Korean word that has begun to find some circulation in American English, *han*. As Elaine Kim explains: "*Han* is a Korean word that means, loosely translated, the sorrow and anger that grow from the accumulated experiences of oppression. Although the word is frequently and commonly used by Koreans, the condition it describes is taken quite seriously. When people die of *han*, it is called dying of *hwabyong*, a disease of frustration and rage following misfortune" (1993, 215). What is most suggestive to me about this word is the way feeling and bodily harm are so closely linked, so much so that to be afflicted with han means equally to be subject to a physical wounding that can literally kill, *hwabyong*. Such a close linkage between, if not the simple impossibility of separating, feeling and body is exactly what is figured in the metaphors I discuss above. Indeed, among some critics interested in the concept of trauma, one important intellectual task has been to demonstrate the ways in which sudden violence both afflicts the psyche and the brain where the psyche is thought to be located, a lesion in other words in tissue and affect (see, especially, van der Kolk and van der Hart 1995). With tongue only slightly in cheek, perhaps we might think of the cultural moment I have tried to give flesh to here as something we might call *han*ism.

ALTHOUGH THE SCOPE of my starting claims are obviously quite sweeping, what I wish to accomplish in the following chapters is much more modest. I wish to begin a discussion about the basic features of the moment we found ourselves in during the early 1990s. This was a moment with little optimism about the future, a general sense of futility about the possibility for positive change, and, as such, a *vulnerability* to arguments for greater state repression as necessary defense against the triptych sign of national decline (the diminished economic fortunes of a white middle-class, the daily misery of poor urban blacks, and alien invasion). The 1992 Los Angeles riots were one major historical event that brought this kind of pessimism into violent public attention and set the pace for a decade of neoconservative public dominance during which many of our worst fears seem to come true. As such, the riots have remained fresh in the minds of cultural producers who have wanted to generate meanings that do not lead us back down the same arguments for the simultaneous need to shrink the size of the state and to increase the punitive nature of our laws. Such arguments, it seems to me, inevitably prepare the ground for a situation in which the redistribution of wealth upward into fewer and fewer hands is made possible by the outright coercion of those who might object. If this is so, the works I am interested in exploring demand us to consider: How will we respond to the losses created by such coercion? How will we mend the divisions endlessly created by these arguments without, at the same time, succumbing to their logic? How can we participate in the shaping of the social changes that are everywhere manifesting themselves in a destructive manner?

Chapter 1 provides a selective historical mapping of demographic changes found in postwar Southern California, with the help of Ray Bradbury, Luis Rodriguez, and Cynthia Kadohata. This chapter sets the stage for considering the historical event that unfolded in the early 1990s and that has since become a cultural-literary event. The specific creative works under investigation in *Strange Future* beyond this first chapter make references to particular aspects of the riots. In chapter 2, the commercial film *Strange Days* (1995) focuses discussion on the question of why the beating of Rodney King by four police officers acquired such immediate iconic status. In chapter 3, the experimental drama of Anna Deavere Smith's *Twilight: Los Angeles, 1992* (1994) points to the difficulty of documenting a historical event that literally involves the wounding of social spaces. In chapter 4, Dai Sil Kim-Gibson's documentary *Sa-I-Gu*

(1993), which tells the story of the riots from the perspective of merchant Korean American women, also tells a story about the difficulty of mourning a loss that feels as if the thing lost is still in the process of being taken away. In chapter 5, the novel *Native Speaker* (1995) moves away spatially from the epicenter of the riots' violence only to encounter this violence as a memory that fuels continued dissatisfaction with the U.S. nation-state and its solutions to social problems. All of these works, by introducing us to particular aspects of the riots as they pertain to the pervasive sense that recent history has robbed the United States of its national momentum, allow us to explore the pessimism that seems to have hijacked the imagination of our collective future. As I hope to make persuasive by the epilogue, this pessimism is not something merely to be wished away.

Racial Geography of Southern California

1

On 30 April 1992, a satellite operated by the National Oceanic and Atmospheric Administration (NOAA) began transmitting an image of an unusual heat source emanating from Southern California. This heat source spanned nearly thirty-three square miles and was as hot as the Mount Pinatubo eruption of 1991 in the Philippines. When researchers processed the image, they realized that what they were looking at was a picture from outer space of the second day of the Los Angeles riots. The heat source was attributed to the fact that "an average of three new fires were started each minute during the three hours preceding the image" (Dousset, Flamen, and Bernstein 1993, 33; quoted in Davis 1998, 421). At the start of the last decade of the twentieth century, technology and urban destruction melded together into an unexpected form of social epistemology. Rather than projecting us outward as it did in the mid-twentieth-century science fiction of writers such as Isaac Asimov, Arthur C. Clarke, Robert Heinlein, and Ray Bradbury, technology turned its lenses back upon the Earth. Rather than presenting us with an image of the Earth as a unified globe in a vast emptiness as successive missions to the moon made famous from 1969 to 1972, technology recorded with digital accuracy the continuous failures of post–civil-rights government policies to promote social acceptance, equal protection under the law, and common economic prosperity irrespective of race.

What this image suggests is that this failure could well have been planned. The whole of Southern California is not a bright uniform orange; nor do orange spots dot the region in sporadic and random places. Rather, the technological representation of burning buildings records a clearly defined area of containment and spatial segregation across a vast multinucleated metropolitan area. Whatever grief or frustration or justifiable political need sparked these fires, these fires were carefully managed to cluster about a subregional, mostly unincorporated grid— what I will call a negative space—defined by economic poverty, ethnic

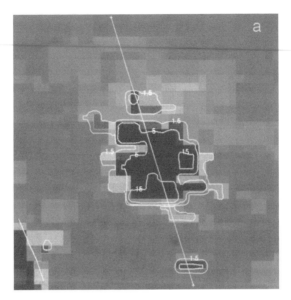

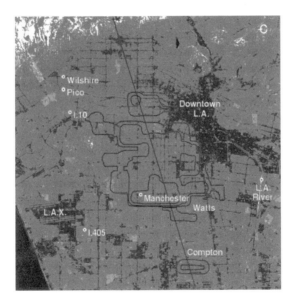

and racial diversity, and a noticeable separation from the other equally managed, incorporated, wealthier, and more racially homogeneous grids of Southern California. The concentration of these fires, made so vivid by the NOAA satellite image, calls into question the *orthodoxy* that often dominates awareness of our built-up surroundings. Orthodoxy refers to the sense that what appears to us as random and haphazard, so succinctly captured in the dismissive term *suburban sprawl*, is actually something that has been carefully organized, that serves specific functions, and that shapes our experiences in a powerful but difficult-to-acknowledge way.[1] It is, to put it simply, common sense that this region should be the way it is. The region's gridlike spatialization seems a natural extension of its geographical peculiarities, almost as if the tract housing, the strip malls, the congested freeways and boulevards, even the economic and racial inequities, are themselves organic growths on the floor of a Mediterranean-climate basin.

What kind of cultural logic was at work in the making of such common sense? How, in other words, has the accumulation of choices made and opportunities squandered come to appear to us, in retrospect, as somehow inevitable? By logic, I refer to the assumptions we might begin with in attempting to interpret cultural phenomena, how our thoughts and actions are guided by these assumptions, and the ways in which such assumptions are subjected to testing and reworking. With this definition in mind, we might say that the orthodoxy of planned communities, incorporated and unincorporated spaces, racial exclusions, and capital flows are built on assumptions of cultural superiority, human progress, and consumer desire. This orthodoxy of assumptions overlapped and at times were at odds with a second kind of cultural logic guiding the interpretation of spatial change by the region's residents. The latter was primarily concerned with the promises of a future that could dissolve current inequities, the looking back when looking forward became impossible, and the desire to start over either by wiping out what was already there or by moving someplace else. This subjective approach to interpreting cultural phenomena found beautiful expression in three creative works of the postwar era. Ray Bradbury's *The Martian Chronicles* (1997 [1946]), Luis Rodriguez's *Always Running, La Vida Loca: Gang Days in L.A.* (1993), and Cynthia Kadohata's *In the Heart of the Valley of Love*

(1992) are arguably some of the most significant literary works to interest themselves in the depiction of this region's cultural contours since the Second World War. Side by side, they provide us with a rich cross section of historical changes as they are lived, brooded over, and reshaped into narrative. Together, they tell a startling story of how looking forward, looking backward, and looking to start over can occupy the same gaze through which to regard the incredible changes that Southern California has experienced in the years between the end of the Second World War and the start of the 1992 Los Angeles riots.

··· NOSTALGIA FOR AN ANTIQUE FUTURE

For the generation who grew up during the heady days of early space exploration and who have largely moved to the homogeneous community developments that have sprung up throughout the United States since the Second World War, the irony of the reversals captured so vividly by the NOAA satellite must seem unusually acute. During the height of the Eisenhower and Kennedy years, advance technology was represented by rocket ships and not the miniaturization of technology, and the future involved manned missions to outer space and not a remote-controlled pixilated abstraction of American residents yet again setting fire to their own cities. In *Ecology of Fear: Los Angeles and the Imagination of Disaster* (1998), Mike Davis comments on the meaning of the pixilated image transmitted by the NOAA satellite for a person of his generation: "Once upon a time—in the rocket summer of my childhood—it was widely believed that Los Angeles's ultimate suburb would be the planet Mars, not a maximum-security prison in the desert. . . . If this now seems preposterous, it is only because our imagined futures have worn poorly over the ensuing years. The 1990s in particular have been a funeral decade, interring many of the hopes and fantasies of the earlier twentieth century" (418). As this passage might suggest, *Ecology of Fear*, much like the other works in Davis's oeuvre, is a radically pessimistic work of cultural criticism where the present is defined by a state that has, like technology, turned inward. This state has become more invested in surveillance, information gathering, and incarceration than in guaranteeing the freedoms associated with the ready availability of employment and plentiful unstructured leisurely activity. This is in sharp contrast with a past when a few were able to enjoy the pleasures of an expansive freedom and could look forward to the future as a continuation of what they already enjoyed.[2]

Ecology of Fear thus occupies an interesting place between the two major genres of literature that primarily concern me in this chapter, science fiction and memoir. Like the former, Davis's book obsesses over a future that has become harder to imagine, and harder still to desire. It seems like a dark place, with little hope, full of biting irony and reversals. At the same time, even this obsession with the future engages in a work of remembrance, as the passage just quoted suggests with its recourse to Davis's own personal memory of his childhood spent dreaming over space exploration. The past is comforting for Davis exactly because it enabled a younger version of himself to look forward to a future that would, unfortunately, never come to pass.[3] To make sense of this duality in another way, Davis's most pessimistic book on Los Angeles engages in its eschatological thinking a surprisingly complex rhetorical trope: nostalgia for an antique future.

According to Svetlana Boym in her remarkable work of cultural criticism, personal memoir, and travelogue, *The Future of Nostalgia* (2001), "Nostalgia (from *nostos*—return to home, and *algia*—longing) is a longing for a home that no longer exists or has never existed. Nostalgia is a sentiment of loss and displacement, but it is also a romance with one's own fantasy" (xiii). When traced to its root words, nostalgia can be defined as a turning backward, a desire for something that may have once existed but does not necessarily have to reflect any recoverable referent. It can also be a yearning for an ideal that brings into sharper clarity through contrast what seems missing in our present moment and place. Nostalgia longs for a home that may not exist except in our fantasies. Indeed, nostalgia is often a fantasy of homecoming that is felt most strongly when home itself lacks clear definition. As such, it can become manifest as a desire to restore what is felt to have been lost or as an occasion to reflect on the conditions of homelessness that give nostalgia its affective sting. "Restorative nostalgia," Boym writes, "puts emphasis on *nostos* and proposes to rebuild the lost home and patch up the memory gaps. Reflective nostalgia dwells in *algia*, in longing and loss, the imperfect process of remembrance" (41). For Boym, restorative nostalgia is always problematic because it fails to recognize itself as nostalgia, preferring instead to see itself as squarely rooted in the real world of practical politics engaged in the construction of nation- and state-building as home. In other words, restorative nostalgia (as found in most of the neoconservative writings mentioned in the introduction) mistakes itself for politics geared toward the future and not a politics preoccupied by the past. It is a form of looking back that thinks of itself as looking forward. In contrast, reflective nostalgia is more modern because it recognizes the impossibility of return and satisfies itself with exploring the makeshift nature of existence as a contemporary retelling of the *Odyssey* without a possible triumphant reconquest of Ithaca. It is a looking back that, in understanding itself as such, acknowledges uncertainty about what lies ahead.[4]

If this is the case, which kind of nostalgia does Davis engage in when he mourns a future that refused to come to pass and that seems now "preposterous" because it is so remote from being actualized? It is the nature of nostalgia to blur attempts to differentiate too sharply between its possible manifestations. This is so because the concept of home upon which nostalgia relies is a feeling that reassures us "that things are in their places and so are you" (Boym 2001, 251). Such feelings have become things to comment upon because the sense of unremarkable ease of being has been more or less permanently disrupted: "In the late twentieth century, millions of people find themselves displaced from their birthplace, living in voluntary or involuntary exile. Their intimate experiences occur in a foreign background" (Boym 2001, 252). The act of looking back in time, intrinsic to our understanding of nostalgia, is predicated on social conditions of rootlessness, exile, and travel that reflect what appear to be the immutable trends of the future.

The future, as it is currently most vividly imagined, is a place defined by the very conditions of relentless mobility and displacement that make preoccupation with a lost home possible. In trying to make ourselves at home in this future, we cannot make a well-defined distinction between the *act of restoration*, which will render the new lands we occupy places we feel secure in, which provides us with a sense of unremarkable identity, and the *act of reflection*, which sees in these new lands only the loss of any secure identity, which tries to accept the out-of-reach nature of home as a concept necessarily tainted by a look backward. To make ourselves at home in a place is to engage in the re-creation of something we have already lost. Since we cannot, however, re-create a perfect replica of the places we have left behind, we cannot expect to feel at ease in these new lands. Whatever homes we might engineer will always be haunted by an absence of ease. In trying to occupy a future that is not simply the uninterrupted continuation of the past, we are constantly engaged in the restoration of a past and a reflection on the inadequacy of such restorations. We cannot, therefore, say with any degree of certainty whether Davis's invocation of "suburbs on Mars" engages in a desire for a return (restorative nostalgia) or in a critical examination of social structures that have relegated such dreams to a future awash in a patina of impossibility (reflective nostalgia). Like all nostalgia, regardless of how we might qualify its various manifestations, Davis is engaged in both. Science fiction and memoir, speculation about the future and rumination over the past, are inseparable because both are about distance from an unpleasant present.

··· **THE DESIRE TO START OVER**

When we follow Davis's nostalgia-laden thoughts to their touchstones, we discover this inseparability. When Davis writes, "in the rocket summers of my youth," he is explicitly gesturing toward Ray Bradbury's *The Martian Chronicles* (1997 [1946]).[5] The latter book begins: "*Rocket summer*. The words passed among the people in the open, airing houses. *Rocket summer*. The warm desert air changing the frost patterns on the windows, erasing the art work. The skis and sleds suddenly useless. The snow, falling from the cold sky upon the town, turned to a hot rain before it touched the ground" (1). As this passage might suggest, there is already something deeply nostalgic about *The Martian Chronicles*, a collection of loosely related short stories and vignettes that roughly follows the chronology of the human exploration of Mars, its colonization, and its eventual abandonment as conditions on Earth turn toward nuclear self-destruction. The book's opening lines juxtapose images of an idealized small-town America that has literally become frozen in time with the icons of an emergent Space Age that melt this tableau in favor of state-funded vertical propulsion, escape, and radical transformation. This opening passage evokes the desire to blast off to a faraway place and to start all over again even as it looks back wistfully at what has been left behind.

Space travel becomes in the early part of *The Martian Chronicles* an unquestioned marker of futurity, a turning point in the linear evolution of human sophistication from prehistory through the division of labor to the colonization of other planets, even when it also becomes a means of critiquing the failures of such progressive modernity to guarantee the freedoms once enjoyed in an anterior (and retrospectively imagined?) moment. The first half of the book is filled with this double-edged romance of exploration, novel technologies, and, most important of all, settlements on Mars, before turning attention more insistently on the problems of overbureaucratization and total war once these settlements take root. What draws Bradbury, and undoubtedly many of his readers, to the romance of space travel and colonization is the sense of freedom that such expansion promised. Breaking away from the bounded spaces of a self-contained, overpopulated, and delimited planet held out the hope of a greater expansiveness of being, the ability to envision new societies that could correct for the failures of the one in which he and his readers found themselves. Breaking away could mean starting over without the material and ideological constraints that often condition the failures of the old world.

Like postwar suburbanization, space travel promised the possibility of, and ambivalence about, a new start to modernity, an alternative form of technology-driven social formation that would not, but perhaps could, make the same mistakes of the past. We can see this most forcefully in the last story in *The Martian Chronicles*, "The Million-Year Picnic," in which a prototypical nuclear family escapes to a deserted Mars on a rocket ship as Earth concludes a protracted genocidal war that leaves the airwaves empty of any signs of human existence. The family in the story is comprised of a father, a mother, and three sons. At the story's end, they await the arrival of another family with four daughters. As if to reiterate my point, the father tells his sons:

> Life on Earth never settled down to anything very good. Science ran too far ahead of us too quickly, and the people got lost in a mechanical wilderness, like children making over pretty things, gadgets, helicop-

ters, rockets; emphasizing the wrong items, emphasizing machines instead of how to run the machines. Wars got bigger and bigger and finally killed Earth. . . . Now we're alone. We and a handful of others who'll land in a few days. Enough to start over. Enough to turn away from all that back on Earth and to strike out on a new line. (266)

As this passage makes evident, there was a clear and obvious utopian impulse behind Bradbury's interest in space travel, one strongly based on a desire "to start over" when the future made possible by technological advancements proved unsatisfactory. There was also, in this interest, a stinging critique of the materialism of this period, where faith was put into machines that would, in effect, absolve us of responsibility to tend to social relations with one another. At the same time, the strength of this critique necessarily leaves us wondering if perhaps such misplaced faith in machines and things can be shaken off by the catastrophic death of a planet. There is, after all, no guarantee that this family will be able to avoid the mistakes of the past in beginning anew.

Unfortunately, the characteristic blend of utopianism and attendant doubt found in this story, and in many works of science fiction from this era, was shadowed, and occasionally overshadowed, by various expressions of irresponsibility, escapism, adventurism, and outright racism. From P. W. Dooner's *Last Days of the Republic* (1978 [1879]), a late-nineteenth-century recounting of how the Chinese planned and successfully executed an invasion of the United States with their immigrants as an advance secret army, to the pulp serialization of Fu Manchu and Flash Gordon adventures and, beyond, to recent racist novels such as David Wingrove's Chung Kuo series,[6] we find that these unpalatable qualities are often, though not necessarily, integral to the genre of science fiction. At least one of these qualities can be observed in the celebration of space travel as futurity. Subtending this fantasy is a progressive hierarchy that literally replicates the thinking behind scientific racialism: the physiognomic organization of peoples along a fixed chain of human development that supposedly reflects their level of civilization and worth, with the concept of whiteness at the vertex of this development.[7]

From one perspective, we might say that Bradbury rejects such thinking when he portrays the conclusion of this kind of historical linearity in

"The Million-Year Picnic" as the inevitability of mutual assured destruction. But from another perspective, it should be chilling to us to consider how easily Bradbury writes off the death of an entire planet, and vests his hopes for the future on a group of castaways who are upper middle-class, heterosexual, and white. Indeed, the narrator seems to revel in the racialized description of this family. The father is characterized as a "man with the immense hawk nose, sunburnt, peeling—and the hot blue eyes like agate marbles you play with after school in summer back on Earth, and the long thick columnar legs in the loose riding breeches" (258). The mother, on the other hand, is "slender and soft, with a woven plait of spun-gold hair over her head in a tiara, and eyes the color of the deep cool canal water where it ran in shadow, almost purple, with flecks of amber caught in it" (259). Both of these figures are caught in a time warp. They are reminiscent images of an idealized couple more likely found in the illustrations of an Eisenhower-era magazine such as *Collier's* than in the people living next door. At the same time, their physical description accentuates the fact that they are white, in an extremely idealized way, while positioning this fact within a tightly wrought network of associations that pulls the reader back into an imagined past ("like agate marbles you play with after school") and that confuses the nostalgic quality of this past with the physical geography of their alien surroundings ("eyes the color of deep cool canal water"). The Martian landscape becomes a mirror through which we can grasp a mercurial image of a half-remembered and racially idealized past, a place of nostalgia that simultaneously propels us to the future and draws us back in time even as it bears witness to the destructiveness of wanting to start over.

· · · **MARTIAN DREAMING**

It is exactly the mercurial nature of Bradbury's Mars that makes *The Martian Chronicles* at once a hard-to-define work of science fiction and an intriguing allegory of postwar suburbanization (and especially the mass suburbanization of Southern California that took place during this period). There is, without a doubt, a deeply underlying antimodern streak running throughout the breadth of *The Martian Chronicles*, one that seeks, in response to the threats of mutual assured destruction made possible by the Cold War, to reject technology and increasing human complexity. This streak makes Bradbury a strange bedfellow to other science fiction writers of his generation, whose pre–Second World War fascination with the technological and scientific advancement of human societies continued unbounded, if not heightened, in the 1950s. Although technology and science often, and repeatedly, proved fatal to humanity in these other works, there was nevertheless an interest in technology and science that crossed into the territory of an established religion. Whatever the future might hold for the human race in the imagination of these writers, we could not get there without ever more sophisticated machines described in loving and scrupulous detail.

Because Bradbury treats technology and science with less reverence than many of his contemporaries (his space ships, for instance, are detailless abstractions), he acts as a mediating figure between two major strains of mid-twentieth-century science fiction. Scott Bukatman describes the first strain as " 'hard' science fiction of vast technical detail and extrapolative power which dates from the 1930s. . . . Hard science fiction has always demonstrated a disdain for more traditional literary values, and certainly the 'cardboard' characters that people the work of Heinlein and Asimov are not only a part of their charm, but an important aspect of science fiction as a genre of philosophical, rather than psychological, concern" (1993, 138). The second strain, which appeared during the 1960s as a new wave of writers, such as J. G. Ballard, Samuel Delany, and William S. Burroughs, became more interested in exploring the inner space of the mind accessible through hard drugs than the outer space of the physical world accessible through rocket ships. "Within the New Wave's transformation of the genre," Bukatman writes, "the predilection of science fiction for the mapping of alternate worlds and reality became melded with an awareness of, and familiarity with, the experience of hallucinogens— trips of another kind" (139).

Bradbury's mediation between these two strains of midcentury science fiction is important to note. Otherwise, the Martian landscape he so lovingly evokes in *The Martian Chronicles* will make little sense. This landscape is a product of hard science fiction, in the sense that we need rocket ships to get there and other technological accomplishments to survive in its inhospitable climate. At the same time, and more important, the surface of Mars imagined by Bradbury, with its water canals, breathable oxygen, and vanishing aliens, cares little for what scientific research at that time could verify, and it is a flagrant violation of the realism that dominated this genre as one of its chief sources of readerly pleasure. As Bradbury admits in an introduction to his book, "If [*The Martian Chronicles*] had been practical technologically efficient science fiction, it would have long since fallen to rust by the side of the road. But since it is a self-separating fable, even the most deeply rooted physicists at Cal-Tech accept breathing the fraudulent oxygen atmosphere I have loosed on Mars" (1997 [1946], xi). The Martian landscape found in Bradbury's fiction is not meant to correspond to any scientifically knowable place, but is rather a mythical geography. This geography plays upon our fantasies and desires for a new life while simultaneously drawing us back to an idealized, and potentially poisonous, past. Bradbury's Mars centers attention on a then-prevalent ambivalence suffered by mostly white suburb-bound families about the cultural status of home in the postwar years in America. Is home a place we can return to? Isn't home a place of constriction we have actively sought to escape in making ourselves suburban? Can we make a new home for ourselves that doesn't start to resemble the homes that we were running away from?[8]

These questions are electric with anxiety in "The Third Expedition," when those lucky enough to go to Mars as early explorers, settlers, and suburban developers arrive only to discover a simulacrum of what they had left behind in their hometowns in Ohio and other parts of the Midwest. I examine this story somewhat closely here because it contains many of the conflicted emotions associated with the development of Southern California as a preeminent example of postwar suburban nostalgia, at once forward looking and caught in the yearning for the past: "The rocket landed on the lawn of green grass. Outside, upon this lawn, stood an iron deer. Further up on the green stood a tall brown Victorian house, quiet in the sunlight, all covered with scrolls and rococo, its windows made of blue and pink and yellow and green colored glass" (44). Where Bradbury's future explorers come from is important because so many white migrants from the Midwest peopled Southern California during its periods of intense suburban growth before and after the Second World War, re-creating in the semidesert climate of the region, so similar to the semidesert climate of Bradbury's Mars, a simulacrum of the idealized hometowns from which they had fled. Like the early Martian explorers in Bradbury's fiction, settlements in the Los Angeles basin expanded at an explosive rate at the end of the Second World War as a series of centrally planned communities that promised escape from the poverty-ridden, overly restrictive and dull life—underscored by extremes in weather—associated with the Midwest. At the same time, these settlements threatened a re-creation of the restrictions that many had hoped to evade. This is the contradiction that Davis works out at the end of *Ecology of Fear*: "Like his contemporary, Ray Bradbury, whose *The Martian Chronicles* depicted American subdivisions on the red planet, [Chesley] Bonestell [whose futuristic paintings of interplanetary travel became emblematic of the Space Age] dramatized the 1950s moral and imaginative equivalence between the utopia of space conquest and the utopia of suburbia. In his painting, the counterpoint to the ballet of soaring rocket planes is the perfect euclidean geometry of Los Angeles's future suburbs as they probe the desert along the routes of new freeways" (1998, 419). If we take the logic of this passage further, we might begin to think of an imaginary colony on Mars not as the extension of suburban developments plotted out in Los Angeles, as Davis suggests in this passage, but, rather, Los Angeles itself as the prototype of a planned Martian development that attempts to break away from the patterns that mired more traditional forms of urban and rural dwellings.

The gridlike, planned nature of a quickly suburbanizing Los Angeles in the postwar era, evoked so longingly in Davis's remembrance of Bonestell's illustrations and Bradbury's fiction, was a sharp departure from the developments that have characterized the growth of urban areas in the east, and the model upon which Bradbury imagined colonization of Mars. As Greg Hise points out, "Through institutions such as the Urban Land Institute and the Community Builders' Council, mass builders forged a regional vision; they thought in terms of a coordinated metropolitan system, a network of integrated communities. They did not dichotomize the urban landscape into a core and periphery, a city and suburb" (1997, 11). The critical task that this observation sets out for us is to find a vocabulary that can capture the complexities of a cityscape that, starting from the postwar period but with important continuities with past experimentation in housing and civil engineering, is such a sharp departure from the cityscapes associated with Europe and the East Coast. In Los Angeles, the growth of suburban developments that trailed behind the ex-urbanization of white-collar work led to the disappearance of a traditional core. Thus, a city without a core cannot be said to have a periphery. Hise is especially adamant on this point: growth that appears "as unplanned, chaotic sprawl" is in fact "the product of a planned dispersion of jobs, housing, and services throughout metropolitan regions" (4). Suburban growth was not simply predicated on white flight and middle-class rejection of traditional forms of urban living for an idealized melding of country and city. It was also significantly led by the movement of jobs outside whatever might pass as the center of a traditional city in Los Angeles and a state-funded system of transportation that took advantage of the already decentralized nature of work, housing, and shopping facilitated by the now-defunct interurban railways. Bedroom communities sprung up near these new places of work even as work moved to follow the outflux of white-collar employees.

Such a dance of work and employee migration has led, in the intervening years since the publication of *The Martian Chronicles*, to the formation of what Joel Garreau calls "edge cities."⁹ Edge cities, according to Garreau, are created by corporations who follow their workers out into previously undeveloped land, where they can operate cheaper and closer to their employees. In the process, new urban centers form that are more spatially spread out and dependent on the automobile than were previous urban centers. Hise understandably criticizes Garreau for making such "ahistorical" claims (1991, 215). Garreau is often oblivious in his prose to growth that has been intensely planned for, thought out, and realized in a carefully laid-out logic of spatial expansiveness, infrastructure construction, and infilling that often preceded by decades the actual growth of the communities which they were designed to support. Often, according to Hise, the planning for such spatial expansiveness was conducted with the blessing of corporations who immediately perceived the benefits of moving their offices and workplaces out of traditional urban centers. However, while certain parts of Southern California and later other regions of the United States followed this model of development—the city of Irvine in Orange County is perhaps the most salient example—there were other parts of Southern California that have grown without such planning and that have certainly not been as well managed as Irvine. And even for Irvine, planning has not prevented overdevelopment, environmental deterioration, and clogged roadways. Edge cities are not new because they have no important models in the past or because they have sprung up out of nothing. They are new because they create problems that are hard to predict and even harder to resolve. The development of edge cities could have been anticipated when the first plans for an extensive system of interstate highways were drafted—and could even have been seen in Los Angeles with the expansive urban development enabled by its early twentieth-century system of streetcars. At the same time, edge cities develop along their own lines of logic that refuse to conform to the logic of their utopian developers.[10]

The emergent postwar Southern California cityscape was, and continues to be, dispersed, resistant to generalization, and full of the capacity to remake itself continually according to the pressure of capital investments.[11] Like the blank matrices found in many popular science fiction movies about virtual reality (as in, most recently, *The Matrix* [1999] and its sequels), the gridlike structure of Southern California acts as a near-invisible staging ground for the performance of nostalgia and is therefore aptly reminiscent of the all-purpose semidesert climate of Bradbury's Mars. Nostalgia itself is a kind of distraction that draws attention away from the invisible grids of capital flows, pursuit of jobs, and maximization of profit upon which such nostalgia is based. In the landscape, we see shimmering before us the pursuit of half-realized, indistinct, and evanescent figures that remind us, perhaps, of something we have lost. It is an expressive urban environment of dreamy wonder that can hide the deeply entrenched hierarchies of social and economic inequity, concentrations of power, and the manipulation of desire that helped to transform a climate devoid of water, prone to natural disasters, and distant from the nation's traditional centers of power into the second-largest city in the United States.

If this is so, and we decide to interpret Davis's dark prognosis of the poorly worn "imagined futures" of his youth through Bradbury's fiction, what we discover is that these imagined futures have actually come to pass: Los Angeles is Mars's substitute, a ready example of what can be accomplished if we are allowed to start over in a new land far away from the restrictions that have defined where we have come from. Simultaneously, in accordance with the tenets of the era that gave us both the Space Age and mass suburbanization, what we find in Bradbury's fiction is the presence of the state as a central engine of change. It is the state—centralized, powerful, coordinating, paranoid—that accelerated the race into space, built powerful rockets that could propel men into orbit and propel missiles carrying nuclear warheads to the other side of the planet, constructed the superhighways enabling the fulfillment of the spatial dispersal imagined by developers, and made contingency plans for the destruction of the planet in a game of nuclear brinkmanship.

What is disappointing in *The Martian Chronicles*, however, is that Los Angeles-as-Mars has turned out to be too much like the rest-of-the-United-States-as-Earth its inhabitants had hoped to leave behind. What the explorers in "The Third Expedition" discover is that the simulacrum of home re-created for their benefit on Mars is only that, an illusion: "Suppose these houses are really some *other* shape, a Martian shape, but by playing on my desires and wants, these Martians have made this seem like my old home town, my old house, to lull me out of my suspicions. What better way to fool a man, using his own mother and father as bait? And this town, so old, from the year 1956, long before *any* of the men were born" (1997 [1946], 63). The early explorers to Mars in this story are almost of the same generation who imagined they would explore Mars and reshape it into their own image, as Davis tells us many young boys of his generation imagined they would someday get to do. What makes this story and the many others in *The Martian Chronicles* unique is the way this desire to escape Earth and to start anew someplace else also draws upon a reservoir of nostalgia. What we desire as new, to put it another way, cannot escape the pool of associations and ideals that we already collectively know as a fictive place called the past.

Interestingly, "The Third Expedition" ends as a chilling but predictable Cold War allegory (reminiscent of the 1956 classic *Invasion of the Body Snatchers*): "And wouldn't it be horrible and terrifying to discover that all of this was part of some great clever plan by the Martians to divide and conquer us, and kill us? Sometime during the night, perhaps, my brother here on this bed will change, melt, shift, and become another thing, a terrible thing, a Martian. It would be very simple for him just to turn over in bed and put a knife into my heart" (1997 [1946], 64). This ending can be read as a subtle commentary on the history of the political and social climate that gave birth to our contemporary notions of Southern California. This history cannot be restricted to one region or nation. Interpreted from the perspective of the Cold War, and its many skirmishes in East and Southeast Asia, this passage starts to sound much like a warning against U.S. adventures abroad, where we might come into contact with natives who appear friendly and who pretend to share our values but who will stab us in our sleep if we let our guard down. This was a real enough threat at the height of the Cold War, as the United States increasingly found itself having to negotiate a more complex terrain of foreign relations in which friends and foes were hard to differentiate.

It did not help, of course, that American diplomats were, like the men in "The Third Expedition," often guided by their own assumptions about what everyone else would want, namely, to be just like them. As one of the explorers in Bradbury's story exclaims at the prospect of being stuck in a foreign place such as Mars, "If there was any way of reproducing every plant, every road, every lake, and even an ocean, I'd do so. Then by some vast crowd hypnosis I'd convince everyone in a town this size that this really was Earth, not Mars at all" (1997 [1946], 53). As the port of choice after the Second World War that linked the continental United States to Asia, Los Angeles could easily be imagined as a place of threat, at once a part of the United States and at the same time a part of another extraterritorial region, which we now call the Pacific Rim, with interests that might not converge with the rest of the nation's. This is especially underscored by the fact that the midcentury growth of Los Angeles was sustained through a "series of Pacific Wars—the Second World War, the Korean War, Vietnam—that propelled the Los Angeles region into a primary position within what President Dwight D. Eisenhower would call, warning people of its power, the American 'military-industrial complex'" (Scott and Soja 1996, 9). At the same time, the "Second World War and the Korean War were periods of intensified social tensions that brought back to the surface the long history of white American racism and xenophobia in Los Angeles" (Scott and Soja 1996, 9). The city might resemble places like the burgeoning outskirts of New York and Chicago, but it was also eerily different in its newness, layout, and geopolitical importance, giving rise to a reaction to growth that manifested itself in the form of internal racial purges, such as the Zoot Suit Riots of 1942 and the evacuation of Japanese Americans to concentration camps after the issuance of Executive Order 9066 in the same year. The question arises, Were our settlers in Southern California re-creating what they had left behind, or were they being infiltrated by aliens secretly plotting something else that we could not penetrate because of their guise of familiarity? Even the settlers themselves seemed unsure during this period about how to answer this question.

As in my reading of "The Million-Year Picnic," I insist that the future "The Third Expedition" is concerned with is also an Anglo one that cares little about the fate of other racial groups. Since all the characters in "The Third Expedition" are clearly white, and the town they discover on Mars is a re-creation of an idealized small-town America populated exclusively by all the signs and symbols of whiteness in the United States, especially visible to us because these signs and symbols are powerfully associated in our contemporary minds within the temporal domain of the 1950s (Brown 1995, 61), we need to wonder who the native Martians are who have taken on the familiar signs of the settlers in the story and who are secretly plotting their demise? In addressing this question, I wish to note that all the stories in *The Martian Chronicles* imagine Mars itself as already a settled, but dilapidated, land. Like the myth of Spanish mission California, Mars in Bradbury's imagination is populated by only a few of its original inhabitants—vanishing ancient natives and a more recent congregation of disappearing indigenes whose differences are situated conceptually somewhere between the ancients and the newest arrivals—and is littered with the artifacts of a civilization that is now in permanent ruin.[12]

What the early white settlers to Mars discover, to put it plainly, is the exact racial geography that supposedly greeted the early settlers of Southern California: vanishing American Indians and a mestizo Californio population whose rule was long past its ascendancy. The ruins belonging to both groups act in California history as a quaint local background for the serious business of constructing a new society. As such, the Martian landscape can be celebrated by Bradbury's characters much in the same way as Southern California's nostalgia-imbued past can be celebrated by the descendants of its Anglo settlers. Carey McWilliams, one of the shrewdest historians of this region, observed the same year *The Martian Chronicles* appeared in print: "All attempted revivals of Spanish folkways in Southern California are similarly ceremonial and ritualistic, a part of the sacred rather than profane life of the region. . . . The residents of Santa Barbara firmly believe, of course, that the Spanish past is dead, extinct, vanished. In their thinking, the Mexicans living in Santa Barbara have no connection with this past. They just happen to be living in Santa Barbara" (1983 [1946], 82–83). What Bradbury could not imagine, however, when he penned his stories in the immediate postwar era, was how radically Los Angeles and the rest of Southern California would change demographically in the next five decades. The presumption of Anglo dominance that is present everywhere in his stories no longer holds true in the more mature metropolis of Los Angeles, when the utopianism of postwar suburban planning has become a nightmare of containment, spatial segregation, and resettlement—what Davis calls, above, the signature of a "funeral decade."

· · · **NEGATIVE SPACE**

It is important *not* to see the gradual transformation of rhetoric from nostalgic utopianism to funeral decade as applying uniformly to all who live in this region. Because this utopianism explicitly sought to create new, integrated, and fully rationalized habitations of housing, work, and shopping for *whites*—repackaging a fictive past in the process to sell mostly Anglo homebuyers on the desirability of suburban living and making "Los Angeles the most segregated city in the country" by the mid-1960s (Fulton 1997, 10)—nonwhite Angelenos found themselves occupying the negative spaces of the city to which planners and developers had not yet turned their attention in the 1960s and 1970s. In *Always Running, La Vida Loca: Gang Days in L.A.*, Luis Rodriguez's emotionally difficult memoir of his days as a member of a Chicano gang in the Lomas neighborhood during these years, we are offered a vivid description of one of these negative spaces:

> Unincorporated county territories were generally where the poorest people lived, the old barrios, which for the most part didn't belong to any city because nobody wanted them. Most of Watts and East Los Angeles were unincorporated county territory. Sometimes they had no sewage system, or paved roads. . . . In the mid-60s, South San Gabriel included both flat areas and what we called the Hills, or *Las Lomas*. . . . The Hills were unseen. Cars flew past north of here on the San Bernardino Freeway into Los Angeles, but most of the drivers never imagined such a place existed, a place you could have found in the Ozarks or the hills of Tijuana. (1993, 38–39)

The negative spaces on a developer's map of Los Angeles did not recognize the existence of the communities that had formed in them, but rather, like Rodriguez's imagined drivers on the San Bernardino Freeway, ignored the presence of those who made a home there and, without much thought, marked such places for future development. As the various established communities were shaped, and major highways linked them to one another, a process of infilling occurred in the later years that *Always Running* recounts. This process continued to build the gridlike zones of habitation that defined the rationalized spaces of white Los Angeles, and with the help of new capital from other places pushed those living in these negative spaces into more rigidly defined and embanked communities of exclusion. "New tract homes," Rodriguez writes, "suddenly appeared on previously empty space or by displacing the barrios. In later years, large numbers of Asians from Japan, Korea and Taiwan also moved into the area. . . . The areas that weren't incorporated, including Las Lomas, became self-contained and forbidden, incubators of rebellion which the local media, generally controlled by suburban whites, labeled havens of crime" (41).

The developments rapidly altering the look of the city during these decades both resembled suburban growth in the rest of the country and at the same time represented a departure from the patterns that defined this growth. As Nayan Shah points out, in San Francisco, a similar kind of segregation and containment of nonwhites occurred earlier in the century, resulting in similar kinds of race relations: "The rationale of nuisance law underwrote the cultural logic of residential covenants. In the upper-middle-class residential developments, real estate developers defined the public good narrowly. . . . In contrast to the mixed-use heterogeneity of older districts such as Chinatown, the new residential districts sought to create a homogeneous, bucolic world by denying entrance to 'undesirable neighbors' and strictly controlling the appearance and type of buildings constructed" (2001, 72). Just as in early twentieth-century San Francisco, Los Angeles was also constructed with the same "cultural logic" of hygiene, rationalization, and control—the complexity of which we explored at some length above in our discussion of Bradbury. The suburban developments that began to appear in corporate boardrooms before the Second World War, modeled on what already existed in Southern California, intentionally sought to re-create a pastoral ideal of stand-alone houses sitting on top of perfectly defined green rectangles, outfitted with the latest conveniences in home technology, each street and row of houses resembling the next, with cosmetic variations in height and facade, all of which were constructed along ruler-straight lines that curlicued into pointless cul-de-sacs and were emptied of those who might taint this ideal. Suburban developers were literally answering the call to start over by tearing down old neighborhoods and decimating fragile ecosystems in the relentless pursuit of an ideal.

The difference, however, between a place such as San Francisco and Los Angeles is that the former had a long-established downtown area while postwar Los Angeles began with a suburban ideal in mind. This means that for developers in San Francisco, rationalization entailed the expulsion of older, less maintained, nonwhite communities from the city's borders (as successive but failed attempts by politicians and labor unions to remove Chinatown from San Francisco's city borders suggest) and the growth of suburban developments outward in concentric circles from the newly rehabilitated center. In this way, San Francisco resembled the growth of an older, more established city such as Boston, which has for a long time been known as "the Hub" for its clearly defined wheel-spoke shape if not also for its anachronistic pretensions of being the cultural center of the country. Los Angeles, however, had long before dispensed with its traditional center, making the territory defined by the city limits over time a patchwork of negative and rationalized spaces.[13] From the early twentieth century, Los Angeles development was spatially dispersed, with multiple centers of business and social activities, each center in turn remaining semiautonomous from the others, and suburban growth spread out from these centers to run into one another in the not-yet incorporated negative spaces that provided the room for developers to practice their trade. When infilling no longer became possible, new centers of work and shopping would emerge in the deserts and farmlands surrounding Los Angeles, and the process would continue. The metaphor of center and periphery, or any conceptualization of Southern California's urban space founded on such a neat dichotomy, does not therefore make sense. From the start of the twentieth century, during its first wave of population growth, the region of greater Los Angeles was conceived of as a suburban whole, an array of planned communities intentionally without a traditional urban core. There are, therefore, only rationalized spaces and negative spaces, with some rationalized spaces suffering from urban blight. The contrapuntal movement of nonwhites and the economically enfranchised set off, during the years in which *Always Running* is set, a vicious cycle of capital flight, white-collar work dispersal, and property devaluation, and as a result led such formally rationalized spaces to lapse into negativity. These were rationalized again years later by disaffected suburbanite youths, now grown into adulthood, and followed by more middle-class professionals, some of whom were recent immigrants from Asia—all in a craze of gentrification.

··· **PROPERTY AND VIOLENCE**

The narrative of *Always Running* dramatizes what life was like for the forgotten and displaced populations that inhabited these increasingly self-contained, and spatially more gerrymandered, negative spaces—the spaces, in other words, necessarily outside the cultural logic of progress, reflection, and starting over—and is thus an important corrective to the seductive play of the Anglo imagination found in Bradbury's planetary metaphor of postwar suburbanization. The most important characteristics of this life are property and violence. The early part of *Always Running* is structured by these characteristics, as the narrator relates how the narrator's life was constrained by the need to respect the racial boundary between rationalized and negative spaces. As a child, Rodriguez recalls, his mother took his siblings to a park; when they sat at a bench to rest, an "American" woman and her children reproached them for occupying space that did not, in her mind, rightly belong to them. "Look spic, you can't sit there!" the woman tells them. "You don't belong here! Understand? This is not your country!" (1993, 19). The verbal violence of this encounter is followed, in another scene from his early childhood, by physical violence when Rodriguez and his brother venture across the train tracks that define their (non)place in Los Angeles from the places belonging to their white, working-class neighbors: "'What do we got here?' one of the [white] boys said. 'Spics to order—maybe with some beans?' He pushed me to the ground; the groceries splattered onto the asphalt. I felt melted gum and chips of broken beer bottle on my lips and cheek. Then somebody picked me up and held me while the others seized my brother, tossed his groceries out, and pounded on him. They punched him in the face, in the stomach, then his face again, cutting his lips, causing him to vomit" (1993, 24–25). Finally, in another scene, Rodriguez and a friend sneak into their school's basketball court for a late-night half-court game, only to be interrupted a short time later by the arrival of the police. Their access to this semipublic space has thus been restricted. When they try to run away, the officers give chase, which tragically results in the death of Rodriguez's friend when the latter falls through a rooftop skylight (1993, 37). All three of these examples demonstrate the violence emanating from all levels of social control, from the informality of interpersonal expressions of racism to the formalized enforcement of property boundaries by the police, that disciplined Rodriguez and his cohorts, keeping them separate from the rationalized spaces of postwar white Los Angeles and shutting them out from the expansive freedom that others, not so racially marked, enjoyed.

Given the corollary cultural logic at work in these three examples, the necessary exclusions that seem to attend yearnings for ideals, it should be no wonder that the children growing up in racially restrictive negative spaces respond by forming gangs. These gangs, as Rodriguez understands them, replicate the logic of property rights and the need for their violent protection by anchoring membership to geography. As gang membership becomes more mature in *Always Running*, evolving from simple protective cliques that Chicano boys (and to a lesser extent girls) formed to protect themselves from the violence that swirls all around them in grade school, the gangs themselves consolidate into two dominant organizations in their neighborhood: the Sangras, who occupy the plains, and the Lomas, who represent the residents on the Hill. In a play that Rodriguez writes in school, as he becomes more politicized through involvement with community activists and self-study groups, he reveals an impressive awareness of how much the territorialism of these groups replicates the overarching logic of property rights that marks all of their lives. Even as these gangs seek to take informal ownership of land through imitative violence, this overarching logic continues its relentless drive to rationalize, and take away, this very territory: "The play begins with someone from Sangra crossing out Lomas on a huge piece of white paper pasted on the wall. Then the action moved toward a point when the dudes from both neighborhoods go at each other. The upshot is as the two barrios fight, local government officials are on the side determining the site of a new mall or where the next freeway will go while making plans to uproot the very land the dudes were killing each other for" (1993, 177). Ironically, no one wants to play the part of the Sangra who will initiate the plot of the play by crossing out a Lomas symbol. Even as the play reveals the ways in which gang conflict reenacts a larger logic of spatial segregation that only symbolically vests members of conflicting gangs with a sense of ownership, the importance of this sense of ownership is such a powerful force in their lives that to pretend to disrespect the self-enforced rights of another group risks actual violence.

While *Always Running* makes abundantly clear that logic predicated on property rights and violent protectiveness of these rights is at work throughout the different layers of social interaction it narrates, property rights themselves are predicated in this book on racial demarcations. Common ownership of public spaces still exists, though this too slowly erodes during the course of the memoir, but common ownership is restricted to membership in a particular race. Those without the requisite racial markers and the willingness to engage in violence are severely reprimanded for trespassing on such communal public spaces. We see this in the examples just given, when Rodriguez and his family are forcibly removed from park, street, and schoolyard, all public spaces that belong to, are under the control of, and are heavily regulated by a logic of power founded on the prerogatives of whiteness. The rise of Sangra and Lomas in the book, then, appears as an imitative reaction, their territorialism following the same model of communal ownership and violent protectiveness as found in the overarching structures of power that define their lives. But because the rise of such gangs is founded on powerlessness, the violence gang members have learned from those in dominance is not turned against the dominant but is instead directed against each other. This understandable response re-forms a set of vindictive relations that parallels but does not attack, or question, the prevailing cultural logic of dominance, namely, the equivalence of property with violence. Thus, I want to insist that to view gangs as somehow intrinsically embodying a resistance to power and race oppression is to romanticize their social limitations, for these gangs (at least in Rodriguez's memoir) seem to replicate—primarily because they can do little else—the same cultural logic that leaves them powerless and oppressed.

At the same time, this refusal to read resistance insists that the cultural logic dictating the lives of the youths depicted in *Always Running* cannot be separated from the same cultural logic shaping the cultural and spatial imaginary of white Los Angeles. Rather, their behavior reflects back to us the pathology of violence and racial segregation that underlie the drive toward rationalization motivating postwar developers. Rodriguez, in other words, never lets us forget the violence—often predicated on normative gendered identities—that is required to maintain such segregation. The police, especially, are the most visible agents of this violence: "In the barrio, the police are just another gang. . . . Sometimes they come up to us while we linger on a street corner and tell us Sangra called us *chavalas*, a loose term for girls. Other times, they approach dudes from Sangra and say Lomas is a tougher gang and Sangra is nothing. Shootings, assaults and skirmishes between the barrios are direct results of police activity" (1993, 72). Under the guise of a utopia pursued, the forces of rationalization depend on deeply ingrained relations of power and violence to demarcate the rational from the irrational. Upon closer inspection, then, what seems irrational is actually shaped by the same reason that reigns over the rest of suburban Los Angeles. What seems like disjuncture is, in fact, contiguity.

Only later in *Always Running* do we begin to see a glimmer of an alternative way of thinking that seeks, haltingly and with uncertain footing, to reverse the polarity of values that victimizes the lives of Rodriguez and his friends. In the second half of the book, we encounter the rise of identity-based political activists who are involved in the antiwar movement, who return after college to the places where they have grown up to run community-based organizations, and who begin to channel the self-destructive energy of Chicano youths toward artistic expression and student protest. Chente Ramirez, a young activist who runs a community center in the neighborhood, exerts a special influence on Rodriguez, encouraging the latter to quit drugs, to return to school, and to study with a group interested in revolutionary theory. This study group explicitly expresses a desire to resist the cultural logic shaping its members' lives. "The group aimed to train a corps of leaders," the narrator explains. "Unlike others in the Chicano Movement who strove to *enter* the American capitalist system, it prepared for a fundamental reorganization of society" (1993, 184). As naive, perhaps, as such sentiments might appear at the other end of the civil rights era—when the protection of what gains we have made in terms of access to heath care and higher education, the curtailment of police powers, and greater electoral involvement seem almost beyond our collective reach, despite how marginal and incomplete these gains have been—Rodriguez's involvement in this group sets off a chain of self-transformative events. It leads him to become politically active in school, to pursue his artistic ambitions, and to challenge the authority of the Lomas's leaders in the hopes of brokering, and then maintaining, a truce between the gangs. When this truce breaks down after a suspicious drive-by shooting of two Lomas gang members (a shooting, it is suggested by the narrator, perpetrated by the police to prevent the two gangs from ending their self-destructive feuding), Rodriguez argues before his fellow Lomas, "We have to use our brains. . . . We have to think about who's our real enemy. The dudes in Sangra are just like us, man" (1993, 208). Although Rodriguez is punched in the face for saying this, and ultimately fails in his attempt to stop a planned act of retribution, the fact that he could articulate such an argument suggests the possibility of undoing a cultural equation that leaves so many of the author's friends emotionally scarred, physically injured, and dead.

Another example from *Always Running* dramatically illustrates the complex nature of the intellectual work Chente and his fellow activists perform in reversing the destructive polarity of values found in the lives lived in their community. As we have seen, a significant way in which Rodriguez learned his place in Los Angeles's power structure was through his forceful exclusion from public spaces. On 29 August 1970, Rodriguez relates, protesters, organized by activists and angered by the fact that the Vietnam War has claimed a disproportionate number of Latino lives, march on Laguna Park "in the heart of the largest community of Mexicans outside of Mexico" (1993, 161). The march claims the kind of right to public spaces that Rodriguez and his family has been denied throughout the book. Instead of protecting territory from other Chicanos, this moment revels in an oppositional cultural logic that seeks to free up the spaces that have become semiprivatized by race, and to engage in a form of civic involvement that is an alternative to the power taking that has led to the self-destructiveness of the Sangra and Lomas feud. Unsurprisingly, the forces of the state intervene, revealing in the ensuing melee the investment that the state itself maintains in preventing just such a form of civic engagement: "A deputy in a feverish tone shouted for me to move. '*Chale*, this is my park.' Before I knew it, officers drove my face into the dirt; there was a throbbing in my head where a black jack had been swung. On the ground, drops of red slid over the blades of grass. The battle of Laguna Park had started" (162).

Even as this scene is rendered to us as a clearly defined struggle between organic intellectuals exerting changes in political thought among a disenfranchised population and an impersonal state interested in maintaining the prevailing dominant values, it should be kept in mind that these intellectuals could not have done their work without the help of the state. "New government programs," Rodriguez notes, "existed then for agencies like the Bienvenidos Community Center, which ran the youth center; Chente tapped into some of these funds to provide Lomas its first and only recreational facility" (1993, 146). With one hand, the state provides the limited means by which intellectuals such as Chente could do their work with a community that receives little from the state, and it is under the cover of these means that such intellectuals struggle to challenge the underlying logic lending the state its conservationist stability. At the same time, the state exerts an even greater pressure on the same community through heavy-handed modes of policing, surveillance, and containment that willingly resort to violence to keep people literally in their places. The state is at once a possible facilitator of change and, more the case in *Always Running*, a repressive defender of the status quo. As we enter the 1980s, the glimmer of state tolerance for community autonomy offered by Rodriguez's memories of his youth becomes extinguished as the state itself, guided by neoconservative ideas, turns more and more to its police and juridical apparatuses to quell social disquiet.

··· **CAPITAL EVAPORATION**

In 1985, Mayor Bradley appointed an impressive group of civic experts to study the city of Los Angeles and formulate a vision for what it might become within the next fifteen years. Their final report, submitted in 1988, is a slick document with beautiful graphics and an attention to style that is more reminiscent of a fashion magazine than a government-sponsored report. LA 2000: *A City for the Future* articulates a promise: Los Angeles will become a future multicultural metropolis that prospers because of its position at the crossroads of North America, Latin America, and the Asian Pacific.[14] In the tradition of rhetoric espoused by prior city officials and business leaders, this document engages in the fantasy of starting over. It promises that through proper management and a massive infusion of capital from Japan and the newly industrialized countries of East Asia, Los Angeles could become a city that would define the brave new world of an increasingly global economy, a privileged nodal point in a vast regional trading bloc that would circle around the peripheries of the Pacific Ocean and that would magically produce wealth wherever the new transnational productive capital passed through. The dream of a postwar white Los Angeles, so lovingly captured in the pages of *The Martian Chronicles*, gives way in the pages of this report to the official acceptance of a particular corporate-led multiculturalism. The face of the future, it seems, was to become demographically heterogeneous to reflect the changing nature of capital influx, but oddly at the same time homogeneous in that the various ethnic (and not racial) groups would occupy the same clearly defined and regularized mosaic of respected, and mutually recognized, boundaries.

While the disparity between the rich and poor, suburban "sprawl," and environmental degradation figure largely in their assessment of the city's problems, the report's authors are adamant that strong economic growth would be a guaranteed cornerstone of efforts to combat such urban plagues. What makes officially multicultural Los Angeles a place of diversity without conflict, to put it simply, is affluence. The authors provide three reasons why Los Angeles's economy would continue to experience exponential growth: "First, Los Angeles is the largest aerospace center in the world, with more high-tech industries, scientists, engineers, mathematicians and technicians than any other place in the United States; Second, Los Angeles has many craft industries—for example, motion pictures, fashion, and automotive design; Third, industries that rely on an abundant supply of entry level workers find the Los Angeles labor force attractive" (*LA 2000* 1988, 60). On the one hand, the report could be surprisingly candid about the disturbing inequalities defining Southern California's economy: "Los Angeles is rapidly becoming a bimodal society as the number of mid-level jobs fails to keep up, widening the disparity between high-skill, high-paying jobs and low-skill, low-paying jobs. At the same time, we are seeing a widening gap between the rich and the poor in the quality of health care, education, and housing" (1988, 20). On the other hand, the report is quick to minimize such disparities in its vision of the future. By building more roads and increasing commercial rail traffic between the ocean and the rest of the state, by improving schools and providing more money for better police protection, by attracting new corporate investments (especially from Japan and other parts of East Asia) and promoting cleaner fuels, by sponsoring more civic arts events and creating venues for celebrating the region's unparalleled diversity, the city of Los Angeles could make it possible for its urban poor to share in the wealth of an ever-expanding economy. Thus united, the report promises, the city would proceed into a new era of multicultural prosperity. Even the apparent widening of the gap between rich and poor was cause for optimism, since it created a large pool of cheap labor that would attract manufacturing to the region.

Just as these promises were delivered to Mayor Bradley in handsomely bound duplicate volumes, something perverse occurred in the region's economy. Southern California began to feel the effects of the Cold War's end with the onset of a severe economic collapse. Major industrial plants run by long-established companies, which had done so much in the previous decades to move the working class into a semblance of middle-class affluence, began to close. By the time the riots began in 1992, Los Angeles was in the worst recession since the Great Depression, in part led by a mass reduction of manufacturing jobs within the aerospace industry. The group most harshly affected by these job losses were the Latino and black residents of South Los Angeles who were living near the traditional industrial zones of the city. By 1990, "approximately one in three South Central residents lived in a household with an income below the official poverty line, a rate over twice that for the county as a whole. In 1990, only 59 percent of adults (ages 20–64) in South Central worked, a figure 16 percent lower than the rate for the county" (K. Park 1999, 63). Even when the economy began to recover in the early 1990s, most of the jobs created were service related. Such jobs usually paid less than $25,000 a year; barely one in ten new jobs paid more than $60,000 a year (Valle and Torres 2000, 6).

With the collapse of government spending on defense in the late 1980s, coupled with the movement of many manufacturing jobs overseas in search of cheaper labor, Southern California had to rely on its other industries to reverse a disastrous, and unexpected, economic trend. In Los Angeles, this meant a reliance on the increasingly technology-dependent business of manufacturing culture—movies, music, fashion, industrial design—for an increasingly global clientele, and the labor-intensive business of manufacturing garments in ethnically marked sweatshops and the flipping of burgers in fast-food restaurants. The first kind of businesses were staffed by highly educated and well-paid professionals, who lived in segregated preplanned communities in the suburban hinterlands of greater Los Angeles, while the second kind of businesses were staffed by a large influx of new immigrants willing, or more likely forced by circumstance, to work for little. Just as the report delivered to Mayor Bradley in 1988 predicted, when the production of war machines was being (temporarily as it now seems to be turning out) deescalated in the economy, what remained were craft and service. The first provided a life of leisure for the predominantly white upper middle-class suburbanites of the West Side and the relatively new developments surrounding the city, who were spatially set apart from those caught in the older, dilapidated, and increasingly isolated suburbs of South Los Angeles and the Inland Empire (Riverside and San Bernardino counties, and also the eastern tip of Los Angeles county). The residents of the latter places often found themselves incapable of escaping a life of hard work, politically despised for their structurally regulated destitution, and victimized by deteriorating social services. These conditions were exacerbated by the continued effects of Proposition 13, which prohibited the city and state from increasing property taxes without a two-thirds majority.

To make matters worse, the racial hysteria that gripped California in the wake of the riots led to a series of civil rights setbacks: in 1994, passage of Proposition 187 would have deprived—if it had been upheld in the courts—undocumented immigrants of basic social services, such as health care and education; in 1996, the passage of Proposition 207 ended affirmative action in the state, depriving many African Americans and Latinos access to, among other things, the institutions of higher education their tax dollars help fund; and in 1998, Proposition 227 ended bilingual education in California's public schools. Not only were those working in the service economy increasingly separated from the wealthy, spatially and financially, the law institutionalized social mechanisms for strengthening such separations. Wealthy suburbanites had literally voted to secede from the poor.

Economic recovery, it seems, did not fully inter the fears generated by recession, rioting, and growing demographic diversity. Instead, many who belong to a professional-managerial class grew more paranoid and aggrieved. "For the first time since the thirties," Norman Klein notes, "with the debacle in aerospace, the Anglo middle class was hit harder by a downturn than the rest of the country. The resulting anger seemed confirmed by images of white neighborhoods like West Hollywood being looted in 1992. The anger has contributed to a drop in real-estate prices, up to 60 percent in areas even faintly associated with the 'Riots,' cavernous drops in neighborhoods that did not participate, and are not necessarily more dangerous than others, but look poor" (1997, 118). The result of such feelings and of the proposed voter initiatives that gave such feelings statutory form was the undermining of the state's role as the central engine of prosperity that LA 2000 implicitly endorses. The state became in the years after the Los Angeles riots less a tool for properly managing the city, providing necessary social services, and planning for an equitable future, and more a regime of incarceration, retributive justice, and increased surveillance. All throughout the 1980s and 1990s, residents of the city of Los Angeles could read the signs of this regime in the many police helicopters hovering overhead, disturbing their sleep with their circling noise and bright spotlights.

The year 1992 might thus be seen as a flash point in the concretion of Greater Los Angeles's "bimodal" political economy and in the rising commitment to a police state that would patrol the boundaries of this economy. By the time a Simi Valley jury acquitted the four police officers in the videotaped beating of Rodney King (discussed at greater length in the next chapter), South Los Angeles was ripe with understandable economic grievances. Many, especially young men, who had been gainfully employed in relatively high-paying industrial jobs, were out of work. What remained was service-sector employment attractive only to the newest and poorest arrivals, who had little choice but to occupy the economic niches made available to them, especially if these arrivals lacked proper documentation. At the same time, the other kinds of jobs were reserved for the most educated, and many residents of South Los Angeles were so poorly educated in deteriorating, underfunded, and overcrowded schools that some—like Rodney King—could not even read. Furthermore, residents were politically disenfranchised, especially the many newly arrived Salvadorans and Guatemalans who had just escaped U.S.-sponsored political terror in their home countries (Hamilton and Chinchilla 2001, 30–33). Illegal activities were often the only possible avenues for living out the fantasy of escape from such conditions and illicit drugs a powerful way to self-medicate the depression such conditions inflamed. At the same time, such activities, even at a time when criminality was quantifiably on the wane, became the rationale for the construction of more jails and tougher sentencing guidelines. By the time a crowd had gathered at Normandie and Florence to protest the Rodney King verdict on 29 April, LA 2000's worst fears seemed to have already become reality for many South Los Angelenos, and the bright future it and its many predecessors had promised far out of reach. Like the rain that never ceases in Ridley Scott's *Blade Runner* (1982), the loss of so many jobs in a short period of time seemed an improbable happenstance of nature: what would Los Angeles be without its sunshine and its always dependable economy?

If we can, for a moment, try to re-create the mood created by such a freakish economic downturn among the residents of Southern California, the near future that Cynthia Kadohata's *In the Heart of the Valley of Love* evokes does not seem as unlikely as it might first appear. Set in the year 2050, when demographers predict the United States will no longer have a white majority, this novel envisions a future America that looks much like the recession-gripped Los Angeles of the years before and immediately after the riots. The planned-for civic projects by the state have been permanently put on hold; the government has become an alien force in the lives of most of the nation's residents, hassling and arresting those it deems suspicious with a startling disregard for any concept of due process; the rich have become as remote and untouchable as the agents of the state, shutting themselves off into spatially differentiated suburbs; and, most ominous of all, finance capital itself has disappeared. "Before everything ran out of money," the narrator Francie relates, "back at the beginning of the [twenty-first] century, the government had started to build something in Southern California called the Sunshine System, an ambitious series of highways and freeways that would link the whole area and eliminate traffic jams. They never finished the Sunshine though, and the truncated roads arched over the landscape like half of concrete rainbows. . . . We snuck up an abandoned rainbow and leaned over the edge where a road abruptly stopped. We felt as if we'd reached the end of the world" (1992, 2–3). Reading these words, we might easily wonder, Where did the money go? This is exactly the question that many in Los Angeles might have been asking themselves as investments from Japan began to dry up, in part because of a depression-level financial crisis from which that country has still to recover, and as investments from other parts of Asia failed to materialize. Unlike the last half of the twentieth century, when a series of Pacific wars boosted the economies of America's burgeoning sunbelt, the end of the twentieth century witnessed an Asia failing in its historic mission to keep prosperity afloat in Southern California.

In the imagined continuation of such economic deprivation, the state in *In the Heart of the Valley of Love* becomes ever more remote, oppressive, and unresponsive to the needs of the city's residents. Its workings, like the workings of finance in this novel, are mysterious and foreboding. People are simply vanished and apparently imprisoned, as happens to Rohn, one of Francie's de facto caretakers at the start of the novel. "Just about everybody broke laws all the time," Francie tells us, "the Consumption Law, the black-market laws, the licensing laws. There was probably nobody in the entire country, except a few chirps, who couldn't be arrested for *something*. Occasionally, the police arrested a randomly chosen person, and if you went searching for him or her, they might arrest you, too" (1992, 13). Despite the dangers of seeking out lost attachments, Francie nevertheless ventures later in the novel to find out where Rohn has been taken. In the process, she comes across lines of trucks rumbling into the desert, depositing unknown quantities of goods and potentially people into gigantic holding facilities for the government, and feeling the whole time the menace of asking too many questions. As one kindly truck driver tells her, "I only drive as far as they tell me to drive. I don't drive past that. But I've heard that some of the truckers carry prisoners. I've heard there are prisons out there, past where I drive to. Prisons like warehouses" (198). To make matters worse, the police, never a symbol of friendliness in Southern California for the poor and nonwhite, are corrupt. When they approach people for simple traffic violations, they are in fact asking for a bribe to look the other way: "Rohn reached for his wallet. I knew it pained him to give them anything. . . . He handed each of them a ten-gallon gas cred, and they took the creds as nonchalantly as Rohn had pretended to be as he handed them over. The men hopped on their bikes and were gone" (5). Everyone, it seems, is potentially a criminal and subject to arrest. One of the characters in the novel observes, "But one thing I learned is that they like you to break laws. . . . They like to have something on you" (201). Criminality has become, as it had for many young male residents of South Los Angeles (especially after Operation

Hammer), a form of social control.[15] The arbitrariness with which arrests are made simply accentuates the degree to which the enforcement of crime has become, in this novel, the exercising of such control.

At one level of interpretation, then, *In the Heart of the Valley of Love* can be read as an exaggerated chronicling of social conditions brought about by an unusually severe economic recession. Without money, the usually disguised policies of the state become more naked and the rich themselves become vulnerable. In the ruins of the future promised by LA 2000, Kadohata imagines Southern California as reversing the trends explored in *The Martian Chronicles* and *Always Running*. The nostalgia that greases the workings of capital in the manufacturing of the region's built-up spaces is stripped from its pages. What remains is an expansion of negative spaces that threatens, in the wake of capital evaporation, to drown the remaining vestiges of what I have been implicitly calling in this chapter a postwar nostalgic utopianism. The city itself, as in *Always Running*, is imagined in *In the Heart of the Valley of Love* as broken into two parts: a dwindling, racially homogeneous, white bunker of affluence called "richtown," and everyone else. But unlike Rodriguez's autobiography, Kadohata's novel depicts violence as being dictated by a lack of cultural logic and the spaces of rationalization themselves dissolving in the proliferation of random violence: "I don't know what I thought of the riots; you got used to them. They'd become so commonplace, I didn't think much about them at all. But a few days ago there's been a big riot in richtown. That frightened me and thrilled me at the same time. When richtowns across the country started to fall, I knew there would be changes" (1992, 116–117). As a chronicle of what economic recession can lead to, if extended too long, *In the Heart of the Valley of Love* suggests the polarization of the population along class and racial lines, the complete hegemony of a repressive state regime that announces its own vulnerability the more repressive it becomes, and a largely residual class of wealthy white folks verging on self-destruction. The state, while mindful of the interests of the wealthy, is incapable of producing wealth and as a result exists as a capital-independent defender of a stagnant social order.

On another level of interpretation, then, *In the Heart of the Valley of Love* surprisingly predicts the rise of a form of socialism in the midst of capital evaporation. The state becomes the primary, if not always adequate, dispenser of life's necessities. Credits are provided to the residents of the future for the acquisition of such necessities as water (crucial in the semiarid climate of Southern California) and gasoline (the lack of which has left the streets of Los Angeles virtually empty). What leaves so many of the region's inhabitants criminalized, it seems, is the desire to engage in unfettered business enterprises, black-market exchanges of goods and services that are necessary for the supplementation of government hand-outs. No wonder, then, that richtown is itself in revolt. For what good does it do richtown's residents to have access to money when money itself cannot help one to purchase more of the necessities of daily living, and when the policies of the state are as likely to make them criminals as anyone else?

According to Francie: "I learned later, when I met some students who'd attended universities, that what mostly separated us from the students at universities was they held expectations of the world, whereas what we had was hope" (1992, 34). The difference in perspective outlined in this passage between the heirs of richtown, who attend universities, and the rest, who attend state-funded schools with open admission, is crucial here. "Expectation" suggests an assumed right to privileges which, as the pages of this novel amply describe, is dangerous to assume in a world that can barely provide water and fuel for its denizens. "Hope," on the other hand, suggests that despite not being able to assume a life of privilege, one can nevertheless strive for something that will give one's life meaning. In the latter case, one is less likely to be disappointed, while in the former one seems destined to be dissatisfied in an era of material scarcity, no matter how much worse others around oneself might be suffering. It is on the basis of this difference that Francie can claim the future for her own kind, as opposed to those who live in relative, but unsatisfying, affluence: "It was starting to become clear to us, if it was not to them, that someday it would be our children and not theirs who would be inheriting this country, if there was a country to inherit" (82). The prospect of capital evaporation in *In the Heart of the Valley of Love* turns out, upon closer inspection, to be a fantasy of class reversal, a situation in which the rich must face a loss of expectations without the sustaining tradition of hope that has, for a long time, fueled the struggles of working-poor peoples.

If, as Francie claims, "we" are destined to inherit whatever mess is left over once the privileges enjoyed by richtown are finally eroded and undermined by the contradictions of a capital-scarce economy, it seems valid to wonder whom Francie has in mind when she says, "we"? This is the question that has drawn Viet Thanh Nguyen, in his recent critical reappraisal of Asian American cultural politics, to focus his attention partially on Kadohata's novel. In the conclusion to *Race and Resistance: Literature and Politics in Asian America* (2002), Nguyen argues that Asian American intellectuals have been too fixated on the idea of Asian Americans as "bad subjects," members of a racial minority who resist the pull of whiteness and of the inequality its supremacy is founded upon. In the study of bad subjects, Asian American intellectuals occupy, or at least wish to occupy, a field of cultural production that seeks to maintain autonomy from the field of class relations, if not also the field of power, by maintaining its own system of consecration. This system, founded on the valuation of bad subjects, rewards cultural producers and intellectuals alike for reversing the polarity of values founded in the larger dominant fields.

With this criticism in mind, I wish to trace out two possible readings of Kadohata's novel that relate to the questions raised in the previous paragraph. Because this novel is set in the future—one of the few examples of Asian Americans writing sci-fi—it enables the fictive exploration of a crisis of capitalism that simplifies a crisis of racial ordering just beginning to become visible by the early 1990s. This crisis of racial ordering, I wish to stress, hinged in large part on the ambiguous position of Asian Americans as a fast-growing, heterogeneous, and increasingly visible group. In creating a crisis of capitalism, then, *In the Heart of the Valley of Love* brings into sharper contrast the possible representational choices that might help us to understand more clearly the divergent futures awaiting us as the meaning of racial difference, in the midst of rapid demographic change, becomes pluralized.

At one level, Kadohata seems to endorse the view that autonomy is not desirable for Asian Americans, in lieu of a more expansive embrace of a cross-racial and minoritarian discourse. The potential problem with this endorsement is its failure to address the ambivalent class position of Asian Americans in the current social order. Thus, in his reading of *In the Heart of the Valley of Love*, Nguyen emphasizes the ways in which Kadohata's depiction of the near-future splits the racial geography of Los Angeles, as a synecdoche of the country as a whole, along a simple line of demarcation. Richtown is comprised only by white subjects, while the disenfranchised rest are made up of nonwhites and poor whites. Nguyen concludes, the "ambiguities of racial and class alignment are erased. Asian Americans, for example, are not mentioned as such (the category is never used) and instead cast as nonwhite and non-rich, while contemporary experience would seem to point toward a future in which some Asian Americans will be included in categories of wealth and (possibly) whiteness" (2002, 151–152). What such reductions erase is the ways in which Asian Americans, along with the rise of a substantial stratum of black and Latino middle-class subjects, make problematic the conflating of racial and class categories. Richtowns are no longer entirely white, and whiteness itself as a result, as Nguyen argues, may be experiencing a transformation of meaning, the terminus of which is still as yet unclear. As Lisa Duggan suggests, one possible terminus of such a transformation might be the mainstream embrace of "an emergent rhetorical commitment to diversity, and to a narrow, formal, nonredistributive form of 'equality' politics" by former "civil rights lobbies" and "identity politics organizations," which would have the effect of aligning groups representative of Asian Americans, Latinos, African Americans, and gays and lesbians with neoconservative policy goals (2003, 44). Such ambiguity is ignored by Kadohata, who depicts instead through the figure of Francie, who is racially Japanese, Chinese, and black, a romanticized vision of an interracial nonwhite coalition unified in the yearning for an alternative social order not founded on the depredations of capitalism and white supremacy.

There is also a more generous way to interpret this novel. The rigor with which Kadohata avoids discussing the tensions between racial minorities suggests an embedded utopian vision in what might otherwise seem only dystopian. By deepening and temporally extending the economic recession of the early 1990s that gripped the United States and was so powerfully felt in Los Angeles, Kadohata creates a fictive crisis of capitalist development that enables groups who might otherwise fail to see common cause with one another to comprehend how emergent repressive state apparatuses negatively affect everyone. The remoteness of the state itself, which seems increasingly to operate independently of class-based and race-based interests in the pursuit of social stability for its own sake, deprives the residents of Los Angeles from participating in the governance of their own lives and leaves everyone, including residents of richtown, desperate for some form of autonomy from the repressive state apparatuses that prey on them. The springing up of riots in richtown as well as everywhere else in the city suggests that richtown residents have finally been forced, because of capital evaporation, to come to terms with the fact that circumstances are reducing them to the level of those they disparage. Their ingrained expectations are proving to be unfounded.

If, then, the disenfranchised—the nonwhite and the poor white—are destined to inherit what remains of the country once the state collapses underneath the weight of an economy that can no longer sustain itself, this is only possible because richtown itself as the last bastion of privilege is on the verge of losing its own autonomy from the fields of dominance that frame everyone's lives in Kadohata's Los Angeles. The residents of richtown are becoming poor whites, who in turn have accepted in the subtly utopian world of this novel the necessity of coalition with nonwhites. Of course, the richtown residents do not accept the prospect of their lost autonomy with grace, and as circumstances worsen they seem to be invested more than ever in maintaining their relative affluence. But as the novel winds down, Francie reads in the ferocity and simultaneous aimlessness of richtown's own dissolution—everyone, she says, now riots not for "change" but simply for "destruction" (1992, 190)—the prospect that with the imminent end of the current social order, something else must emerge. "Also, I knew that something was ending," she tells, "which also means that something was beginning. I don't know whether, a hundred years from now, this would be called The Dark Century or The Century of Light. Though others had already declared it the former, I hoped it would turn out to be the latter. I thought the question might be resolved within a decade" (190). What *In the Heart of the Valley of Love* imagines is the end of whiteness itself and of the social order it founds. With the end of white rule, what appears like destruction might prove, over time, to be the necessary precondition for an as-yet inconceivable postracial world. As in *The Martian Chronicles, In the Heart of the Valley of Love* gives voice to a yearning to start over somewhere else, to be rid of the baggage of the past in favor of a radical new future. Indeed, this future is so radically new that it cannot be imagined until all the vestiges of the old order and its nostalgia-ridden promises have crumbled to the point of disappearance. The fact that such a prospect, however, is greeted by the narrator, and presumably by the prospective reader as well, with uncertainty, even in some cases with horror, suggests the investment in whiteness that many of us undoubtedly possess, often without acknowledgment.[16]

Oddly, to suggest that Kadohata sees in capital evaporation the prospect of whiteness's demise is also to foreground the very ambiguity of Asian Americans in Los Angeles's racial geography. This is so because the crisis of capitalism envisioned by Kadohata is possible only with the sudden disappearance of Asian capital investment in the region, and in the country as a whole. Foundational to *LA 2000*'s optimistic assessment of Los Angeles's future, for instance, was the continued flow of investments and trade with the other side of the Pacific Ocean. This government report needed to imagine Los Angeles as an officially multicultural city exactly because this would place the city in the way of capital flows emanating from the burgeoning economies of East Asia, making Los Angeles in the process a main beneficiary of free-market ideologies. Demographic change figured capital realignment on a global basis, and this in turn leads us to wonder at the racial ambivalences such change might stir. In the 1990s, racial geographies became more and more difficult to map in Southern California, potentially remaking in the process what we mean by whiteness into something still wholly unpredictable.

AS WE HAVE SEEN in this literary prehistory to the 1992 Los Angles riots, the racial geography of Southern California is not a place only defined by notable landmarks; easy-to-identify boundaries; or static sedimentations of rock, sand, and soil. Racial geography is also a place produced by the imagination, which, in its striving to make sense of social experiences and extant social relations, contributes to the continual shaping of what is already there. The NOAA satellite image, with which I began this chapter, is merely a snapshot of what imagination has helped to produce thus far:

a stark social reality that pits many racial and classed groups against one another in a strictly confined zone of the city, while other parts of the city are insulated from this zone by armed guards, visible and invisible walls, and repressive state apparatuses of every conceivable variety. Even as this social reality grows ever more difficult to understand in racial terms, there is something of value in recognizing how we interpret this difficulty through a gaze comprised of our hopes for the future, our remembrances of the past, and our revolutionary desires to separate hopes and remembrances from one another.

Following Mike Davis's lead, I first looked at Ray Bradbury, who illustrates the most dominant way in which this gaze—formed by progress, reflection, and starting over—has made sense of a city-building project that has been from its inception also a cryptoracial project. Luis Rodriguez's memoir gives testimony to the social costs incurred by those who were overlooked by this project, those raced peoples who occupy the negative spaces of suburban growth. Even if they were overlooked, many of these peoples continued to interpret their interaction with their surroundings and with others through the same gaze. Progress was insisting that space owned by others could nevertheless belong, in a more intimate way, to those who occupy it. Reflection existed in the memory of difficult lives that were nevertheless once lived in relative freedom from the new encroachments of capital-driven developments. If this is so, we might say that Rodriguez concludes his book with the question, What would starting over mean for the peoples he writes about? One provisional, though not wholly satisfying, response to this question can be found in Kadohata's *In the Heart of the Valley of Love*. Starting over for such people can only occur if the gaze, through which the dominant has become accustomed to interpreting lived geographies, self-destructs. In the wake of such a crisis of meaning, we may have opportunity to enter what might appear, in retrospect, as a "Century of Light." But barring the kind of economic disaster Kadohata imagines and putting aside for a moment the worrisome possibility that her narrator is wrong to place her hopes on a postracial world, what social force has the power to initiate such a light-bringing crisis? And if we had command of such a social force, wouldn't we first want to ask ourselves whether we must—to paraphrase Virginia Woolf—break all the windows to get a breath of fresh air?[17]

Soon after midnight on 3 March 1991, "a 25-year-old high school dropout and part-time Dodger Stadium groundskeeper" by the name of Rodney King went on a joy ride with two of his friends (Los Angeles Times 1992, 33). King had recently been released from prison the previous Christmas for trying to rob a Korean American–operated convenience store with a tire iron. The owner of the store he tried to rob, Tae Suck Baik, later claimed that "he felt sorry for King" after beating him with a weapon kept near the cash register for just such an occasion (34). King was soon caught by the police. One wonders if the car King used in his failed attempt to escape from Baik and the police in 1989 was the same Hyundai Excel that Melanie Singer and her husband, Tim, spotted when King drove past their California Highway Patrol (CHP) cruiser on the freeway in 1991. According to officer Singer, he was driving at speeds of 110 to 115 miles per hour in this vehicle (Cannon 1999, 25). By the end of the chase that followed, "more than two dozen law enforcement officers—21 from the LAPD, four from the CHP and two from the Los Angels Unified School District—converged" on King's Korean import (Los Angeles Times 1992, 33–34).

What perhaps stretches credibility more than the possibility of a three-year-old Excel, which retailed at under $8,000 in the late 1980s, reaching speeds of over 100 miles per hour is the image of Rodney King, six feet three inches tall and 225 pounds heavy, squeezed into its tiny white frame. What doesn't stretch credibility, however, is the scene where King is being beaten by four Los Angeles police officers caught on tape by George Holliday, an Argentinean-born plumbing supplies salesman who happened to have a camcorder handy when he was awakened by the sound of police sirens and a helicopter. More than a decade later, it is still easy to recall what Holliday's camcorder recorded. King is surrounded by four police officers, who are surrounded by twenty-five more police officers, and who are in turn surrounded by awakened neighbors and stopped traffic. Overhead, a police helicopter makes its presence known by the bright circular light it rains down on this scene. The footage is grainy, but it is still easy to make out the slashing motions of the batons and the foot that seemed to come down on King's neck after he was subdued. The reason this scene does not stretch credibility is because it has been reproduced during the rest of the 1990s and beyond on book covers, in movies, in art exhibitions, and even in comedic spoofs. As a result, this scene has become an icon, a shorthand and simplified visual representation that conveys a singular meaning with powerful immediate recognition.[1]

Over the years, the Holliday videotape has become the source of a preferred *tableau vivant* of police misconduct: a man on the ground, one arm stretched outward to protect his face, a circle of light illuminating uniformed figures wielding steel batons against him. Other sensational cases of excessive police violence have caught the public's attention since this primal scene was first enacted and reproduced on our television screens ad nauseam. None of these cases, however, resonated quite so powerfully with, nor dug quite so deeply into, a common store of national symbols to produce an icon that seemed economically crafted to circulate in American culture and beyond.

The word *store* seems particularly apt here. It denotes at once a place where something is held in reserve, from which we can draw meaning, and at the same time a place of commercial exchange, where meaning is bought and sold. In a similar way, we might think about how this icon has found continued circulation a decade after its initial production by following the double logic of its availability as national symbol (something held in reserve for many to access) and as commodity object (something that needs to be exchanged and its value haggled over). The first suggests immediacy, shared experience, and commonality. It draws the viewers of the videotape into close psychic proximity to one another, making the nation in effect a space of surprising domestic intimacy. The second, however, suggests relationships that are mediated by a market, that require arbitrary and fluctuating valuations placed on items negotiated interpersonally, and that are therefore defined as divided, separate, and lacking in firmly established attachments of meaningfulness. Is it possible that in the second meaning of the word, we might extract something more than what is commonly identified as the Rodney King beating? Is it possible, in other words, to find in the facts that King had just been released from prison for trying to rob a Korean American small business and was caught speeding in a Korean-made automobile the germ of another story embedded in the one that we are so acculturated to hearing?

In trying to address these questions, I focus my attention on the troubled zones of meaning opened up by the wide but uneven availability of the icon of the black body in pain made famous by the Holliday videotape. To help fix this attention, I look at one example from popular culture that has taken part in the forging, the circulation, and the reception of this icon, Kathryn Bigelow's *Strange Days* (1995).[2] This film helps me to argue that the icon of the black body in pain, as emblematized by the image in which King is being mercilessly beaten by four police officers, was a national trope of waxing cultural significance in the early 1990s. After decades of dizzying demographic change, porous national borders, economic restructuring that has taken place on a global scale, and uncertainties about the trustworthiness of America's political leadership, this trope gained in circulation because it was so familiar. It rendered social complexity into easy-to-read social positions based on a long-standing racial difference between blacks and whites. Consequently, all conflict seemed to emerge as a result of a single axis of difference defined by the opposition between these two discrete camps. And because the difference between these two camps was deeply entrenched, the existence of conflict was made to appear equally entrenched and hence, for all intents and purposes, permanent. By fixing the coordinates of our hatred, the trope of the black body in pain also helped us to hold onto what is familiar. The film *Strange Days* takes center stage in this chapter because its many narrative failures—its weirdly pointless plot twists, its half-hearted attempts to make connections with others unlike oneself, its fawning deference before police power—and its repetitions of the Rodney King beating demonstrate how strong this need to hold onto the familiar can be.

··· A PARADOXICAL TROPE OF NATION

In a provocative essay that takes the Holliday videotape as its starting place, Elizabeth Alexander wonders about the status of the black body in pain as an icon of both racial conflict *and* American national unity.

"Black bodies in pain for public consumption have been an American spectacle for centuries," she writes,

> This history moves from public rapes, beatings, and lynchings to the gladiatorial arenas of basketball and boxing. In the 1990s, African-American bodies on videotapes have been the site on which national trauma—sexual harassment, "date rape," drug abuse, racial and economic urban conflict, AIDS—has been dramatized. . . . White men have been the primary stagers and consumers of the historical spectacles I have mentioned, but in one way or another, black people have been looking, too, forging a traumatized collective historical memory which is reinvoked, I believe, at contemporary sites of conflicts. (1994, 92–93)

In this meditation on the meaning of King's body in pain, Alexander asks us to think about the ongoing history of racial violence against which this meaning unfolds. In this history, black bodies are acted upon, defiled, and treated with abuse as a form of normative disciplining, the very reproduction of the image of the black body *yet again* in pain inevitably alluding to a repetition of traumas inflicted on blacks by whites over a long period of time. The black body in pain thus seems a powerful trope of racial unease and anxiety about national identity that finds its greatest meaning explicitly, and exclusively (?), in the United States.[3]

As this quotation suggests, it is the almost theatrical repetition of a single kind of trauma that maintains an acute awareness of the differences between black and white bodies in this country, the former put on a stage while the latter pull the ropes and sit in the audience. Black witnessing of this repetition interprets its meaning as the ground upon which, no matter how sophisticated, complex, or nuanced our theoretical understandings of identity, a notion of "a people" is based (Alexander 1994, 92). This interpretation, furthermore, is not available to whites. The latter cannot feel in quite the same visceral way the impact of the blows falling on King's body—as if those blows were beating down on their own bodies. Whites consume without feeling, or, if they do feel, they do so by reading the object of violence as also its cause: "King was described as 'buffed-out' 'probably ex-con,' 'bearlike,' 'like a wounded animal,' 'aggressive,' 'combative,' and 'equate[d] . . . with a monster' " (93). The black body somehow deserves the pain inflicted upon it, and, worse, if the black body is not disciplined in this way then it will project violence against white bodies. The icon of the black body in pain is an affective shibboleth. It divides individuals into two distinct groups: those who feel separated from, and even protected by, the pain inflicted on a black body, and those who feel this pain as potentially inflicted on their own bodies.

A closer look at Alexander's essay, however, reveals ambiguity about the role of the black body in pain in maintaining such a sharp division. This icon is, after all, an explicitly "American" spectacle. Over centuries, this spectacle has come to define what it means to be part of a national community, a subject who can immediately recognize the historical context against which the beating of King by four white police officers must be understood to have meaning. The differences in responsiveness to King's pain that separates blacks from whites also cast both blacks and whites as primary actors in a national drama that continues, unabated into the 1990s, to reenact a singular scene of unifying violence. Other than the medium, in other words, little has changed since Frederick Douglass recalled in print in 1845 the beating of his aunt by her legal owner and saw himself subject to the same terrible power (Alexander 1994, 96–97). As an icon of national recognition, the black body in pain is part of a subject-forming scene that has only two characters, the one inflicting the pain and one suffering the pain. Because of the reductive nature of this scene, the actual actors playing these two characters do not matter so much as the structural relationship they enact between them. Even identification—am I the one inflicting pain or the one suffering the pain?—becomes a form of nationalism. No matter how one answers this question, one sees oneself as being part of a continuous narrative about what it means to be an American.[4]

· · · WAXING SIGNIFICANCE

There is something deeply anachronistic about this reading of the black body in pain as national trope. We clearly no longer live, if we ever did, in a society that can sustain the easy-to-read racial dichotomy that renders the black body in pain such a persuasive trope of nationhood. The latter part of the previous chapter explored the increasing complexity of racial difference as it has increasingly been lived and understood in Southern California. The current chapter's focus on the videotape of the King beating and its connection to the riots adds another layer to this sense of increased complexity. For instance, we might pause to consider the fact that one of the four officers indicted for beating King on the Holliday videotape, Theodore Briseno, has a father who is Mexican American (Skerry 1993, 9–10; quoted in Abelmann and Lie 1995, 8).[5] Or, as Todd Gitlin relates, we might consider how stories about the riots often hinge on the confusion of identities created by racial boundaries that refuse to hold firm: "In Berkeley in 1992, during some minor local rioting triggered by the Rodney King verdict, a blond student told me how frightened she had been when some black youths surrounded the car in which she was riding, rocked it back and forth, and screamed and cursed her before letting her and her passengers move on. Her surname was Lopez. Somewhere there are rhetoricians and political strategists grouping her and her assailants together as 'people of color'" (1995, 117). To concentrate our attention on the Holliday videotape compels us, as these two examples prompt, to consider the ways in which whiteness itself can no longer be said to operate in the darkness created by the brightly lit stage upon which the scene of the black body in pain is performed. Mere visual inspection hides from view the meaninglessness of whiteness as a racial and national category. Those who seem white may turn out to be of foreign, and/or of nonwhite, origin. Like all racial categories, white contains a heterogeneity that hints at fractious internal histories, contradictory inclusions and exclusions, and boundaries that are blurry at best. And furthermore, being white, like being nonwhite, guarantees nothing about how a person will behave in any given situation.

Perhaps this may explain why so many critics of what might be called a cultural Left, as Gitlin's observation illustrates, have been perplexed by the growing popular usage of racial categories such as Latino and Asian American.[6] As Gitlin writes about the latter: "What does it describe? Race—a substitute for the widely disliked term 'Oriental'? If it describes the continent of national origin, should immigrants from the South Asian subcontinent be classified 'Asian American'? If the category is cultural, does it make sense to group third-generation Japanese Americans with Hmong tribesmen, educated Koreans, and the newly arrived Hong Kong poor?" (1995, 162).

This criticism is well deserved. Racial categories such as Latino and Asian American do betray an obviously violent reduction of meanings. These categories also, simultaneously, betray the violence at the heart of racial categorization itself, especially in its substantiation of a white racial identity that so often has been allowed to operate, uninterrogated, as synonymous with a national identity. If the bringing of so much diversity, defined in a number of dizzyingly different ways, together into these categories and the treatment of these categories as if they name sameness appears absurd to us, then so should the racial category white (not to mention the category black), which also treats differences as shared commonality. However, because Latino and Asian American have not yet become orthodoxy, it is easy to sneer at the use of these categories without interrogating the use of other taken-for-granted terms of group identity.[7] They name the strange that disrupts the neat dichotomy between black and white, which the trope of the black body in pain affirms. The more these others become visible, the more this trope may seem to wax in importance as a way to hold more tightly onto a vanishing social world.

Hence, we might consider in a new light the claim that attention to Latinos and Asian Americans as distinct racial categories distracts attention away from the plight of African Americans, toward whom all Americans—regardless of their background—owe a special racial and historical debt. "In fact," Gitlin writes in support of this claim, "one result of the ethnic revival was to eclipse the uniqueness of the African-American experience" (1995, 163). The history of slavery; the betrayal of promises made during postbellum reconstruction; Jim Crow; redlining; and now wholesale imprisonment, economic de facto ghettoization, and a life expectancy that rivals the life expectancy of any third-world nation are surely facts that should not be overlooked in any discussion about race. The Nobel Prize–winning economist Amartya Sen observes, "the point is often made that African Americans in the United States are relatively poor compared with American whites, though much richer than people in the third world. It is, however, important to recognize that African Americans have an *absolutely* lower chance of reaching mature ages than do people of many third world societies, such as China, or Sri Lanka, or parts of India (with different arrangements of health care, education, and community relations)" (1999, 6). But why does the pain these facts point us toward deserve our undivided attention? Do discussions of high rates of Latino imprisonment, the deportation of American-raised Cambodian refugees, the economic desperation of small, predominantly white towns in the Midwest and Great Plains make us forget what has happened, and is happening, to African Americans? Another way to respond to these questions, then, might be to continue Gitlin's thought for him. If "the uniqueness of the African-American experience" is eclipsed, the black body in pain as national trope might no longer be available to shore up a crumbling notion of a once-dominant national identity. The displacement of attention might, in turn, disrupt the meaning of whiteness itself as referring to those who remain in the dark, snap the whip, initiate the action on the stage, and by extension remain in control over the political and social life of the United States. The apparent concern over the loss of attention that African Americans might experience, should we turn away from a simple black-and-white model of racial difference, seems to be a concern as well about the loss of a particular racial identity for whites.[8]

There was, to put it another way, as much attention paid during and after the two King trials to the whiteness of the officers as there was to the blackness of King's body, to make us rethink how appropriate it is to insist the Holliday videotape is only a spectacle of a necessary hyper-visible blackness. Given the kind of social changes at the background of the Holliday videotape, it is not too far-fetched to argue that the black body in pain encoded both the disciplining of a raced body and the fear that made such an act of disciplining necessary. No longer, the message seems to be, could such acts of disciplining take place unnoticed. It would also mean something that before could be assumed. Indeed, it is tempting to read in the excesses of this scene the trembling menace of a boundary that has become more difficult to maintain. The more violently the "white" police officers beat Rodney King, the more they seemed to be struggling to maintain the integrity of their own racial identity against the alien threat represented by the many Latino observers—like the one secretly filming them—who surrounded them further in the dark and, even, by the one among their ranks whose ancestry might disrupt the racial sameness of their esprit de corps.

At the same time, despite the apparent complexity such observations point us toward, it would be a mistake to dismiss out of hand Elizabeth Alexander's spirited response to the scene of King's beating by four police officers. This response was the most mainstream by far. Indeed, to push this point home a bit further, this response may well define what it means to be mainstream. As Victor Valle and Rodolfo Torres argue, newspapers and television news coverage in the wake of the riots participated in rendering—if not simply participating in the reiteration of a preexistent understanding of—the violence following the not-guilty verdicts in the first King trial as part of a familiar national story of racial conflict. White-on-black violence led to black-on-white violence, the verdict in the trials being the primary, if not the only apparent, reason why so many darker-hued people took to the streets, set fire to buildings, and targeted other less-hued people. "Through sheer force of televised repetition, images of King's beating and court trial and, later, images of young black males beating white truck driver Reginald Denny," Valle and Torres write, "the riots had been framed between the horrifying bookends of white-on-black violence and black-on-white violence" (2000, 46). What became obscured from view by such "televised repetition" were alternative explanations that would have to take into account economic restructuring leading to joblessness, commercial divestment from black and Latino neighborhoods, lack of educational opportunities, demographic changes taking place on a multinational scale, and a history of pervasive police misconduct in what were, and are, perceived as crime-ridden areas. In these explanations, the anger over the acquittal of the officers involved in the King beating must be seen as a condensation of anger emanating from multiple and systemic sources.

While critics such as Valle and Torres are persuasive when they argue that the news could have been more self-conscious about the ways in which race limited reporters from exploring these other explanations, it also seems to me that the preeminence with which race—as the difference between blacks and whites—figured in coverage about the riots served the function of making familiar what was scary because so unfamiliar. The images of Latino protestors and looters, the shadowy figures of gun-toting Asians, and the lack of gang affiliation among many African Americans involved in the rioting opened a window to a social world that many perhaps had not been aware existed, and thus the obsession with black bodies as the target of rage and fear could also be a kind of "screen" that distracted from the strange.[9] The black body in pain became an important, if paradoxical, trope of national unity in the early 1990s because the meaning of the nation itself seemed to be coming apart. This trope increased in importance in response to a historical moment of troubling social complexity.

· · · THE PERMANENCE OF UNREST

More than any other film produced during the mid-1990s, *Strange Days* wrestles with, indulges in, and tries to exploit the waxing significance of the black body in pain as a paradoxical national trope. It does so by depicting the near future (now recent past) as the perpetual reenactment of urban unrest and revelations of police brutality that gripped the city of Los Angeles in 1992, showing us at its opening the supposed results of the Rodney King incident after its first trial results were made public. Only then does the film go on to dramatize the iconography of the incident itself. The apparent reversal of chronological order, however, is no accident. Bigelow's film deliberately begins with scenes of rioting because this is the social problem which the later thinly disguised reenactments of King's beating will solve. Not catalyst of violence, the recording of a black body in pain is made in *Strange Days* to appear as an instrument of redemption, an awakening of numb hearts to the divisions that spark open racial and urban conflict.

Thus, one of the first sequences of the film depicts the main character, Lenny Nero, portrayed by Ralph Fiennes, driving through a dystopian urban space in a Mercedes sports car. As he drives, the camera tracks alongside the car, capturing in its frame several white women chasing a man in a Santa costume. The chase dissolves out of sight behind a tank flanked by national guardsmen. This sign of a militaristic state presence is further emphasized by the scene of a police officer pushing a man against a gated storefront. Other figures, mostly African American, are seen running with merchandise still in their boxes. In an image reminiscent of grainy news footage of Korean Americans armed with rifles patrolling the rooftops of their businesses, two East Asian men, perhaps father and son, protect another store with machine guns.[10] Next to them, another police officer in riot gear arrests a man in an alleyway. Lenny soon comes upon a roadblock, where more police are checking each driver's identification card. Over the radio, we hear a sardonic announcer responding to a woman's voice predicting the arrival of the rapture. Even as the disc jockey mocks her religious fervor, his bravado is undercut by the scenes we are witnessing and by the woman herself, who speaks with a finality that makes her seem more aware of these scenes than the disk jockey. "I pray for you all," she says. Throughout this sequence, Lenny is engaged in behavior usually associated with the living room—eating pizza, making deals on a mobile phone, fiddling with the knobs on his dashboard—and stops only rarely to ponder what he sees.

We the audience have no way of grasping the causes of this spectacle, because we witness it from Lenny's perspective. This sequence literally begins with a close-up of Lenny's eyes. In comparison to the confusion outside, the camera lingers on the shiny reflective skin of the car's flawless steel body and the soundproof bubble in which we travel. Our attention is drawn to surfaces and glassed-off interiors that prohibit everything but visual contact with the events taking place on the street, while disembodied voice transmissions struggle to narrate what we see with contradictory messages. The violence seen from this perspective replicates the experience of watching the Los Angeles riots as it took place on television, another glass screen separating us from the events that we witnessed. As in this sequence, watching the riots on our televisions often involved having to listen to announcers and interviews with people on the streets speaking past each other as they vainly attempted to fit events into familiar frames of reference. Like Lenny, we could have easily watched while being distracted by our own lives, talking on the phone, eating, switching channels with our remotes. We might pause at a particularly sensational image, but we could continue with our lives uninterrupted in the safety of our living rooms. The future that Bigelow's film evokes borrows from this experience. Her future is an urban landscape stripped of safe public spaces. In this landscape, people engage in violent, moblike behavior without motivation or regret. Security is found in the shielded privacy of

our private interiors, which insulate and prevent us from understanding the spectacle, normalized in the film as a permanent part of the social background.

What this sequence emphasizes is both the quotidian nature of the rioting it depicts and the lack of causality that might explain the riots' outbreak. It thus tears us out of the flow of a *diegetic* narrative, the orderly sequence of cause and effect where a character's behavior is rooted in some ultimately detectable set of motivations. This sequence shoves us into the middle of a scene of violence and death without any knowledge of character, situation, or plot. Indeed, the first opening sequence of a botched robbery is not even a part of the plot, but only a sensational spectacle meant to introduce us to the film's social world. As a result, this second opening sequence's portrayal of what appears to be a typical street in the near future deepens an already-established mood where perception cannot be trusted, where violence occurs randomly, and where order is maintained only through the use of brute force—such as by police officers giving chase to criminals and vigilantes guarding their storefronts with automated weapons. Rioters riot in this sequence because their identities as such define who they are and dictate how they will behave. No more explanation for why they are rioting is necessary. In addition, because they are rioters, they will always riot so long as they remain with these identities. Given the irreducibility of their identities, nothing can be done to curb their behavior except to delimit the damage they might cause.

A police state is therefore necessary to contain the rioters' intrinsic lawlessness, either by arresting them and, in the process, evacuating public spaces of their destructive presence or by cordoning off those spaces where they are concentrated to protect other spaces from their lawless presence. As Steve Herbert tells us in his ethnography of the Los Angeles Police Department, based on fieldwork conducted in the mid-1990s,

> Most significant police actions involve some sort of enforcement via the movement of people in space. This is most obvious in the power the police most frequently threaten and often carry out—the power to jail. But it is crucial to managing interpersonal disputes and other mundane ongoing challenges the police face. It is crucial to keeping

business owners free from the sight of homeless people bothering their customers, to keeping residents of a neighborhood free from the fear of clusters of young people on their lawns. Indeed, it is only in the capacity to control and clear space that the police are in many situations able to restore the order they are presumed to maintain. (1997, 6)

These are the tasks that the police and the national guardsmen perform in this sequence. They are, respectively, arresting rioters and setting up roadblocks to delimit a space of rioting from the other areas of the city that are not ravaged by such violence. Because hard identities, as envisioned in this sequence's portrayal of urban unrest, preclude causality, foreseeable change, or even agency (whether individual or collective), the police and other militarized agents of state power are needed to protect the law abiders from the law breakers by spatially keeping the two groups apart.

While the spatial separation between law abider and law breaker imagined by Lenny's nighttime drive might seem free of racial meaning, I wish to argue that this is in fact not the case. As Paul Gilroy points out, even a seemingly structural, and therefore potentially provisional, distinction such as law abider and law breaker depends on the positing of a more deeply held incompatibility. It is this deeper lying incompatibility that makes an identity hard. The distinction between law abider and breaker is, of course, unavoidably social, insofar as the law itself is by definition a social construction. However, the permanence of this distinction on display in the second opening sequence of *Strange Days* suggests a deeper force at work. The behavior of the rioters, in its lack of causation and therefore in its apparent randomness, points to a naturalism that drives the law breaker's behavior forward, an impulse springing up from what they are and not from the circumstance of their existence. As a result, the law breaker becomes what Gilroy calls an "absolute identity," which is often evoked "to account for situations in which the actions of individuals and groups are being reduced to little more than the functioning of some overarching presocial mechanism" (2000, 103). When this happens, Gilroy continues,

Identity ceases to be an ongoing process of self-making and social interaction. It becomes instead a thing to be possessed and displayed.

It is a silent sign that closes down the possibility of communication across the gulf of one heavily defended identity of particularity and its equally well fortified neighbor. . . . When identity refers to an indelible mark or code somehow written into the bodies of its carriers, the other can only be a threat. Identity is latent destiny. Seen or unseen, on the surface of the body or buried deep in its cells, identity forever sets one group apart from others who lack the particular, chosen traits that become the basis of typology and comparative evaluation. (2000, 103–104)

In other words, an identity such as law breaker does not have to be visibly marked as racial to operate as a racialized distinction of identity. These markers can be found, instead, in the microscopic, the body's racial meaning implanted beyond the eye's ability to see as surface marker but still interpretable as behavior, propensity, and culture. For identities to become hard, as they seem to be in the second opening sequence of *Strange Days*, such identities must find an anchor in some marker, visible or not, that suggests both durability over time and presocial causative function. The most obvious place to find such a marker is on, or in, the body, which promises in its seemingly stable materiality to guarantee meaning. The link between bodily marker and behavior does not have to be explicitly established, though, since our understanding of human difference has penetrated down to the chromosomal, the invisible codes of the body's operations that exist out of sight in the deep cellular recesses of tissue and blood.

It is not, therefore, too difficult to understand why we must look for such guarantors of meaning beyond the eye's unaided ability to see. In an age when social certainties are destabilized, when the nation itself as a basic unit of global political division seems under threat by crisscrossing and hard-to-fathom forces, and when dizzying technological advancements revise and revise again perceptions of our own body's materiality, the belief that racial meaning can be found buried somewhere out of sight, perhaps in our cells or our DNA, only to resurface in indirect ways, for instance, in one's likelihood of breaking the law, is the only way to fix difference into two large opposing categories such as white and black. The categories of law abiding and law breaking become hard, then, when these categories are seen, however veiled, as symptomatic of a deeper, more basic behavioral trait rooted in some unseen racial difference (coded categories of gendered, sexually desiring, and classed identities might also similarly seek their verification on the body as essential but not necessarily easily observed physical differences). The voices that can be heard coming out of Lenny's radio cannot explain what is happening for this reason, because there is no explanation for a social phenomenon that divides individuals into two large groups of spatially segregated social beings, where one group appears to act without reason or moderation and must therefore be physically restrained, except the one provided by the circular logic of hard identity. No wonder Lenny cultivates indifference to this social world and concentrates his attention on immediate self-interest. No change is possible.

··· **NARRATIVE BREAK**

As the plot develops, Lenny's emotional remoteness—if not our own—is put to the test. We soon learn that a black rap star named Jeriko One has been murdered. Lenny's friend and potential love interest, Mace, played by Angela Bassett, calls the star "one of the most important black men in America" because of his politically explicit and popularly messianic songs. This statement signals the larger significance of his murder in the film. Jeriko One is important diegetically because his presence makes explicit the racial meaning cryptically embedded in the film's earlier scene of societal division, and because he is also the first to challenge the logic of hard identity by offering a narrative that posits racism as one of the causal factors behind the social unrest we have been witnessing. Although his narrative does not challenge the permanence of this sequence's violence, nor does he offer a particularly rich understanding of its possible causes, he does offer an explicit critique of hard identity's logic. He sings in a televised music video:

> And you tryin' to make me think that I did this to myself
> When the drugs I smoke
> And the guns I tote
> Both came from your shelf.

The logic of hard identity places the blame for social ills on the shoulders of those who suffer most from these ills, in this case African Americans, because these ills spring from some intrinsic failing in the whatness of this classification. Jeriko One's lyrics counter in a crude but pertinent way that self-blame is not appropriate when the causes of such ills can be traced to other social phenomena, such as the ready availability of illicit drugs and the legally mandated ease with which firearms can be acquired. I insist on the "crudeness" of this response because Jeriko One's lyrics only challenge the lack of causality in the logic of hard identity, not its claim that one can possess a sense of self that is categorically separable, and discrete, from another (and also because contemporary rap and hip-hop have long ago made similar claims with much greater insight and raw force). The reductions of self to category, and category to simple opposition, remain unchallenged.

After registering this incomplete critique of hard identity's logic, the film proceeds to narrate how Jeriko One was murdered and in doing so draws parallels between this murder and the beating of Rodney King. A squad car orders Jeriko One and his friends to pull over in what appears to be a random case of racial profiling. A verbal altercation ensues. One of the officers summarily shoots Jeriko One in the head. The others are also murdered except for a prostitute named Iris, who succeeds in running away. Iris, as it turns out, has been wired with a new kind of recording technology called a SQUID, an acronym for "super-conducting quantum interface device." This technology, to which we were surreptitiously introduced in the first opening sequence of the film, is comprised of a webbing worn on the head that somehow connects through the skin to the cerebral cortex below. Whatever the wearer experiences can be directly recorded onto a minidisk operated by a remote player roughly the size of a large compact disk walkman. Other people can relive the exact same experience by playing the disk. This technology positions the wearer within the physical subject-position of the recorder. We do not see events unfold so much as experience them through the sensations of the other's body. Thus, we learn how appropriate Iris's name is in the film, since hers are literally the eyes and the lenses that have recorded this murder in intimate detail.

If the recording Iris has made gets out, the rioting that has marked the

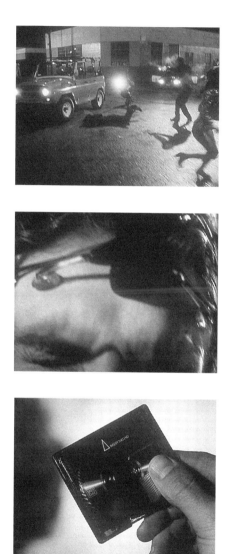

opening sequences of the film is likely to flare up and lead to what Mace calls an "all out war"—though it is difficult to ascertain how such an all out war might differ from the scenes of rioting and seemingly motiveless violence to which we have already been compelled to bear witness. Just as the second opening sequence implicitly references the Los Angeles riots, this plot development replicates popular accounts of the Rodney King beating. According to these accounts, often mistaken in fact, King was pulled over in a random traffic stop and, when he offered resistance to his arrest in a minstrel-like performance (he supposedly "danced about, grabbed his behind, and laughed crazily" [Baker 1993, 42]), was beaten by enraged police officers who demand nothing but complete compliance from their suspects. When a videotape of what happened became available, and when those who were responsible for the crime walked free, a riot broke out.

It is around the recordings of Jeriko One's death and the King beating, however, that the plot of the film diverges from the events that reputedly led to the Los Angeles riots. Although it is generally assumed by everyone in the film, as it was in the trial, that the meaning of these recordings was self-evident, the videotape of King's beating failed to live up to these expectations. When the jurors in a Simi Valley courtroom decided to acquit, critics had to scramble to understand why. Judith Butler asks what was perhaps on the minds of many: "The video shows a man being brutally beaten, repeatedly, and without visible resistance: and so the question is, How could this video be used as evidence that the body being beaten was *itself* the source of danger, the threat of violence, and, further, that the beaten body of Rodney King bore an intention to injure, and to injure precisely those police who either wielded the baton against him or stood encircling him?" (1993, 15). What the verdict revealed was obvious: the medium of video is vulnerable to interpretation. What one thought actually happened could be shown to demonstrate the opposite. The distance between referent and sign, as many poststructuralist critics had been asserting for years, seemed irrefutably and perilously wide when the riots began. But the reason for such distance between sign and referent in the first King trial did not involve a simple built-in gap in language, one that is universally true in the operation of all languages. Nor did it involve a universally true slippage of meaning, where multiple witnesses clashed in their accounts of what they witnessed with *Rashomon*-like (referring to Akira Kurosawa's 1950 film by that name) disagreement.

Neither explanation goes far enough to account for the surprise that greeted the Simi Valley verdict. Even for the most theoretically sophisticated, the verdict seemed to violate a surprisingly untheoretical confidence that what we saw on screen was an indisputable approximation of what had actually happened. Clearly, any explanation of this verdict needs to involve, as Butler goes on to discuss in her essay, the question of whose interpretation of the events captured on video would be accepted by a jury. How much did the jury's prior preconditioning and fears regarding matters of race affect their receptivity to certain interpretations? How much was interpretation contingent on the jury's ability to feel a connection with King's suffering, as opposed to identification with the police officers' symbology of protection from such violence?

These questions all seem to revolve around the differences between the terms *sympathy* and *empathy*. In short: one can be sympathetic to another's pain without feeling the danger of being in the same kind of pain oneself. The main affective component of sympathy is pity. One cannot, however, be empathetic to another's pain without feeling the possibility that that pain might be inflicted on oneself. To feel empathy, one must identify with the person in pain. One must literally see oneself as being just like that other person. The difference between sympathy and empathy might thus be thought of as the difference between identifying *with* and *as*. In literary terms, as Marianne Noble points out, sympathy is closely aligned with sentimental literature and empathy with the Gothic. "While the reader of the Gothic is an active participant, so that the identification produces anxiety and fear," Nobel writes, "the reader of sentimental literature is sidelined, unable to help but forced to watch. These differing perspectives on a common core of violence account for the differing reader responses: heart-pounding terror for the Gothic reader, heart-wrenching tears for the sentimental reader" (2000, 72). Like readers of nineteenth-century American sentimental literature, many felt sympathy for King during his famous videotaped beating, but, in a Simi Valley courtroom, what sympathy the twelve jurors in the King trial might have felt *with* the abused did not allow them to identify *as* the person in pain—to see themselves in his place, to act on his behalf, to risk the danger of having what happened to him happen to them. As a result, they voted to acquit the four officers charged with the use of excessive force. The accounts available to us from this trial, for the many who were shocked by its outcome, suggest that the jurors, while sympathetic to King's pain, felt empathy with the four officers who were called upon by civic necessity to perform an unpleasant but necessary task. Rather than feel the terror of being made an object of their violence, as in Gothic fiction, the jurors preferred to see themselves as the perpetrators, finding in them protection from a different kind of terror. Given the option between identifying themselves with a brutalized King and a brutalizing force, they unsurprisingly chose to align themselves with the figures wielding the police batons.[11]

Unlike the Holliday video of the Rodney King beating, then, the SQUID recording of Jeriko One's death found in *Strange Days* collapses the distance between sympathy and empathy. The SQUID recording is the symbolic means by which, in this instance, the imagination compensates for the disappointments that exist outside of its made-up world. If the Holliday video cannot grant us the kind of unmediated access to past events we long for, *Strange Days* proposes to invent a new medium that can. In doing so, the film gives expression to a longing for something that might be called civic virtue, namely *the ability to identify with the pain of another not like oneself that compels one to act to relieve that pain as if it were one's own.* The film implicitly envisions civic virtue as the ability to empathize, and not only sympathize, with the plight of those who are unlike oneself. I intentionally use the somewhat antiquated term *virtue* here because the film's narrative is specifically about ethics. It struggles with the question, as many critics of a cultural Left have done throughout the 1990s, of how to position oneself socially so as to benefit a greater good than oneself, a commitment to a civic spirit in an age represented by the film's dystopian rendering of a riot-torn and demographically divided city that seems to present little possibility for such a spirit to flourish.

The word *virtue* is further appropriate in this context because *Strange Days* can only imagine (one of its narrative failures) the possibility of such an ethics as emanating from individual actions. When the world seems devoid of order and civil behavior, what remains is the struggle of lone actors to conduct themselves by a higher standard than the one that shapes the behavior of those around them. Thus, virtue refers specifically to a rising above a historical moment, a differentiating oneself from a crowd or a mob, and an internal struggle between one's baser impulses and higher aspirations that is separate from collective engagement. To borrow from the language of Saidiya Hartman's provocative reflections in *Scenes of Subjection: Terror, Slavery, and Self-Making in Nineteenth-Century America* (1997), "At issue here is the precariousness of empathy and the uncertain line between witness and spectator" (4). Virtue, in its stress on what is abstractly right in negotiating a set of interpersonal relations that is by nature ever shifting and resistant to the regularized workings of principles, potentially spurns the motivation of others who might not recognize the rightness of such abstraction. It does not encourage dialogue nor reflection, but rather insists on what should be unproblematically self-evident to everyone.

Like virtue, civic virtue as imagined in *Strange Days* does not do away with the individualism that is so highly prized. Rather, it seeks to activate that individualism into behavior, away from the position of spectator to that of witness. At the same time, however, civic virtue also entails the ability to place oneself in another's position that may blur the lines that gives individuality its autonomy. While on the surface, such a desire for civic virtue may appear reasonable given the circumstances, it is a desire that cannot escape its own logical inconsistencies. For if empathy is founded on identification as someone else, it presumes the subject-position being identified with is just like oneself. Empathy necessarily entails seeing oneself as just like another. It is necessarily founded on the notion of a shared commonality that can suspend whatever disparity that might exist between variant subjective experiences in favor of a perceived sameness.

In this way, empathy as it relates to the civic engages in a deeply homogenizing political project. This project, infused with a nostalgia for an unmarked past, makes citizens out of an allegiance to an ideal that gains more power by being assumed. The unmarked past refers to a historical moment, actual or only retroactively imagined, when the middle class, the white, and the properly gendered and sexually oriented were simply thought to reflect the nation's populace, a reflection that one could assuredly expect to view without irony on the movie screens of classic Hollywood (or, as we saw in the previous chapter, in the pages of

Ray Bradbury's stories). It was so much a part of the background that it did not invite commentary. The current political problem arises from what appears to be an apparent social fact, that such icons of an American way of life are now no longer unmarked, but visible, and specifically visible as *cultural identities*. As in the growing circulation of terms such as *Latino* and *Asian American*, the once invisible racial moniker *white* now requires a defensive posture. What does it name? Who is included and excluded? Why? Under such scrutiny, the integrity of any given cultural identity must necessarily buckle.

The emphasis on empathy as a civic virtue can therefore be seen as the desire for an impossible return to a historical moment of untroubled communality, material plenty, and expansive expectations about the future based on an assumed, and of course often largely fictive, national and racial identity—in short, yet another manifestation of a nostalgia for an antique future (see previous chapter). Such virtue, Lauren Berlant writes, "does not involve starting with a view of the nation as a space of struggle violently separated by racial, sexual, and economic inequalities that cut across every imaginable kind of social location" (1997, 4). We might call the ideal represented by a virtue that rejects such an unsettling starting place "unconflicted personhood," what Berlant describes as "to be American," a way of life that entails inhabiting "a secure space liberated from identities and structures that seem to constrain what a person can do in history" (4). While *Strange Days* begins exactly with the "view of the nation as a space of struggle violently separated by racial, sexual, and economic inequalities," its focus on individual virtue leads it to what can only be described as a disappointing ending. This is so because the problem of civic virtue as it is explored in *Strange Days* is also exactly predicated on the need to elicit police intervention. The solution, in other words, to the rioting, the destruction of property, the hearty displays of anger, and the pervasive cynicism found throughout the film is *more* policing.

··· **A PERFECT LANGUAGE**

Circumstances depicted in this film, to be sure, have not devolved into complete civil meltdown. There are negative spaces of permanent rioting, but these are contained by police checkpoints, and the rest of Los Angeles seems functionally rational if somewhat impaired. In this way, the film already implicitly endorses the view that the police, as an agent of social stability, is more necessary than ever before. The threat posed by the recorded murder of Jeriko One, then, is the possibility that a functional policy of containment will fail. The zones of permanent rioting is at risk of spreading and overlapping into the spatial boundaries placed around it as a precursor to civil meltdown. The reason for this threat is the rot found within the police itself. The police appear as part of the problem. The police seem another formation of hard identity, banding together against others who threaten their rule and becoming in the process the facilitators of violence rather than its cure. The police have proven themselves, as they seem to have threatened in the wake of the Holliday video, to have failed their role as virtuous and impartial defenders of the good, out of touch with those whom they are suppose to protect from the forces of hardened evil, incapable of differentiating, in fact, between the good guys (law abiders) and the evildoers (law breakers), and as a result prone themselves to become the kind of person they are sworn to restrain. At one point in its narrative, the film toys with the possibility of a wholesale corruption by hinting at the covert (and officially sanctioned?) existence of death squads within the LAPD who seek to murder those who question the police's power—only to dispel this idea as a cruel hoax, something to distract from the actual activities of lone madmen.

In order to correct a failing that might make the idea of LAPD death squads seem possible and to cut through the barriers to power that those in charge of the police have set up around it, *Strange Days* offers us the SQUID recording. In this film, a SQUID is the medium of a perfect language uncorrupted by subjective difference through a temporary suspension of such difference. It offers those wired to its technological apparatus a moment of pure empathy that can compensate for the loss induced by the demographic diversity on display throughout the film and that can make effective an appeal to the authority in charge of the police. In Butler's reading of what happened in Simi Valley, she suggests that the mostly white and middle-class jury was offered a series of subject-positions with which to identify. These include King, the police beating him, the police standing around the scene in a circle, the observers at a greater distance, and the camcorder recording the incident. The defense convinced the members of the jury that they should identify *as* those protected by the circle of police, the police doing the protecting, and surprisingly with King himself—"but whitewashed: the blows he suffers are taken to be the blows they *would* suffer if the police were not protecting them from him" (Butler 1993, 19). In all of these possible identifications, King remains the source of social disruption and violence from whom the jurors must be protected. In *Strange Days*'s reenactment of these choices, the viewer of the videotape, now a SQUID recording, is brought into an identification that imagines King not as the source of disruption but as the sufferer of police violence. The camcorder and the witness are collapsed, and are brought into the circle of the police as a potential victim of its use of force. The rationale for such force is neutralized, since the viewer is no longer protected by this circle from a racialized source of violence. The viewer instead is this circle's target.

The SQUID recording of Jeriko One's murder is offered to us, then, as a way to bridge the walled-off security and its attendant lack of comprehension dramatized by the opening sequence of Lenny's drive through the lawless streets of Los Angeles.[12] Rather than pass safely through a corridor of violence protected by an omnipresent police state, we are forced outside the bubble of his automobile and thrust into the swirl of unchecked violence denoted by scene after scene of multiracial crowds pushing against each other and against the police, who can barely contain them. The multiracial character of this violence is further accentuated in the final scene, when a giant flashing sign wishes the crowd happy New Year in English, Arabic, Korean, and so on. Through a temporary suspension of difference, SQUID technology is presented in *Strange Days* as a way to induce empathy with another not like oneself by making its users imagine the fate of another as potentially their fate. All that is necessary is that the recording find an audience with a figure in the seat of power.

The question remains at this point in the film's narrative, Can this artificial empathy lead to an identification between power and powerlessness that can, in turn, lead to social action? Before we address this question, however, we need to acknowledge how surprisingly limited by race even this artificial empathy is in the film. All the SQUID recordings in *Strange Days* are made from the perspective of its white characters. Not once are we treated to a sequence that depicts the perspective of a SQUID

recording made by a person of color. Even Jeriko One's execution is recorded by Iris, and thus we experience Jeriko One's murder at a distance and he himself remains a remote icon of black rage. The only cross-racial act of artificial empathy that takes place in this film is from black to white, when Mace is forced by Lenny to experience Jeriko One's murder from Iris's perspective. This is a kind of identification we are already well accustomed to making without the aid of an as-yet-to-be-developed prosthesis for producing proper feelings. Mainstream television and films have long asked their audiences—regardless of their race, ethnicity, or nationality—to identify with the hopes, fears, and predicaments of mostly white characters, and for the most part their audiences have had little difficulty meeting this request.[13]

Thus far in this chapter, as this last point highlights, I have been considering in my interpretation of *Strange Days* the problem whereby people in dominant positions have to make identifications with others who are in more vulnerable situations—and, more explicitly, with black bodies. Toward such others, people in dominant positions are accustomed to feeling pity but not empathy. The limits that race places on an empathy artificially enabled by new technology in *Strange Days* suggests, however, that all of us have been asked to, and have become accustomed to, identifying with, and as, those who are in power, whose ideals codified by a black/white racial binary are constantly paraded in front of us, and whose long shadow has demanded the eclipse of those who cannot approach this ideal. Empathy has not been difficult when it refers to our identification *as* holders of the dominant position. For those in vulnerable situations, in positions that lack power or proximity to an Anglo-ideal (at least in, though not necessarily limited to, this country), empathy with this ideal has long been a description of and not a solution to our lack of civic engagement.

Strange Days's ending calls attention to such stark subjection. It portrays the two officers responsible for Jeriko One's murder as chasing Mace through a crowd that has gathered at the foot of the Bonaventure Hotel to celebrate the end of the twentieth century. When she resists and subdues the rogue cops, other officers perceiving her as a threat to the social order they represent come to the two officers' aid and begin to beat her with their metal batons. The tableau of Mace on the ground and surrounded

COURTESY OF PHOTOFEST

by a ring of violent police officers is easily the film's most direct, and equally hard to watch, reenactment of the King arrest and ensuing rioting. A young African American boy, enraged by the violence he is witnessing, attacks one of the officers. He is soon joined by more multiracial celebrants. It appears for a moment as if the Los Angeles riots will again break out—or, continue to break out, given the scenes of violence that begin the film—and spread, until the deputy police commissioner arrives with the recording of Jeriko One's murder in his hands. Luckily, Mace had been able to deliver the recording to him before her beating takes place. The deputy commissioner flashes it like a badge, and the violence promptly abates. The two rogue cops responsible for the murder are quickly brought to justice in a predictable shootout. The countdown toward the New Year ends at this moment, and all traces of the previous scene of mob violence are erased as people hug and kiss each other in exuberant celebration. We are treated to a glimpse in which a member of the mob deeply kisses a police officer in full riot gear as Lenny leads a bloodied Mace away from the crowd.

The lawlessness initiated, at least implicitly, by the outcome of the King trial has finally ceased in the film, once authority, with the aid of SQUID technology, is made to see what the camera alone cannot capture. Once the deputy commissioner experiences what is on the recording of Jeriko One's murder, he feels compelled to intervene and discipline the officers under his charge. He halts the beating of Mace and punishes the ones actually responsible for her pain. In this way, the promise of apocalypse made throughout the film and even in its prerelease trailers, and imagined as a more widespread reenactment of the Los Angeles riots, is defused as the rapture's allure loses its charm in the midst of a new social experience. Change seems possible without the advent of an end to everything once the outlaw elements of the LAPD are exorcised. Those officers who do live up to their mission as moral protectors can now continue to protect and maintain social boundaries that have come too close to collapsing. This happy conclusion is made possible through a direct appeal to authority with a tool that forces a figure of authority to take responsibility for the misbehavior of those under his command. Interestingly, this appeal must be made on the basis of yet another black body in pain, this time properly identified as pain by a figure of authority with the power to redeem a scene that has found too much circulation.

The conclusion of *Strange Days* comes across in its sudden jubilation as a filmic version of LA 2000, where racial and economic differences suddenly become a reason for celebration without the fear of conflict or further violence. But unlike LA 2000, this conclusion predicates such jubilation on the necessity of the black body in pain that must be recognized as such before commonality can be achieved. While we might interpret this outcome as a form of civic virtue, because the deputy commissioner has finally been forced to identify with the pain of another not like himself and to intercede on her behalf, we must not lose sight of the fact that such virtue is still founded on the need for a strong police state whose repressive presence is felt everywhere in the film. While the film presents us with a tantalizing definition of civic virtue founded on the disruption of an unquestioned logic of hard identity, such virtue remains wedded to the perpetuation of a police state that is the antithesis of civil society. As *Strange Days* narrates, the only way to appeal for justice in such a state is in the spectacle of our bodies' pain; the only outcome for which we can hope is that someone in power will care enough not to remain a spectator.

ODDLY ENOUGH, if *Strange Days* is remembered by filmgoers, it will not be because of its thinly disguised re-creations of Rodney King beaten by the police. Instead, it will be because of this scene: a serial killer records his rape and murder of Iris with a SQUID while simultaneously wiring her to the same unit. In this way, Iris feels what it is like to rape and murder just as she herself is being raped and murdered. According to Lenny, who inadvertently "jacks into" this recording, "She sees what he sees." She is, in other words, forced to be her own victimizer as well as victim. While many people I have spoken with about this film have understandably expressed their dislike for this scene, I wish to insist that this scene's very graphic difficulty can alone make *Strange Days* worthy of study. This scene comes closer than any other in the film to capturing the obscenity that is at the center of the heightening significance of the black body in pain. For those who could already place themselves psychically in King's

COURTESY OF PHOTOFEST

body, to see the Holliday videotape over and over again on television was to find themselves drawn, like Iris, to seeing this event as the officers saw it while simultaneously feeling their blows raining down on their own bodies. What makes this scene so difficult to watch, in addition to its ugly portrayal of rape, is the way it makes explicit a psychic process that usually occurs in a mental background.

We are forced to see what they see. We are at once victim and victimizer. We are at once in the bodies of those who are being lacerated by the enforcers of state power, and in the bodies of those who are the enforcers of this power. In the outrage we feel that the four officers directly responsible for King's beating were not punished in the Simi Valley trial, to the outrage we feel that the police did not do more to stop the rioters as they looted and burned Korean American stores, to the outrage we feel that the four black teenagers caught on tape beating Reginald Denny during the riots were ultimately exonerated of criminal behavior, we find ourselves in collusion with the jurists in the first Rodney King trial, who presumably saw themselves as being protected from the violence of a black body out of control by the officers who savagely beat him with their police batons. At the end of that beating, according to the Los Angeles Times book *Understanding the Riots: Los Angeles before and after the Rodney King Case* (1992), "One of King's eye sockets was shattered, a cheekbone was fractured, a leg broken. His flesh was bruised by the repeated blows. A concussion and painful facial nerve damage complicated his other injuries" (33). If *Strange Days* provides us with some clues as to why the trope of the black body in pain waxed in cultural significance during the 1990s, can this film also tell us about the fragility of all human bodies under the violence we find ourselves horrifically retreating behind in the name of what is familiar?

While it took Anna Deavere Smith only four days to conduct all the interviews for her one-woman play *Fires in the Mirror: Crown Heights, Brooklyn and Other Identities* (1993), about a riot that took place in Brooklyn in 1991, "the more than two hundred interviews for *Twilight* began in the fall of 1992, extended through the actual performance [at the Mark Taper Forum in Los Angeles] in the summer of 1993, up through the present performance [in New York's Public Theater] in 1994" (Kondo 1996, 318).[1] Obviously, the Los Angeles riots presented Smith with a much larger aesthetic challenge than the one she encountered in Brooklyn, where conflict was localized to a specific neighborhood. While the violence in Los Angeles began locally as well, at the corner of Normandie and Florence, it spread quickly, pushing north into Koreatown and the Mid-Wilshire district. The level of destruction was, of course, unprecedented.[2]

Even today, when one drives down Vermont, a street at the epicenter of violence, one still sees burned-out empty lots enclosed by metal fences. The only difference is that the camera crews have long ago vanished and the streets are now eerily silent. Even in the middle of the afternoon on a workday, there is hardly anyone walking outside. Traffic is light. The road seems absurdly wide for the few cars, fewer pedestrians, and more numerous police vehicles who travel on it. There is no shade because the trees have been chopped down. Only a few stores seem to be open. There is a Ralph's grocery store. There is an occasional gas station and convenience store. Although the ashes have largely been swept away from what remains as material testament to the riots, grass grows where buildings once stood.

To her credit, Smith does not respond to the stark destruction that still seems to echo down this quiet street by focusing on only a handful of sensational characters. The published version of *Twilight: Los Angeles, 1992* (1994), which will be the focus of this chapter, contains over forty-five interviews, each of varying length. The interviewees are from every conceivable background. Some are public figures, others well-known

academics or local activists, and many unfamiliar names even to those who may know the area well. They are each presented in a unique format that maintains the pauses, stutters, mispronunciations, grammatical errors, and staging clues (presented in parentheses) that replicate on the page the dramatization Smith performed on stage. We are thus invited, as we read their words, to listen to the way the interviewees might speak if they were in the same room with us. If we pay attention to this format, we might note that what directs Smith's editorial choices are those moments in a person's self-presentation when her or his speech breaks up, loses its coherence, leaves the speaker hunting for a word or a phrase that might help with regaining the thread of thought suddenly come undone. To ensure that this format remains foregrounded, this chapter quotes from the published play as if the text were verse. This means that when the text is too long or too awkward to quote as it appears in the original, it appears here with slashes where line breaks should be. In addition, I quote particular passages as they appear in the original to emphasize the formal quality of the textual presentations, in large part because these are the moments when the play sheds the most light on the culture of wounding inhabited by its many speakers.

By wounding, I mean a metaphor for the distress found in our social interactions with one another in public spaces. This metaphor hinges on a double meaning. First, wounding imagines a site of contact between the isolation of one's body and the social world beyond. Wounding might therefore be understood as the expression of a yearning to transgress restrictive boundaries, to enable freer intercourse with those not like oneself, and ultimately to found a greater sense of community than what is already permitted. Second, wounding imagines this kind of contact as always accompanied by severe pain. The body's isolation from the exterior beyond its limits cannot be penetrated without the separation of skin, the shedding of blood, the tearing of tissue, and the sharp shooting pain of nerve endings discharging messages of alarm to the brain. Similarly, a person's social isolation cannot be penetrated without the always palpable, and palpitating, possibility of rejection, stigmatization, even physical violence. Wounding, to put it another way, expresses a desire for interaction with other people and peoples at a time when, and in a culture where, such interactions are fraught with likely dangers. In addition, we know such interactions can lead to pain because it has already happened to us. Previous encounters with others have left us recalling the sting of rejection, social stigmatization, and even physical violence, the crystallized memory of which I will be calling injury. Injury teaches us to be wary of placing ourselves yet again in such a vulnerable position.

In dramatizing how people cope with the apparent pain that accompanies the pursuit of a desire for the social, *Twilight* highlights three strategies employed by its interviewees in trying to make sense of their immersion in a culture of wounding, the feeling of being enveloped in a situation where isolation is the norm and relating to others unlike oneself an act of frustrating, and often painful, difficulty. These strategies are naïveté, identity politics, and professionalism. This chapter examines each strategy in order, starting with the way Smith imagines Reginald Denny's character. The appearance of this character in *Twilight* is particularly revealing because he was so often represented after the riots as being a pure victim, one who innocently stumbled into the violence without any other kind of ulterior investment and was therefore unfairly attacked by crazed black youths whom he later so generously forgave. The chapter proceeds to explore several characters who seem representative in the play of specific racialized identities. These characters are explicitly invested in identifying themselves with their particular racial or ethnic identities, and therefore we might be justified in reading their accounts of the riots as emanating from a politics rooted in such identities. At stake here is the difference between wounding as frustrated desire for social interaction and injury as law-mediated anger over social abjection. Finally, the chapter turns to the many professionals in the play, who enact both the promise and the limitations of their socially proscribed roles. To whom can we turn, this section asks, when contact with others not like oneself seems inevitably to lead to pain and stigma? In what ways can we ourselves participate in the formation of a public sphere that will go beyond the descent into ressentiment and a self-mounting horror at our participation in a culture of wounding, as found in *Twilight*? The sequence of this chapter's exploration of Smith's play begins with a concentrated focus on one character and proceeds to discuss a multiplying number of characters. In this process, it becomes more fragmented in form. This is meant to capture the ways in which Smith opens up to view a social body that is, and remains, deeply wounded. My formal mimicry of the play's own formal experiments is mean to highlight the inconclusiveness that Smith's theatrical experiments emphasize. In *Twilight*, to put it simply, Smith does not allow us to remain spectators safely removed, somehow, from the scenes of interpersonal conflict to which her characters give such generous witness. At the same time, she offers us precious little direction for how to respond to the scenes of conflict she unleashes through their words.

· · · NAÏVETÉ

About two-thirds of the way through the PBS adaptation of *Twilight*, Smith appears on screen as Reginald Denny.[3] Denny is the white truck driver whose telecast beating by black teenagers at the start of the riots became almost as notorious as the Holliday videotape. He had blacked out just as the attack began and woke up days later at the hospital with disfiguring physical injuries. The first person to visit him in his room was Jesse Jackson:

> and I'm thinkin':
> not this guy,
> that's the dude I see on TV all the time.[4]

Smith's face lights up when she says these words, with a long pause after the first line, a stress on *this* in the second line, and a louder pronunciation of the last word on the third line that underscores the end of this thought. Speaking at this moment with nasally vowels, an uncontrolled excitement, and exaggerated facial expressions, Smith seems to reveal some closely guarded insight about Denny. The childlike wonder that suffuses Smith's face when she says these words on screen suggests a lack of sophistication, an inability to guile, a credulity bordering on the simple-minded. He is naive.

Not particularly flattering, this apparent insight nevertheless grants Denny an appealing personality that draws the viewer into feeling great sympathy for what he has had to endure. Denny's naïveté stands out as somehow unique, genuine, and likeable, especially when compared to the knowingness of the other interviewees. It is hard not to feel sorry for him.

A more worldly person might have viewed Jesse Jackson's visit with cynicism, as another public figure looking for a good photo-opportunity. But the awe with which Denny says he greets this personage suggests that he has maintained a lack of sophistication which renders him both artless and unable to discern ulterior motives in others. This is a lack that others have long ago shed, but which Denny somehow holds onto, ineluctably, despite all that has happened to him. As such, he seems impervious to a culture of wounding that warns social contact may come at a painful price:

> Someday when I, / ugh, / get a house, / I'm gonna have one of the rooms / and it's just gonna be / of all the riot stuff / and it won't be a / blood-and-guts memorial, / it's not gonna be sad, / it's gonna be a happy room. It's gonna be . . . / Of all the crazy things that I've got, / all the, / the / love and compassion / and the funny notes / and the letters from faraway places, / just framed, placed, / framed things, / where a person will walk in / and just have a good old time in there. (110–111)

How can he remain so optimistic about his own future after the beating he has endured? And why do we find ourselves so attracted to this quality? I focus on this interview because, far from being somehow outside the culture of wounding found in the pages of *Twilight*, Denny exemplifies a powerful strategy for coping with its contradictoriness. He insists on a political naïveté that leaves him impervious to recriminations against those who attacked him. Unfortunately, this naïveté also made him unaware of the dangers to which he had originally exposed himself when he made his fateful turn onto Florence, right into the middle of an angry crowd at the start of the Los Angeles riots.

When we turn to the published version of Denny's interview, which is comparatively longer than many of the other interviews in the book (suggesting its relative importance for Smith), it reinforces the initial impression made by Smith's performance of his character in the PBS version. Denny's account of his beating and subsequent stay at the hospital starts with an emphasis on the quotidian nature of his existence before the riots: "Every single day / I must make this trip to Inglewood—no problem— / and I get off the freeway like usual, / taking up as much space as I can in the truck" (103). Denny thus introduces himself as someone who has to work for a living and who, because of this fact, has no choice but to turn off the freeway onto a neighborhood street. Immediately following these lines, he says, "People don't like that. / But I have to" (103). Already, in this suggestive description of the everyday, we are at once asked by Denny for pity *and* clued into a buried social tension. Denny must work and, in working, he must make a turn daily that blocks traffic, makes noise with a large semi-truck, and intrudes upon a space that otherwise might be thought of as residential and therefore off-limits to more commercial vehicles.

In what ways, a less naive perspective might ask, did "people" make their dislike of his presence known? Were there verbal altercations; annoyed and hostile stares; honking car horns; pedestrians who intentionally jaywalked slowly in front of him; or the many other sullen, subtle, and not-so-subtle ways in which a person can make another feel unwelcome? For a moment, we are afforded the smallest of glimpses into the way the residents in this neighborhood might have viewed Denny's truck making its loud lumbering way past their houses, trailed by the inevitable smell of diesel and smoke: "That little turn onto Florence / is pretty tricky, / it's really a tight turn. / I take two lanes to do it in" (103). We are also given a glimpse into Denny's own limited work life. He has no choice but to make this turn and intrude on the lives of these people, who perhaps don't care enough about what he has to endure. If they did, they would accept his daily intrusions with more understanding.

Later in his interview, however, this reference to necessity falls into the background as Denny speaks of what he usually finds when he makes this turn onto Florence:

Strange things do happen on that street. / Every now and again police busting somebody. / That was a street that was never . . . / I mean, it was always exciting . . . / we, / lot of guys looking forward to going down that street / 'cause there was always something going on, it seemed / like, / and the cool thing was I'd buy those cookies / from / these guys / on the corner, / and I think they're, uh, / Moslems? / And they sell cookies / or cakes, / the best-tasting stuff, / and whatever they were selling that day, / and it was always a surprise. (105)

In this passage, Denny admits to eager anticipation. He looks forward to making this turn because it is a reprieve from the repetition of his daily routine, one which contains few surprises. The only time he can break free of the deadening familiarity of this kind of existence is when he drives down this street. There is danger there, as well as unexpected social opportunities. In addition to the predictable scenes of police officers going about their business—a kind of excitement that has in any case already been so exploited in television and movie dramas too numerous to mention that it can no longer be considered a surprise—there is the much more extraordinary exchange between Denny, a white truck driver, and the black Moslems selling tasty treats, presumably to raise money for their advocacy of self-help and exclusionary moral uplift.[5] We can imagine the pleasantries Denny and the nameless religious adherent might share, the smiles on faces usually turned impassive and unapproachable toward him, the physical communion of trading money for cookies and homemade cakes at a moment of hasty but nonetheless friendly contact. All of these social activities might understandably seem sweeter to Denny than the actual treats he stops to purchase.

For some, this admission of pleasure might suggest that Denny is not being exactly candid when he says he has to make this turn. Perhaps he could choose an alternative route, or alternate the routes he takes. Certainly, the gridlike layout of Los Angles would have allowed him a number of different ways to make this trip. Indeed, we have only his word that this turn was a necessity for him. Also, when we are told this turn is made by "lot of guys," this should raise alarms about the intensity of the buried social tension in this narrative. Denny is not the only one who makes this dangerous and inconvenient turn onto Florence every day. There are others, a daily repetition of many trucks that block traffic, make loud noises, spew black smoke into the air, shake the walls of one's house. It must certainly be an index of political powerlessness that the residents near this corner could not halt such a parade of trucks. We could certainly imagine that if such a parade of loud, noisy, hulking commercial vehicles were to take place in a more affluent neighborhood such as Brentwood or Beverly Hills, the local residents would know how to put an end to it quickly. At least one interviewee in *Twilight* wondered about what Denny's truck was doing on Florence when it was stopped. Allen

Cooper, aka Big Al, an ex–gang member and an activist in the national movement to bring about and maintain a truce between rival street gangs, asks: "Are they [the government] sure that truck belonged in that area? / Did they check to see if that truck qualified to fit on that city street? / No, they didn't check that" (99). Here is a question that was not asked by many other commentators on the riots, in part because it is inappropriate given the level of suffering that Denny has had to endure: was the violence against Denny completely random, or was there already a history of local and buried social tension that acted as a catalyst for anger turned physical?

We might counter this question with another. Even if Denny's actual reason for making this turn is to seek out the "surprise" that might await him on this street, is this reason enough to condemn him for his behavior? Is necessity, in other words, the only acceptable rationale that can excuse his intrusion into the lives of the people in this neighborhood? Denny's account of why he takes this turn day after day, even when it evokes dislike, suggests a yearning for the strange: the unscripted surprise of social contact with others not like himself, the excitement of lurking dangers that could also yield the pleasurable moment of buying sweets from a stranger, the prospect of an encounter with an Other whose difference might free him from the too-sameness of his own life. What I am suggesting here is that Denny's account of his riot experiences emblematizes double meaning of wounding as social metaphor, the desire for interpersonal contact with Others unlike oneself that cannot be acted on without the all-too-real prospect of rejection, if not actual physical pain. Wounding is special because it visually dramatizes this predicament of desire for interpersonal expansion and the likely prospect of social rebuke.

Because of its visual nature and its subsequent ability to capture viscerally this confounding predicament as it exerts itself in our daily lives, wounding as metaphor has enjoyed a special place in the way critics and cultural producers have tried to comprehend a creeping sense of pessimism about the future. In a provocative account of what he calls "wound culture," for example, Mark Seltzer tries to explain the spectacles of bodies in pain that are everywhere in popular culture as one possible consequence of this double meaning of wounding: "One discovers again and again the excitation in the opening of the private and bodily and psychic interiors: the exhibition and witnessing, the endless reproducible display, of wounded bodies and wounded minds in public. In wound culture, the very notion of sociality is bound to the excitation of the torn and opened body, the torn and exposed individual, as public spectacle" (1998, 254). Even Seltzer's exaggerated prose in this passage, and throughout his book, speaks to a desire to describe what he sees as a pathological public sphere, an inability to speak and listen in public spaces that is figured, especially in popular culture, as violent, graphically gruesome, spectacular and bodily violated. At the same time, his argument's numbing cross-hatching of quotations, illustrative examples, and brief explications performs on the page, as Smith performs on a stage, the blurring of boundaries that he says is the experience of wound culture, the torn body being a master image of our inability to tell the difference between interior and exterior, private and public.[6] In this way, Seltzer seems to share the same excitement over the social possibilities that "torn and opened" bodies presumably help to generate. Wounding is painful, but also exciting.

Furthermore, the metaphor of wounding (as gerund), as opposed to a wound (a noun), refers to an act that is occurring, an action that is itself always already taking place. Wounding is a sight that wounds as much as the physical violence that tears through flesh, rather than something that has happened—that is, a wound (or as I wish to insist in this chapter, an injury)—and that can therefore eventually find healing. When we catch sight of a deep gash or a puckering scar, we recoil in horror at the sight with the feeling that our minds have also somehow been cut by just looking at such an opening. As Anne Cheng states, "When we turn to the performance [of *Twilight*] itself, the assembly of impassioned, conflictual testimonies repeatedly reminds the audience that there may never be enough expressions of individual or national justice, reparation, guilt, pain, or anger to make up for the racial wounds cleaved into the American psyche—remembered by both the dominant and the marginalized alike as inconsolability itself" (2001, 171). Wounding in *Twilight* thus blurs the protective seal between those on display and those in the audience, between the marginalized and the dominant (however these two categories might be defined, refuted, insisted on, revised), between the inside and outside.

By blurring such a seal, wounding frees one (and not necessarily in a positive sense) from one's limitations, communicating a pain that can be felt almost as if it were happening to one's own body, without, at the same time, any promise of relief from pain. Denny recalls:

> By this time, it was tons of glass and blood everywhere,
> 'cause I've seen pictures of what I looked like
> when I first went into surgery,
> and I mean it was a pretty
> bloody mess.
> And they showed me my hair,
> when they cut off my hair
> they gave it to me in a plastic bag.
> And it was just long hair and
> glass and blood. (109)

Wounding is manifested in this passage by the graphic evidence of the body's suffering. This suffering is made substantial in blood and shorn hair, the weight of his pain practically measurable as bodily remains fitting inside a single clear bag. The materiality of these remains, the "hair and / glass and blood," communicates visually the breaking of skin, the oozing of blood, the removal of hair to reach vital organs in a desperate race to save his life. In addition, the reference to broken shards of glass evokes the instruments of pain that let us imagine the graphic extension of their qualities—sharp, jagged, brittle, multiple—digging into flesh and producing disfigurement. The dead matter that is nevertheless alive with the memory of violence, pain, and shock carries us back immediately to the moment when this memory was made, and it literalizes an inability to distinguish between private and public by opening up the boundaries of the body's surface, exposing what is inside with the outside. Denny literally holds out the evidence of this blurring by presenting us in his speech with a bag full of his insides (blood), an extension of his outer protection (hair), and the instruments that broke through this protection (shards of glass).

The apparent enthusiasm with which Denny recounts this dead matter suggests, as well, Denny's removal from his own pain, and a certain sense of pleased wonder that it was his body that somehow became the center of so much attention and sympathy. From one perspective, we might emphasize how this narrative fits into our current understandings of how a pain-inducing, physically traumatizing experience is processed by the mind. "But when I knew something was wrong was when they bashed in the / right window of / my truck," Denny tells us. "That's the end of what I remember as far as anything / until five or six days later" (105). Physically incapacitated by violence, Denny became unaware of what happened to him after being attacked. For weeks, he did not know, and was not allowed to know, the kind of physical violence he had had to endure. Indeed, the rest of the country and the rest of the world, enthralled, horrified, disgusted by the images in which his body is being beaten and dehumanized, knew more about what had happened to him than Denny himself did: "It was quite a few weeks after I was in the hospital / that they even let on that there was a riot, / because the doctor didn't feel it / was something I needed to know. / Morphine is what they were givin me for pain, / and it was just an interesting time. / But I've never been in an operating room. / It was like . . . / this is just . . . / I 'member like in a movie / they flip on the big lights / and they're really in there" (106).

Denny learns the truth of his own physical affliction through the same outlets of information available to the rest of the public. News footage, fragmented eyewitness accounts caught on film, and movie clips that can stand in for those scenes that cannot be otherwise graphically visualized became the main ways in which Denny imagines the horror of what has happened to him. Indeed, Denny describes his unlucky turn onto Florence, the "surprise" he found there, as, again, "just like a scene / out of a movie" (103). Even what he sees with his own eyes can only be interpreted by him through the more familiar lenses of a movie screen. Similarly, the very privacy of his pain can only be accessed by him through his pain's public display. At the moment of pain's infliction, there is only a blank, an unconsciousness that is later filled in by how others respond to him; by how others have depicted what has happened to his body; and by how his body, disarticulated into fragments and alienated from his sense of self as something that can be held in a plastic bag, appears to him.

A second perspective expressed by several interviewees in *Twilight*, however, is less interested in the way Denny processes his painful ordeal and is focused more on why it is that the spectacle of Denny's beating by black teenagers attracted such a flood of what Denny himself calls "love and compassion" (111). Why did so many famous people come to visit him at the hospital? Why did strangers send him "letters from faraway places" (111)? Why were there so many thoughtful artifacts that can be "framed" as commemorative of "a good old time" (111)? Paul Parker, about whom we will hear more in this chapter, observes, "Because Denny is white, / that's the bottom line. / If Denny was Latino, / Indian, or black, / they wouldn't give a damn, / they would not give a damn. / Because many people got beat, / but you didn't hear about the Lopezes or the Vaccas / or the, uh, Quintanas" (172). Allen Cooper, aka Big Al, concurs: "That Reginald Denny thing is a joke. / It's a joke. / That's just the delusion to the real / problem" (102). Clearly, not all the interviewees in *Twilight* feel the attraction of Denny's naïveté. Perhaps the reason for this animosity lies not in their disregard for Denny's personal pain, but in their frustration that his pain has become representative of the ways in which whites would be brutalized by blacks if there were no repressive forces holding them in check. Against the image of Rodney King's beating by four police officers, the images of Denny's mute body being beaten by four black youths convey a formal parallelism. As much as the black body might be brutalized by whites, the white body is equally in danger of being brutalized by blacks. Indeed, which comes first, the repressive beating or the pervasive threat of what might happen if such a *preemptive beating* did not occur more regularly? The political naïveté, then, that seems to shroud Denny, and which Denny's interview substantiates, makes him appear a vulnerable civilian who, at a moment of state neglect from its duties to maintain law and order, would easily become the prey of horrible social predators. The more sympathy his suffering attracts, the more justifiable it becomes to inflict suffering on others to whom sympathy is usually denied.

Given the social context against which the meaning of his suffering is produced, it is no wonder that suspicion hangs over Denny's own careful attempt not to blame those who have attacked him. As Denny makes clear in his interview, his anger is directed at other white men: "You take the toughest / white guy / who thinks he's a bad-ass / and / thinks he's better than any other race in town, / get him in a position where he needs help, /

he'll take the help / from no matter who the color of the guy across. . . . / That's the person I'd like to shake and go, / 'Uuuh, / you fool, / you selfish little shit'—" (111–112). Perhaps this principled stance is meant only to maximize the kind of pathos his naïveté generates. As the introductory note to his interview states, Denny is with his lawyer, Johnnie Cochran Jr., when he gives this interview. Cochran, of course, would only a few years later become famous for being the high-priced black lawyer who helped O. J. Simpson get an acquittal. What is less well known is that Cochran represented Denny and several other victims of the riots in a lawsuit against the LAPD for $40 million. Unfortunately for Denny, the lawsuit was dismissed in May 1998 (Sanz 1999, 233). Apparently, whatever sympathy the spectacle of his body's brutalization by black teenagers elicited during the heated moments of the riots and its immediate after-math was not enough to help Denny out personally in the long run.[7]

· · · IDENTITY POLITICS

In many of the interviews in *Twilight*, we encounter the starting assumption that the interviewee occupies a position of radical pain. These inter-viewees are swallowed up by bitterness over the ways in which they possess bodies that are, literally or figuratively, wounded in some terrible way. If not physically mangled or scarred, these interviewees speak about being psychically damaged, of having undergone a humiliating experi-ence that leaves them feeling socially on the outside—marginal, despised, stigmatized, abject.[8] Indeed, most of the interviewees are consumed less by the physical pains they have suffered, often (if at all) long ago in the past, but by an emotional pain that draws upon the figurative meaning of physically hurt bodies. The bitterness caused by such emotional pain, in turn, speaks more to what I have been calling injury than to wounding.

The concept of injury, as Carl Gutiérrez-Jones explains, is inextricably bound up with the law and with the state that provides the muscle to enforce the law: "Like the verb form 'to injure,' injury marks an act against 'jur,' against the law, rights, and accepted privilege" (2001, 24). Hence, this concept suggests the ways in which injury reifies a feeling of having been wronged within social, and bureaucratic, institutions that may or may not require some kind of mandated compensation. Another way to imagine this concept is to consider injury as denoting a site of social contestation, yet another nodal point where cultural politics must struggle over the articulation of pain in public. But unlike other nodal points, this articulation is also accompanied by questions of blame and recompense. Who caused the injury? In what ways might we enumerate a just compensation for the suffering caused by such injury? Is one's injury even a valid hurt to which one can make claim? Can one maintain the meaningfulness of such claims when everyone seems to have the right to claim one kind of injury or another—when, in other words, everyone seems to feel somehow as if they are adjected by a state that they cannot help turning to for succor? Who will adjudicate between such claims, and decide not only blame but blame worthiness? These are the questions with which many of Smith's interviewees, in expressing their feelings of having been injured, struggle.

There is, for instance, Rudy Salas Jr., the first interviewee in *Twilight*. An artist who as a young man was savagely kick in the head by white policemen during the Zoot Suit Riots of 1942 and who as a result has impaired hearing, Salas struggles with his hatred for all white policemen: "I don't like to hate, never do, / the way that my Uncle Abraham told me that hate is to / waste / energy and you mess with the man upstairs, / but I had an insane hatred of white policemen. / I used to read the paper—it's awful, it's awful— / if I would read about a cop shot down in the street, / killed, / dead, / a human being! / a fellow human being? / I say, / 'So, you know, you know, so what, / maybe he's one of those motherfuckers that, / y'know' " (3–4). In the midst of a powerful anger that makes him indifferent to the pain of another, Salas seems to struggle in this passage with the recognition that another person is actually in pain. Although this other person represents a social force that has repeatedly done damage to him, demeaned him, and in turn threatened his own son (we learn in this interview that a police officer pulled a gun on his son during an apparent racially motivated stop), he still tries to maintain some sense of common ground with this other person. Not exactly forgiveness, the sense of commonality he tries to maintain is more an attempt not to become the kind of person that might take pleasure in the suffering of another.

In a way, Salas engages in a paradoxical refusal of commonality when he seeks to recognize commonality, since he seems to see in the representatives of state power a person who would enjoy the pain another might suffer: "I turned around I threw a punch at one of 'em. / I didn't hit him hard, / but that sealed my doom. / They took me to a room / and they locked the door behind me / and there was four guys, four cops there / kicking me in the head" (3). In trying not to take pleasure in the death of such a representative, Salas expresses his desire not to become like that representative. In trying to rise above the anger that he cannot help feeling, he seeks to differentiate himself from the conditions of his life which keep pulling him into racially charged encounters. He says at one point,

> Damn, man,
> I'd like to kill their dads. That's what I always think about.
> I always dream of that—
> break into their houses and drag their dads out.
> Well, you see, that relieves me.
> But, you see, I still have that prejudice against whites. (5)[9]

Salas has severely been injured, and those close to him continue to be injured in similar ways. As a result, he tells us, he feels an anger that requires someone to blame, a wish if not an act that someone will suffer as much, if not more, than he has suffered.

The powerful awareness of having an injury that does not stop hurting also begins Mrs. Young-Soon Han's interview. A Korean American merchant whose store was destroyed during the riots, Han observes about the televised celebrations that took place after the second Rodney King trial, when two of the officers responsible for his beating were found to have violated King's civil rights: "What about last year? / They destroyed innocent people. / (*Five-second pause*) / And I wonder if that is really justice / (*And a very soft 'uh' after 'justice,' like 'justicah,' but very quick*) / to get their rights / in this way. / (*Thirteen-second pause*) / I waseh swallowing the bitternesseh, / sitting here alone / and watching them" (247). A little later in this interview, Han attempts a softening of this position, finding that past African Americans struggles have made life easier for other racial minorities as well. Still, by the end, she finds herself unable to feel as the celebrants being broadcast on television seem to be feeling: "But after the riots / there were too much difference" (249). As in Salas's interview, Han also struggles, and doesn't quite succeed in overcoming, a feeling of having been grievously wronged. She feels this wrong so keenly that feelings of sympathy, much less empathy, have dried up even in the witnessing of another's suffering or apparent recompense for suffering.

Similarly, Paul Parker, whose brother was tried as one of Denny's assailants during the riots, refuses any sympathy for those who would deny him and his kind an equal amount of concern first: "They basically feel that if it's a black-on-black crime, / if it's a nigger killin' a nigger, / they don't have no problem with that. But let it be a white victim, oh, / they gonna . . . they gonna go / to any extremes necessary / to basically convict some black people. / So that's more or less how . . . / really what made me bitter" (171). Parker makes it clear in his speech that he too has suffered an injury: "You know, like I said before, we innocent. Like I said, / you kidnapped us, / you raped our women, / you pull us over daily, / have us get out of our cars, sit down on the curb, / you go through our cars, / you say all right, / take all our papers, go through our trunk, / all right, / and drive off, / and don't give us a ticket" (173–174). Interestingly, this injury is traced back to a larger history of slavery (he later also makes reference to the television miniseries *Roots*) and is generalized to an "us" that still suffers from random and violating police stoppages. It's not clear in this passage if such a stoppage has ever happened to Parker himself, but nevertheless he insists that he feels such injustices— which undeniably occur daily—in a personal way, almost as if every stop were happening to him. He also insists that this feeling makes it impossible for him to extend sympathy to anyone who cannot, like himself, share in this injury's historical intrusions into the present: "The Koreans was like the Jews in the day / and we put them in check. / You know, we got rid of all these Korean stores over here. / All these little liquor stores" (175).

Side by side, Parker's anger at the "Koreans" and Han's anger at "Blacks" reflect each other, mirror images of a feeling anchored to a strong sense of having been wronged. They both even use the word *bitter* to describe this feeling. Despite themselves, both seem driven to lash out, to inflict as much pain as they themselves feel, without special care against whom this pain is directed. If, as Cheng concludes, Parker reveals himself as a "person who, having himself been discriminated against, is now demanding racial allegiance in equally absolute terms and does not seem to see the irony or horror provoked by his echoing bigotry" (2001, 176), a judgment in kind might also be made of Han's expressions of anger. She too echoes a bigotry that she cannot overcome, no matter how much she seems to try in her interview, in part because the injury that she suffers from has grown to consume all other considerations or outward-directed identifications. Her interview begins with the proclamation, "Until last year / I believe America is the best. / I still believe it" (244–245). After this reclamation of a nationalist sentiment that cannot, somehow, be repudiated for too long, she lists all the ways in which she has become a "victim": "as / the year ends in '92 / and we were still in turmoil / and having all the financial problems / and mental problems. / Then a couple of months ago / I really realized that / Korean immigrants were left out / from this / society and we were nothing. / What is our right?" (245). These cries of pain are transformed, as in Parker's interview, into an acrimonious moment of racial repudiation:

> Many Afro-Americans
> (*Two quick hits*)
> who never worked
> (*One hit*),
> they get
> at least minimum amount
> (*One hit*)
> of money
> (*One hit*)
> to survive.
> We don't get any! (246)

Both Parker and Han, then, seem to validate an observation that Elaine Scarry made famous in *The Body in Pain: The Making and Unmaking of the World* (1985): "Either [pain] remains inarticulate or else the moment it first becomes articulate it silences all else" (60).

Finally, this observation can also aptly describe Judith Tur, a reporter for the Los Angeles News Service who shows Smith a videotape in which Denny is being beaten. While the tape is running, she comments on what is occurring there. In the process, she starts to get very angry and begins

to call Denny's assailants names: "Okay, here's another animal / videotaping this guy. / These people have no heart. / These people don't deserve / to live. / Sorry for getting emotional, / but I mean this is not my United States anymore. / This is sicko" (96). The references to those involved in the beating as being beastlike, heartless, and "these people" obviously perform the function of refusing an identification with persons she abhors. They are nothing like her. But there are many similarities in this passage that are hard to ignore. She is screening a videotape made by reporters like herself, and in this videotape there is another person making a similar kind of videotape. When she calls that person an "animal" for taping this beating, what is the distinction she makes from the reporters filming this scene? As if to reinforce such a similarity, an identification that is made even at the moment of its most strident refusal, Tur reflects:

> We've all had a rough time in our life. / I've had major rough time. At forty-two years old / I left my husband. / Never got divorced 'cause he died four months later. / You know what Judith Tur did? / I used to be a clothing manufacturer. / My husband was major gambler, / blew everything. / I was penniless. / I got a job from ten until three in the afternoon working in a doctor's / office making minimum / and from four until midnight every day / working in a market as a cashier. / I mean, from living on Bel Air Road to . . . / I hadda do it.(97)

As in Parker's and Han's interviews, these reflections on an injury that has been inflicted prior to the interview lead to a heated racial diatribe:

> But I would never think of going on welfare.
> I would never think of robbing a market,
> holding
> somebody at gunpoint.
> I hate guns.
> But you know what?
> I don't hate them anymore.
> If I'm threatened, my life is threatened, I'm not even
> going,
> going to hesitate. (98)

Despite the fact that Salas, Parker, Han, and Tur are separated from one another by numerous axes of difference (race, gender, class, English-language fluency, and so forth), a formal pattern emerges in all four of their interviews. There are (1) the reference to an injury that they still suffer from; (2) a feeling of anger that seems connected to this injury; (3) a directing outward of this anger at members of another racially defined group; and, finally, (4) a pervasive sense of sadness that they are somehow disconnected from others.[10] What accounts for these startling similarities in narrative construction? One credible response traces these similarities to a loss of faith in the fiction of progress—the belief that we are marching in lockstep toward an inevitable future of ever-increasing prosperity, fairness, and commonly shared enlightenment (a nationalist version of this fiction might assert that the United States leads this march and is therefore responsible for exhorting those who have fallen behind to catch up, even at the point of a gun). This loss of faith has occurred because we cannot maintain this belief in progress without, at the same time, turning a blind eye to the ecological disasters, the racial and gendered divides, the gulfs of access to the material necessities of human life that are everywhere forming and widening around us. These inequities appear to many, especially those who have suffered the most, as constituent to narratives of progress. Therefore, a calling attention to particular identities as injured, as an expression of "desire for recognition," is also a demand that progress recognize its abject, the conveniently marginalized that reveal the lies upon which optimism about the future is built.

Judith Tur, then, can be heard giving voice to the fear generated by the unraveling of narratives of progress in the face of minorities who want special recognition for their racial injuries: "and what's happening, the white people are getting so angry / now / that they're going back fifty years instead of being pushed ahead" (98). Implicit in this observation are the kinds of questions that began this section: Having accepted the testimony of the abject, what remains of the future? Don't we all end up retreating into our personal tales of suffering and pain, as Tur does in her interview, demanding in some way that another's personal injury is no bigger than our own? If we are all somehow suffering from an injury, as these interviews seem to testify, how can we pay more attention to some expressions of suffering more than others without seeming arbitrary and insensitive, if not simply accusatory? As Tania Modleski admits in her reflections on Anna Deavere Smith's drama, when everyone seems to have a story of personal abjection, it is hard not to feel left out when one story is given preference over another. "I must confess," Modleski writes, "that I was disturbed by Smith's choice of a woman [Tur] to be the voice of racism— after all, we live in a white patriarchy, not a matriarchy. . . . I did not initially consider my privileged relation to women of color, but rather thought primarily about my own oppression. I even briefly considered withdrawing my article from this collection. If Smith was not prepared to acknowledge my oppression as a woman, I felt, I would not recognize hers as an African American" (1997, 70).

Furthermore, as Wendy Brown argues, the ever-increasing political strength of identities formed from injury leads to a parasitic dependence on the very fiction these identities putatively repudiate. These identities must continue to insist that such a fiction exists (whether we call it white supremacy, capitalism, or patriarchy), that it remains dominant, and that as a result it continues to make them abject. Brown names this process "ressentiment," Friedrich Nietzsche's keyword for "the moralizing revenge of the powerless" (1995, 66). Ressentiment "produces an affect (rage, righteousness) that overwhelms the hurt" felt by those whose unrecognized identities seem to have been selected for them by outside forces, "produces a culprit responsible for the hurt," and "produces a site of revenge to displace the hurt (a place to inflict hurt as the sufferer has been hurt). Together these operations both ameliorate (in Nietzsche's term, 'anaesthetize') and externalize what is otherwise 'unendurable'" (68). We see these operations at work in the four interviews mentioned above. Salas, Han, Parker, and Tur insist on a "hurt" which is caused by some "culprit"—white policemen, "Afro-Americans," "like Jews in the day," and "these people," respectively—and, in response, engage in a logic of escalating recrimination. Because one of your group (the culprit) injured me, it is all right for one of my group (or anyone else for that matter) to injure one of your group back even more. While each of these interviewees exhibits varying degrees of self-awareness about their participation in these operations, they nevertheless cannot exempt themselves fully from its ameliorating, but temporary, effects.

What these expressions of ressentiment register, at least implicitly, is the ways in which these interviewees occupy what I have been calling a culture of wounding. Brown gestures to this culture when she observes, "the characteristics of late modern secular society, in which individuals are buffeted and controlled by global configurations of disciplinary and capitalist power of extraordinary proportions, and are at the same time nakedly individuated, stripped of reprieve from relentless exposure and accountability for themselves, together add up an incitement to *ressentiment* that might have stunned even the finest philosopher of its occasions and logics. Starkly accountable yet dramatically impotent, the late modern liberal subject quite literally seethes with *ressentiment*" (1995, 69).

Can there be any doubt that the four interviews we have examined above "seethe" with a search for someone to blame for the sense of separation, vulnerability, and worthlessness their speeches vent? Don't these four interviewees make personal a subjection that is occurring more broadly, at an abstract level, which defies easy diagnosis? And do they themselves not also wonder if the anger they cannot seem to help but direct against a group of other people or peoples will only give them a temporary, and minor, relief from their feelings of being abject? The predicament of finding oneself immersed in a culture of wounding might thus be characterized as the enactment of ressentiment. But if this is true, what the juxtaposition of so many competing but formally similar interviews in *Twilight* suggests is that such an enactment is accompanied by a sense of horror. In addition to the nursing of an injury, the resulting anger, and the turning outward of anger against another group, Salas, Han, Parker, and Tur collectively register sadness over the fact that the social space they share is full to bursting with interpersonal pain.

··· PROFESSIONALISM

What do the professionals in *Twilight* add to the narratives we have already examined in this chapter? By professionals, I refer to those who occupy positions of authority by virtue of their specialized training and/ or their consecration by a state-recognized institution. These are the media personnel, elected representatives, and public officials who are supposed to work in public for a public good, who more or less occupy some post of dominance in a given field of power, and who might therefore be expected to shed more light on the riots than the less epistemologically privileged interviewees in the play. In their ideality, professionals (as I am defining this term rather narrowly here) will serve these functions unencumbered by personal prejudice or concern for self-gain. These are the subjects to which the injured turn in their desire for recognition, succor, and protection. Even in their less-than-ideal manifestations, professionals occupy such a position of authority that they should be incapable of viewing themselves as abject. They cannot, in other words, claim to be left out of the circuits of power in the way that the other figures I have examined in this chapter can. Indeed, these figures might be said to be an essential part of any circuit of power that might form a (at least politically) dominant class, the group or groups of people who shape public discourse and who in turn insist that they serve the public. While no single person, nor group of persons, can be said to have all the power in such a dominant class, the following certainly participate in the process by which power is produced and exercised in the United States.[11] The representatives of these different professional groups in *Twilight*, however, more often than not fail to live up to these expectations, often refusing even to admit any special access to the levers of the state, and thus professionalism itself seems in *Twilight* as inadequate a protection as naïveté or identity politics against the double meaning of wounding.

Media Personnel

The media personnel found in the published version of this play are Otis Chandler (a director of the Time-Mirror Company and the former editor of the *Los Angeles Times*), Anonymous Man #2 (a Hollywood agent), and Judith Tur. As the inclusion of the last name on this list suggests, being classified as a professional does not automatically exempt one from feelings of abjection; nor does it entail a disinterested perspective. Rather, abjection seems the product, at least in Tur's case, of having been dislodged, even temporarily, from the world of social privilege that is itself normally cut off from the daily struggles of working people. Anonymous Man #2 refers to this world in his interview when he recalls his experiences of the first day of the riots: "Bunch of us hadda go to lunch at the / the Grill / in Beverly Hills. . . . / All the, / frankly, the / white / upper class, / upper middle class— / whatever your, / the / definition is— / white successful . . . / spending too much money, / too, ya know, too good a restaurant, / that kinda thing" (134–135). More to the point, however, is the presence of the surname Chandler on this list. This name points directly to the uppermost echelons of this world of social privilege, as *Chandler* refers to the famous Los Angeles family whose patriarch Colonel Harrison Gray Otis, along with his son-in-law Harry Chandler, founded the *Los Angeles Times* and reaped a fortune by, among other things, participating in the region's numerous twentieth-century real estate expansions (Davis 1992b [1990], 25).[12]

Throughout the rest of his interview, Otis Chandler speaks about the "hope" (220), "leadership" (220), and "commitment" (221) needed to solve long-term problems, all of which will lead, "someday, / whether it's five years or ten years," to the creation of a "pleasant city / for everybody" (220). Unsurprisingly, what this booster rhetoric foregrounds is the familiar fiction of progress that I earlier suggested was confounded by the demand for recognition emanating from abject identities. However, though Chandler is willing to recognize that problems exist, he nevertheless insists that in the long run these problems can be solved. The solutions he offers, besides fine rhetoric, are unsurprisingly neoconservative: "It's gonna cost all kinds of money. / (*four counts of pause*) / I think businesses should give some, / government should give some, / and I think we're gonna have to be taxed. / Hit us all on / sales tax / or gasoline tax / or something / and take a cent or two from everybody / and build up some kind of fund" (222). We might note in this passage the long pause, which suggests Chandler's reluctance to lay out a specific proposal that might indeed entail a public commitment on his family fortune's behalf toward social spending. And when he does provide specifics, he advises the imposition of flat taxes—taxes, that is, on consumer items that do not take into account the payer's income. Indeed, since consumer items are often more expensive in poor urban neighborhoods such as South Los Angeles than in the suburbs, where more competition and greater sales volume contribute to lower prices, any increases in sales taxes usually lead to the implicit regressive demand that those least able to pay must pay the most. As opposed to the view, then, that abject identities must somehow prop up a fiction they cannot do without even as they overtly subvert it, Chandler's unreflective neoconservatism suggests that this fiction

needs no propping up because it is quite capable of adaptation and self-preservation on its own.

The media personnel in *Twilight* thus appear as full of ressentiment as the play's other interviewees do, or so out of touch that they obliviously mouth narratives that should have long ago started to sound implausible to a skeptical public. Katie Miller, a bookkeeper and accountant who resided in South Los Angeles in 1992, sums up this opinion when she recalls:

> [Paul Moyer]'s a damn newscaster. / He was on Channel 7, / now that sucker's on Channel 4, / makin' eight million dollars. / What the hell, / person make eight million dollars for readin' a piece of paper, / but that's a different story . . . / and I turn on the TV / and here is Mr. Paul Moyer / saying, / "Yeah, / they, they, ugh, / I. Magnin. / I remember goin' to that store when I was child." / What he call 'em? / He called 'em things, / these thugs going / into the store. / I said, "Hell with you, asshole." That was my, my . . . / I said, "Okay, okay for them to run into these other stores," you know, / "but don't go in no store / that I, I grew up on that has . . . / that my parents took me / to that is / expensive—." (132)

Miller thus provides us with a partially contrapuntal perspective to the one that the media personnel in this play offer about themselves. In addition to appearing out of touch or full of ressentiment, those who report and help shape the way news is presented to a general public come across as simply greedy. I characterize this perspective as "partially contrapuntal" because it does not add substantially to the negativity that the media personnel have already shaped about themselves. When we read their interviews in *Twilight* together as representing a particular professional post, they simply appear notable for their lack of professionalism.

Elected Representatives

In *Twilight*, elected representatives also appear to fall short of the ideality of professionalism. Former mayor Tom Bradley recalls how his office had prepared a number of different responses to the first Rodney King trial verdict, one for each possible outcome. "The one that I had put down as just a . . . a precautionary measure," Bradley says, "an acquittal on all counts, / was something / we / didn't seriously think could happen, / but we had a message / and it did happen" (85). The message, as he reveals, was one which called for peaceful demonstration: "do it in a verbal fashion / but don't engage in violence" (86). As we know, this message had no noticeable impact on what occurred after the verdict was announced. Perhaps it is because he was so ineffectual in the first hours of violence that Mayor Bradley sounds so defensive here.

If Mayor Bradley thus comes across in the play as out of touch, unprepared, politically weak, and too ready to defend his actions without much concern for a larger public good, the other two elected representatives in *Twilight* provide solace to varying degrees. Senator Bill Bradley, of New Jersey, speaks explicitly about the need for public institutions to take more responsibility for the inappropriate behavior of another public institution. When a black friend of his from law school happened to be pulled over by the LAPD while visiting the partner's house of the law firm he was interning at, Senator Bradley asks:

> Did the partner call the police commissioner? / Did the partner call anybody? / The answer is no. / And it gets to, well, / who's got responsibility here? / I mean, all of us have responsibility / to try to improve the circumstances / among the races of this country/ . . . The moral power of the law firm / or corporation when / moments arise such as my friend's face in the ground with the gun / pointed at his head because he was in the wrong neighborhood and / black / and the moral power of those institutions have to be brought to bear / in the public institutions, which in many places are not fair. (217)

The problem with this analysis is that it expects the corporation to behave in a fair manner. What incentive does such an institution have? What makes it a public institution, rather than a private one with a strictly defined responsibility only to its shareholders? And perhaps most important, why does responsibility fall on the shoulders of everyone except the lawmaker, whose public duty, one might imagine, would be exactly to craft laws that promote the very kind of social situation he expects corporations and law firms to promote?

Ultimately in *Twilight*, only Representative Maxine Waters, whose district was the hardest hit by the riots, speaks forcefully about the responsibility that elected politicians have toward a broadly defined constituency. She tells the story of a meeting at the White House regarding urban policy, to which she had not been invited. When she learned about the meeting, she forced herself into the meeting room and began to talk about the problems that she believed led to the riots:

> I said, "Los Angeles burned / but Los Angeles is but one / city / experiencing / this kind of hopelessness and despair" . . . / I said, "These young people / really, / ya know / are not in anybody's statistics / or data. / They've been dropped off of everybody's agenda. / They live / from grandmama to mama to girlfriend." / I said, / "We now got young people / who are twenty, twenty-one, twenty-two years old / who have never worked a day of their lives." / I said, "These are the young people in our streets / and they are angry / and they are frustrated." (168)

While this speech is fiery and inspirational, the story Waters tells is not an optimistic one. For the most part, like media personnel, elected representatives—especially the further one moves up the chain of command that hierarchically shapes this particular field of power—appear in this play as too much in a world of rarified social privilege and unable as a result to engage with the crises that triggered the riots. Politicians such as Waters, who seem less a fixture in this world than the two Bradleys mentioned above, are also, because of this, less able to move policy.

Public Officials

Despite the ineffectuality of the elected officials in *Twilight*, Mayor Bradley's tepid call for vocal (as opposed to violent) protest seems the model of stately preparedness when compared to the account that the former Chief of Police Daryl Gates offers of his behavior during the riots. "First of all, I . . . I don't think it was a fund-raiser," Gates says. "I don't think it was a fund-raiser at all. / It was a group of / people / who were in opposition to Proposition F, / We're talking about long-term support" (180). Proposition F was a proposed amendment to the city charter that would have limited police chief tenures and imposed more civilian review over the Los Angeles Police Department (Cannon 1999, 300). In the name, then, of protecting his position and the powers that are suppose to accrue to it,

Gates decided to leave the Parker Center, the main headquarters of the LAPD, to take a long leisurely drive to faraway Brentwood to attend a social function on the afternoon the King verdict was announced. Like Mayor Bradley, the tone of this interview is defensive, suggesting that Gates is more interested still, at the time of his interview with Smith, in maintaining a certain reputation than he is in doing what is best for the public at large. His self-professed actions during the riots attest, however, to the ways in which he placed appealing to his supporters and defeating a proposition that might unseat him in the future higher on his list of priorities than performing the duties entailed by his professional post. Negligence is not noxious enough to describe the impression left by his presence in this play.

However, such dereliction is not indicative of how public officials as a whole come across in *Twilight*. Other members of this group are repeatedly represented as selfless, competent, and thoughtful; by the same measure, because these figures seem to live up to the ideality of professionalism, they also indicate what the shortcomings of such an ideality necessarily entails. For instance, Sergeant Charles Duke, a weapons-tactical expert in the LAPD, patiently explains in his contribution why Laurence Powell, one of the officers responsible for beating King, should not have been on duty that evening: "Powell holds the baton / like this / and that is / not a good . . . / the proper way of holding the baton / is like this. / So one of the things they keep talking about / why did it take fifty-six baton blows. / Powell has no strength and no power / in his baton strikes. / The whole thing boils down to . . . / Powell as ineffective with the baton" (61). At one level, it is difficult not to be swayed by the confidence with which he testifies about Powell's lack of training. We get the immediate impression that if Duke were out on the streets that evening, the whole Rodney King incident would have been over before George Holliday had any time to pull out his camcorder. Duke's very tone suggests a respect for preparedness and training, and an impatience for those who have neither. On another level, however, there is something tragically limited about the focus of Duke's comments on the practicality of subduing a possible assailant. There is no questioning here about what all of his practical training is meant to accomplish, no wonder about why such assailants might exist, and no connection to a social context against which such training is deemed necessary.[13]

In addition to the narrowness of Duke's professionalism, Captain Lane Haywood of the Compton Fire Department expresses the material constraints under which public officials dedicated to their posts must work:

> And I looked up. / I saw a task force of engines / coming from Huntington Beach. / So . . . the task force, / they had three engines / and they had a battalion chief / and they had a police escort, / all white guys, / escorted in, and they had the name of the city, / and they had it blocked off with cardboard. / So they couldn't really tell what city it was from, / but in fire service you know who's who. / They, eh, had the protection / they had the manning, / they had the equipment. / And they started to extinguish the fire across the street, / and I'm standing with four guys / and this big old truck. / No help, no vests, no police, / no nothing. (115–116)

The Compton Fire Department that Haywood represents seems no less competent, and perhaps even more dedicated given the deficiencies of their equipment, than the firefighters from Huntington Beach, a more affluent neighborhood. Haywood's team, however, does seem underfunded, lacking in equipment, and unsupported by the other branches of public officialdom. As such, this segment of the play highlights the economic differences at play spatially throughout the Los Angeles region, and perhaps by extension any urban region. Those officials who serve poorer neighborhoods must do so with less material support than those who serve richer neighborhoods. No matter how scrupulously one's professionalism might be practiced, one seems inevitably limited when working under the kind of scarcity regime that Haywood testifies exists in the less affluent neighborhoods of Los Angeles.

If Sergeant Duke and Captain Haywood give witness to some of the limits of professionalism as an ideal, even if this ideal is upheld by their commitment, it is left to Dean Gilmour, a lieutenant in the Los Angeles Coroner's Office, to give testimony about the results of such limitations. Interestingly, the loss of lives that figures in Gilmour's speech is represented as stretching the limits of speech itself when he attempts to explain that all the people who died did not necessarily leave behind intact bodies to be counted:

> Uh, we . . .
> especially in a hot fire
> you're charred.
> You also, after the fact,
> have animal activity.
> Dogs
> and . . . and other critters come along
> and will disarticulate
> bodies.
> Uh,
> rats,
> uh. (193)

The lines gets shorter, thoughts trail off into incoherence and sounds that are not words, and sentences falter into incomplete phrases, then into individual words, and then into gestural utterances. In this way, these lines highlight the possibility that what cannot be expressed in speech as a finished thought likewise cannot be counted, logged, and published as positive knowledge of the violence's destructiveness. At this moment, we encounter a thorough professional whose job it is to contemplate such matters and to produce knowledge to guide policy makers and government officials. Nevertheless, this professional cannot easily find a proper way to express what is dreadful to explain, and he must take caution with his speech because what he is saying is so difficult to hear. It is exactly these kinds of moments in the play that testify most powerfully to the care one must exhibit in a culture of wounding. Speaker beware. When put too bluntly, talk of pain may cause further damage.

THERE IS A fourth group of professionals in *Twilight* that I have not mentioned so far in this chapter: academics. Perhaps it is because I am an academic myself, or because I admire the academics who find their way into the pages of this play. For whatever reason, I must admit to a reluctance in my acknowledging that the academics who appear in the play are as disappointing as many of the other professionals just mentioned. *Twilight* catches Mike Davis, for instance, ruminating nostalgically about his long-past youth of unencumbered freedom ("I'm not saying that, you know, it was utopia or / happiness / but it was . . . / it was something incredibly important" [30]), Cornel West captivated by his obvious erudition that removes him from any apparent personal involvement in the struggles he speaks about ("Yeah. / No, well, good luck, / good luck / indeed in deed / I'm always pullin' an' prayin' for ya" [47–48]), and Homi Bhabha reiterating ideas that he has shared many times before in different occasions, almost as if the particular occasion itself is of little importance ("This twilight moment / is an in-between moment. / It's the moment of dusk. / It's the moment of ambivalence" [232]).

In a different context, I might find what these figures are saying to be thoughtful, maybe even profound. But in a discussion on the culture of wounding made knowable by the juxtaposition of so many different interviewees in one play, all held together by their reference to a cataclysmic social eruption, their contributions sound merely like a faded echo of what many of the other interviewees in the play express more eloquently: the straining of social relations in an age of neoconservative irresponsibility, the ever dwindling of sharable public spaces, and the isolation that grows more acute the more we find ourselves associating with people who are just like ourselves. Political naïveté is no protection from such social circumstances. Neither is the retreat into particular camps of identity formations or the reliance on the solidity seemingly guaranteed by professional postings. These are mere reactions to problems with a deeper lying etiology, and as such these strategies, as I have called them, are symptoms of a culture that hurts us the more we dare venture into encounters with the strange. These strategies also, and perhaps more importantly, attest to the deep desire for social interaction that persists despite the risks.

The documentary *Sa-I-Gu: From Korean Women's Perspective* (1993) is ripe with vexed political meanings.[1] It reveals a group of Korean American interviewees personally traumatized by a violent event that also tears them away from the certainty of familiar narratives about their place in the world, as immigrants, as women, as small entrepreneurs. Captured on film only a few weeks after the end of the riots, many of the women are shown hovering over still ashen lots where their stores had once stood. They pick through the rubble and attempt to salvage halfheartedly what is lost, almost as if they do not quite believe what they are witnessing. Others are shown in the interiors of their homes, the tight quarters and the close-ups of their faces conveying eloquently the immediacy of an eruption that cups them in a temporal eddy of deep shock. They seem so stunned that their mouths refuse to express what their looks yearn to pour out. Framing this sense of a sudden loss that has not quite yet registered as loss is the further shock of having been abandoned. Slowly but with increasing certainty, the women recall in the documentary how the police failed to show up when the violence occurred, how neighbors pitied them or turned their backs on them but did not join them in the protection of their property, how their hopes and aspirations burned up in a few afternoons with no one willing to testify to what had been destroyed. These women were *not cared for*, in the sense of not having the physical security usually expected from a benevolent state. They were also *not cared for* in the sense of a lack of concern, as if what they had suffered and were suffering did not register as anything that deserved to be mourned, especially when compared to the spectacular images in which bodies were being beaten, of men and women being hog-tied by the police, or to the injustice of four police officers going free after what they had done to Rodney King, and of *their* buildings going up into flames anonymously as part of a mass conflagration that had no particular human referents.[2]

Sa-I-Gu is thus singular in its attempt to provide a forum for Korean

American merchant women involved in the riots to speak about what they experienced. No other forum of its kind existed at the time. This documentary, through the hard work of its director Dai Sil Kim-Gibson, enables a group of women personally and immediately traumatized by a violent event to struggle openly, in their multiple ways, with what has happened to them and with what it has revealed about their place in a social order that had only a little while before seemed benign. They are shown wondering, are those in authority potential heroes or villains? How these women *in particular* navigate between these two possible perceptions is historically significant because their ethnic group had become, if only briefly during the fieriest days of the riots, the center of national attention as the most prominent (if blurry) symbols of an alien invasion tolerated by too-liberal immigration laws and a too-hasty retreat from the policies of assimilation. The fact that they are women, furthermore, is significant because they had become visible only for their ethnicity, leaving hidden from view the way gender operated to leave the heaviest burden of such sudden visibility on their shoulders. If Korean American merchants were seen but not heard from, worried over but largely ignored, Korean American merchant women were profoundly omitted from public discourse even as they—foremost through the figure of Soon Ja Du (see next chapter)—became the most visible faces of racial strife in Los Angeles. Finally, the documentary, in addition to being broadcast on PBS, has been widely and repeatedly screened on college campuses and in classrooms across the country. Its importance as a pedagogical tool and as a historical document cannot therefore be overestimated.

This chapter proposes to pay special care to this documentary. It does so by placing its contents and form next to the ongoing discussion within critical circles about how public mourning can best be facilitated. Like Ann Cvetkovich, I worry that "a significant body of work within American studies has recently mounted a critique of U.S. culture by describing it as a trauma culture" and therefore signified such a "transformation" as "a problem, representing the failure of political culture and its displacement by a sentimental culture of feeling or voyeuristic culture of spectacle" (2003, 15). Not only a problem, "cultural formations that bring traumatic experiences into the public sphere" can also, as Cvetkovich suggests, "transform our sense of what constitutes a public sphere" (15–16). In what ways can we participate in the formation of such a public sphere? This chapter addresses this question in its reading of *Sa-I-Gu*, first (in the section "Assimilation versus Tribalism") by examining the precarious position in which Korean Americans in general found themselves at the start of the 1992 riots, second (in "The Story of Two Photographs") by painting a portrait of the affective frame this documentary places around its subject matter, third (in "The Universality of Grief," "Grief That Feeds on Itself," and "The Loss of Self") by exploring how cultural critics have incorporated an attention to affect in their inquiries, and finally in "The Intransigence of Racial Melancholia" by tracing out the ways in which this documentary's contents add to such critical attentiveness. The introduction of a personal narrative voice in what follows—my copious use of the first person—is meant, if imperfectly, to capture the power of *Sa-I-Gu*'s raw representations, its ability to move viewers to feel something about what has happened to a group of women whose personal losses might seem irrelevant in comparison to the great, grave things occurring in the world all around us. Our ability to think critically about such feelings, it seems to me, can contribute much to any intellectual project that refuses to divorce the study of feelings from the study of culture and society. In addition, an attention to such feelings can help us to question the overly commonsensical opposition between the particular and the universal, between a concern for raced peoples and a concern for all peoples, between the discourse of group rights and the discourse of human rights. Indeed, what I most wish to argue in this chapter is that a concern for the particular, for the raced, and for a single group's plight is a necessary anchor for a concern with the universal that won't simply retreat into platitude and banality.[3]

· · · **ASSIMILATION VERSUS TRIBALISM**

Sa-I-Gu might first be read as a record of Korean American merchant women's responses to the riots and, simultaneously, as an aesthetic response to the challenge of representing a social eruption of incredible social complexity, in which case we should also pay close attention to what it can tell us about the possible rigidity, flexibility, repercussions, and complicity with power entailed by the formation of a Korean American political identity. Before the riots, such an identity was inchoate in its development at best. More than a decade after the riots, it is still not clear if there is one or even several coherently developed positions that could be associated with Korean Americans, though many Korean Americans and their more sympathetic interlocutors have insisted on holding onto the view of this group as victims of "racial scapegoating."[4] *Kyopo* (or overseas Korean) merchants, in other words, have been caught between black resentment against whites and white indifference to black poverty and lack of opportunity. According to the racial scapegoating thesis: out of economic necessity, first-generation adult Korean immigrants opened stores in predominantly black neighborhoods, becoming a de facto representative of white power and substitute objects of justifiable black rage.[5] What would it mean, then, to our understanding of this emergent tendency's implications for both the future of a potentially politicized Korean American identity and the larger realignments in racial meaning that have been occurring over the most recent decades to read this documentary gothically? According to Bonnie Honig, it means replicating the perspective of the people who are governed by a state. They experience the state's laws with ambivalence, never certain whether these laws are an expression of their will or an "alien" imposition that fails to reflect their desires (2001, 9).[6] This uncertainty becomes more acute for that segment of the population who are seen as "alien," new arrivals whose place in American society is not yet settled. Such new arrivals are prone, as Honig argues (75), to be used by our host society to work through its own anxieties about the vigor of its civil sphere.

In the American context, the figure of the foreigner helps shore up arguments about national exceptionalism, the belief that America as a nation is unique because it was founded and populated by immigrants who chose to be a part of this nation. In other words, America the nation is exceptional because its citizens, or at least their ancestors, gave their active consent to being governed in a particular way by a particular state. The recent arrival of Korean Americans, then, can be read as the means by which this sense of voluntarism is reinvigorated. We have chosen to come to the United States, have actively given our consent to be governed by its laws and cultural norms, and as such are the most recent reminders of the happy marriage between the laws and institutions that govern this country and the subjects who willingly submit to these laws and institutions. This particular exceptionalist argument, of course, covers up the history of conquest, slavery, expansion, racial exclusion, and forceful manipulation abroad that has also contributed to the peopling of America's territories.

In addition, the exceptionalist argument keeps from view the fear stirred up by the specter of mass immigration that new arrivals will not, or perhaps cannot (because of their race), give their consent to be governed by their adopted government and its cultural underpinnings. Arthur Schlesinger Jr. succinctly gives expression to this fear:

> Mass migrations have produced mass antagonisms from the beginning of time. Today, as the twentieth century draws to an end, a number of factors—not just the evaporation of the cold war but, more profoundly, the development of swifter modes of communication and transport, the acceleration of population growth, the breakdown of traditional social structures, the flight from tyranny and from want, the dream of a better life somewhere else—converge to drive people as never before across national frontiers and thereby to make the mixture of peoples a major problem for the century that lies darkly ahead. (1992, 10)

The solution to this emerging "problem" offered by Schlesinger is a return to the past. We must affirm our nation's Anglo-European heritage, demand strict assimilation of recent immigrants, and carefully regulate who else will be allowed admission to the United States. Without the repressive measures necessary to translate this solution into practice, "optimism" will fade and we will be faced with the following predicament: "If separatist tendencies go on unchecked, the result can only be the fragmentation, resegregation, and tribalization of American life" (1992, 18).

For perceived foreigners such as Korean immigrants, then, we face a difficult choice. On the one hand, we are confronted by the demand that we accept our ascription into the narrative of American exceptionalism. This entails expressions of gratitude for the economic opportunities that immigration has afforded us and a steady refusal to engage in any activities, especially political, that might spoil such expressions of gratitude. On the other hand, we must live with the day-to-day reminders of the lived history that is repressed by such a narrative. If we are operators of small businesses, for instance, we might find ourselves operating them in the economic niches most available to us, blighted urban districts marred by the signs of economic polarization, capital flight, institutionalized racial oppression, and widespread political disenfranchisement that decades of economic restructuring have left in their wake. Although we operate such businesses less frequently than is widely believed (only 10 percent of Korean American merchants in Los Angeles serve primarily African American customers [E. Chang 1999b, 46]), those of us who do must nevertheless struggle with the question, Do we have an ethical responsibility to address the wrongs we find in our adopted workplaces?

One strategy around this Hobson's choice is to position ourselves as racial scapegoats, innocents who have come from elsewhere and have, through no fault of our own, found ourselves caught between age-old rivalries. We position ourselves as claimants to an American dream that promises upward mobility through hard work, the proper enthusiasm, and a high regard for the law. Those who fail to attain such promises are simply at fault for their own misery. But when crisis strikes, as it did in 1992, we find that the state upon which we have pegged our claims to an American dream is not interested in coming to our aid. Suddenly finding ourselves with few allies, we had to confront a world without the certainties afforded by the racial scapegoating thesis that made us seem, like Reginald Denny, political naïfs simply going about our business and trying to do what everyone else was doing (see previous chapter). Many of us might still cling to this argument as an explanation, but others—for instance, the sociologist Claire Jean Kim—insist that we should take a long, hard look at "the somber reality of racial power in contemporary America." Sounding much like the gothic reader that is Honig's ideal, Kim writes, "I am not sure that understanding an issue leads automatically to knowing how to 'fix' it. I am even less sure that policymakers seek solutions that are fair to all, or that academics who study events ex post facto have anything to teach activists" (2000, 223).

The opening scenes of *Sa-I-Gu* encourage a feeling of uncertainty by leading us to consider the intimacy of the riots' destructive aftermath. It begins with ominous music—deep, slow, synthetic notes—as simple white lettering states that the Rodney King verdict inaugurated the start of the riots and swept Korean Americans into the path of its "upheavals." While the music continues, the lettering fades away to reveal burning buildings in an otherwise black landscape. A voice in Korean speaks with English subtitles translating, "Since he left without telling me, I thought he would come right back. That's the last time I saw him." The pictures of burning buildings disappear in another fadeaway, revealing a shot of a woman sitting straight in a chair with a blown-up photograph of a young man who could be her son prominently on display on the mantle beyond her shoulder. The turbulence of the riots' public violence is thus contrasted sharply with the calm recollecting of its losses within a private intimacy, but the quick shift in perspective also suggests that the calmness of the latter scene hides its own fierce turmoil. This suggestion is partially verified when we learn that the woman speaking in this scene is Jung Hui Lee and the photograph a portrait of her deceased son Edward Lee, the only Korean American fatality of the riots. Through a deferral of revelation about how this scene relates to the previous scene of violence, *Sa-I-Gu*'s opening sequence presents the story of Edward Lee as nestled within the larger story about Korean American involvement in the riots. The mother's words and the orderly setting of the living room leave us with a sense of expectation, as if to suggest that neither story is complete.

This breathless waiting is maintained throughout the documentary by Mrs. Lee's framing narrative, which simultaneously acknowledges and defers acknowledgment of the other losses signified by its multiple narrators. A short while after the opening sequence, Mrs. Lee says, again translated by subtitles, "Because my son left without saying anything, I wait." The documentary ends with her saying, "It's exactly three months, as I told you before; even though I saw the body at the funeral, I don't

PICTURE TAKEN BY KULING CHOY SIEGEL. COURTESY OF DAI SIL KIM-GIBSON

remember it. My mind just won't accept it. I know people think it strange . . . that I wait for my son after seeing his body. He just went out and did not come back." These words are further accentuated by the way Mrs. Lee's narrative is intentionally dragged out over the course of the documentary. Her discourse both begins and ends the narrative, and is interspersed throughout alongside interviews with other Korean American women. Scenes of Lee's burial and the protest marches associated with it are also shown throughout. In addition, the declarative statements in white lettering that punctuate the film, the recurring decontextualized images of burning buildings, the disembodied voices of narrator and interviewees, the slow careful speech of the mother as she tells her story in a room that is in sharp contrast to the ruins of its exterior shots—all these things work to detach the viewer from the events that are being recalled.

The resulting mood makes its deepest impression about two-thirds of the way into the documentary, when Mrs. Lee narrates the belated verification of her son's death:

> My daughter said, "Mom, something has happened to my brother." Then she started crying. I urged her to tell me. "I think the victim yesterday might have been Eddie." My husband and I went to the *Korea Times*. I glanced at that day's paper. . . . The headline read, "First Korean Victim." There was one thread of hope—When my son went out, he wore a white shirt and blue jeans. The man in the picture wore a black T-shirt. This couldn't be my son. I was clutching at straws. The face was my son's, but his clothes were not. He could not possibly have changed them. I asked the man at the newspaper where my son was. I was told he was in the morgue. I went there. . . . I discovered they had nothing to confirm my son's identity. Then he brought out a pair of glasses, two dimes, and a pen. That was all he had when he was sacrificed. . . . About that black T-shirt. . . . In the *L. A. Times*, the picture was in color. What looked black in the Korean newspaper was my son's blood.

As the mother narrates this story, the screen shows the *Korea Times* headline, followed by the picture in black and white, and then in color. No matter how often I see this transformation, as the pictures verify what the mother is saying, I feel overwhelmed with grief. I find it difficult to watch, and even more difficult to talk after. I have shown this documentary to many classes, and have always found it necessary to sit in the back of the room so my students cannot see the kind of emotions it elicits from me, though perhaps such discrete behavior on my part is unnecessary since most of my students are also usually preoccupied by their own efforts to hold back their tears. I cannot say exactly what it is about this scene that affects my students and me so viscerally. Perhaps what touches us is the sense of clinging to a hope that one knows, long before the narration is finished, is an act of desperation, as the mind looks for any possible way not to accept what is being thrust upon it. Indeed, Mrs. Lee readily admits to this desperation as a preface to her story. Or, perhaps what affects us is the sense of belated acknowledgment, the way the delay between the two photographs holds out the possibility of life even as it extinguishes it. Or, again, perhaps this story affects us because the color photograph makes the son's death final in a way that the mother's words alone cannot, sight taking precedence over the residues of one's expressed desires and the meek protestations of loss's refusals.

Such moments of emotional responsiveness are unusual in classrooms. There is an unspoken expectation that students and teacher will maintain a calm demeanor, which in turn ensures rational discussion. The implicit assumption here is that emotion and reason are at odds with one another. When one is being emotional, one is not thinking straight. Only recently, Ruth Behar notes, have emotions been allowed to be expressed in academia, but still there is a great deal of discomfort when it is expressed too openly (1996, 16–19). In order, therefore, to question the assumption that emotions get in the way of reason, I searched through many critical works that might help to make sense of the possible political and intellectual significance of feeling grief at the sight of a picture turning from black and white to color. In doing so, I have been surprised to discover how much the morbid topic of grief, especially in the form of trauma studies, has become the preoccupation of many contemporary critics. Indeed, to point this fact out is already de rigueur in studies of this kind (Ball 2000; Seltzer 1998; Phelan 1997). These studies range from the political claims of trauma specialists to the skepticism of the concept's discontents, from the

PICTURE TAKEN BY KULING CHOY SIEGEL. COURTESY OF DAI SIL KIM-GIBSON

stages of grief schematized by developmental psychologists to the fixation on melancholia in psychoanalysis, from ethnic studies' concern with race to anthropological accounts of grief in other places.[7] What can these studies tell us about a feeling of grief at seeing a picture dissolve into color? What is this grief's connection to the racial context of this documentary? Can this grief have a political meaning for viewers of *Sa-I-Gu*?

··· **THE UNIVERSALITY OF GRIEF**

To address these questions, I start with a general observation. Most of these studies seem to agree that there is something widely shared, if not universal, about the experience of loss. Peggy Phelan, to take one example, is extremely comfortable, and elegant, in writing about the idea of grief-as-universal:

> What psychoanalysis makes clear is that the experience of loss is one of the central repetitions of subjectivity. It may well be that just as linguists have argued that syntax is "hard-wired" into the brain which allows infants to discern that specific sounds are language bits, perhaps the syntax of loss is hard-wired into the psyche which structures our encounters with the world. Severed from the placenta and cast from the womb, we enter the world as an amputated body whose being will be determined by the very mortality of that body. (1997, 5)

In the course of our lives, every single one of us, without exception, will lose something that we have grown attached to, will have to come to grips with numerous different kinds of losses from loved ones to loved objects to loved social fictions, and will have to face the always looming prospect of our own inevitable end. It is difficult to disagree with such pronouncements. I nevertheless share anthropologist Renato Rosaldo's reservations when he writes, "One hopes to achieve a balance between recognizing wide-ranging human differences and the modest truism that any two human groups must have certain things in common" (1993 [1989], 10). While all human groups may well hold in common the need to develop some form of expression to articulate what we all feel, the expression of our grief will likely take different forms, partially in response to different kinds and degrees of losses, and it is unclear how such form taking will affect the meaning we invest in such feeling. The generality that everyone experiences grief, in other words, does little to address the particularity of a loss inflected by racial meaning felt by the viewers of *Sa-I-Gu*.

To focus more directly on this particularity, therefore, I turn to psychoanalysis. Recent psychoanalytic critics have had the most to say about these morbid topics, including their relationship to race, than the other critics I have consulted. Indeed, it seems inconceivable to write about any of these topics without at least a brief excursus through Freudian thought. This said, the fact that psychoanalysis has been the rubric under which the intersection between these topics and race has most been explored is counterintuitive. The argument Sigmund Freud makes about these topics is mostly stripped of references to racial difference. In addition, what oblique references he does make, at least until recently, have been interpreted by psychoanalytic critics exclusively in terms of sexual identities and concerns that can be universalized (Eng 2001, 5). Regarding the topic of grief, for instance, Freud asserts that we all make attachments that inevitably must be broken (loss is a universal experience) and that we go through a process by which, if we are lucky enough to be so healthy, we come to accept such broken attachments. In the midst of loss, we are faced with the difficult task of saying farewell to every single memory associated with a lost object so that we can acknowledge it is indeed gone (Silverman 2000, 41). "Each single one of the memories and situations of expectancy which demonstrates the libido's attachment to the lost object," Freud writes in his often-cited essay "Mourning and Melancholia" (1917), "is met by the verdict of reality that the object no longer exists; and the ego, confronted as it were with the question of whether it shall share this fate, is persuaded by the sum of the narcissistic satisfactions it derives from being alive to sever its attachment to the object that has been abolished" (255). The love of life—our primary attachment to ourselves, to put it crudely—provides delight and leads us to say good-bye to the dead and the many memories that seem to vest the dead with life. In the bereaved self's long search for delight in its own existence, the self passes through a phase that for Freud in his earlier work is part of a process of "normal" mourning. The expectation in this line of reasoning is for a terminal point to grief, beyond which one finds joy—something, it is worth pointing out, that Freud himself began to doubt later in his life (Sanders 1999, 21).

· · · **GRIEF THAT FEEDS ON ITSELF**

What about those who are not so lucky? Freud asserts that the alternative to mourning is melancholia. Anne Cheng offers a useful way to differentiate between the two concepts: "According to Freud, 'mourning' is a healthy response to loss; it is finite in character and accepts substitutions (that is, the lost object can be relinquished and eventually replaced.) . . . 'Melancholia,' on the other hand, is pathological: it is interminable in nature and refuses substitution (that is, the melancholic cannot 'get over' loss.) The melancholic is, one might say, psychically stuck" (2001, 8). Cheng relies on this distinction to make a larger claim about racial identity that draws us closer to what is at stake in differentiating between mourning and melancholia for those who care about the Korean American merchants caught up in the Los Angeles riots. As Cheng continues to explain, melancholia eventually appears in Freud's work less as a form of pathology and more as a form of nourishment for the ego: "Freudian melancholia designates a chain of loss, denial and incorporation through which the ego is born. . . . By taking in the other-made-ghostly, the melancholic subject fortifies him- or herself and grows rich in impoverishment" (8). Such apparently contradictory reasoning—the assertion that one can grow fat on lack—paves the way for Cheng to contend, "Indeed, racial melancholia, as I am defining it, has always existed for raced subjects both as a *sign* of rejection and as psychic *strategy* in response to that rejection" (20). Thus, my acknowledgment of grief at Mrs. Lee's narrative in *Sa-I-Gu* might be interpreted both as a moment of recognition on my part that I am a racial minority, vulnerable to delegitimation as a fully enfranchised citizen of the United States because I am as an Asian American always already an immigrant and perennial foreigner, and as an opportunity for me to accept the loss engendered by such recognition as an impetus to struggle for racial justice as one of the disenfranchised.

David Eng and Shinhee Han provide a thoughtful corollary to this argument on racial melancholia. Inspired by their contact with Asian American college students who suffer from depression, the two—a literary critic and a university counselor—conducted a series of recorded dialogues with one another on the "pressing need to consider carefully methods by which a more speculative approach to psychoanalysis might enhance clinical applications, and vice versa" (2000, 669). Their dialogue revolves around Freud's 1917 notion of melancholia, and it arrives at two conclusions that productively revise Cheng's argument. First, they argue: "Although Freud typically casts melancholia as pathological, we are more concerned with exploring this psychic condition as a depathologized structure of feeling. From this particular vantage, melancholia might be thought of as underpinning our everyday conflicts and struggles with experiences of immigration, assimilation, and racialization" (669).

Like Cheng, Eng and Han want us to consider melancholia as conducive to making sense of how the struggles of minority groups are often shadowed by sadness at the Need—what they identify as "immigration, assimilation, and racialization"—that calls such struggle into being. To recognize the psychic state of racial minorities as infused with melancholia is not to pathologize such minorities. It is, to put it another way, not to place the blame of their depressed mental interiors on some lack emanating from within some deep underlying and flawed mental core that has somehow misrecognized loss as presence. Rather, such recognition is meant to invert the source of such psychic depression as something pushed upon and shaping the mind because of historical, social, and economic causes. To accept racial melancholia as a category of social critique is to target the cause of depression on a "structure of feeling." The reference to Raymond Williams is astute because it calls attention to the way a particular mood that might be felt individually is actually dependent on social and politicoeconomic variables. The term, coined by Williams and explored perhaps most thoroughly in *The Long Revolution* (1961), works to call attention to the fragile balance between these variables organized as a "structure" and the "feeling" that the structure minutely, fleetingly, and personally conditions. What feels most intimately like my own privately endured feeling is actually what is most outside myself, most constructed by a moment in time when different macrosocial forces conspired to produce the possibility of my encounter.

"Furthermore, even though melancholia is often conceived of in terms of individual loss and suffering," Eng and Han write about their second conclusion, "we are interested in addressing group identifications. As such, some of our observations bring together different minoritarian groups—people of color as well as gays and lesbians—from widely disparate historical, juridical, cultural, social, and economic backgrounds. We are wary of generalizing, but we also hope that, in foregrounding theoretical links among these various minoritarian groups, we might develop new intellectual, clinical, and political coalitions" (2000, 669). In this passage, Eng and Han express an important concern with the process by which the enormity of all that has to be grieved in the racial subject becomes so great that the subject can no longer sustain a lasting attachment to national fantasies and must seek the political company of others similarly afflicted. Racial melancholics cannot articulate such a breaking away from these fantasies alone; as individuals, they struggle in silence against the gap between what they feel and what cannot be said. Thus, it is no surprise that Eng and Han propose, as one possible remedy for such mute struggle, the formation of a "public space in which these conflicts can be acknowledged and negotiated. In their ideal form, Asian American studies programs provide this publicity, a physical and psychic space to bring together various fragmented parts. . . . This type of public space ultimately facilitates the creation of new representations of Asian Americans emerging from that gap of ambivalence between mourning and melancholia" (2000, 697). What this last point emphasizes is that the designation *Asian American* as a focus of study takes as its precondition the coalitional nature of this focus. Asian American is a space-providing context to explore commonalities, to wrestle with the deficiencies of widely available discourses, and to chart new modes of expression that address these deficiencies. Once this happens, melancholia-turned-toward-mourning provides us with an occasion for dialogue, solidarity, and meditation.

While this conclusion points us to the potential importance of the institutionalization of academic fields such as Asian American studies and the allocation of university and college resources to serve Asian American students—a crucial point to insist on during an era of neo-conservative backlash against all ethnic studies programs and a general hostility toward any mention of race in public—it is also crucial to insist that there are other equally important sites for the formation of an alternative public space where minority groups, along with others, can come together. These are the various community organizations that are already extant and vibrant. Such groups, in pursuing a radical democratic project, work toward the creation not of a public space but of a public *sphere*. They encourage civic dialogue that can be sustained over time and that is not dependent simply upon established institutional frameworks with their imposed limits and connections with various state apparatuses. They provide the means by which unacknowledged grief might find healthy expression, often simply through collective forms of political activism where the day-to-day difficulties of getting people involved, organizing rallies and protests, coming together in meetings and on social occasions, and struggling toward a common (and commonly perceived as worthy) goal all enable the thorough and practical working out of the issues one cannot anticipate on one's own.[8]

Not adequate in and of themselves to remedy a state of melancholia that often profoundly shapes the daily affective experiences of being a racial minority, ethnic studies programs and community organizations are the most significant visible social forces that create such spaces where mourning can safely and openly take place. These social forces may not, of course, be capable of shaping public policy. Rallies and teach-ins do not often change politicians' minds. Even the most eloquently written book or the most daring of social protests will barely receive any attention outside the immediate circles to which they speak. One would not want to overestimate the political influence of these kinds of social forces. But it is devastating to imagine a future when such forces will have been completely neutralized; when community organizations will have been hounded out of existence by federal agents who overvigilantly produce a phantasmic sense of state security, by highly paid political columnists and reporters who are quick to dismiss their serious intent, and by the sheer accumulated weight of the personal costs afflicted on individual activists, whose time is not unlimited and whose resources are few; and when ethnic studies programs, too often taken for granted, will have been legislated out of existence through the corrosive ebb of budget cuts, conservative denunciations, indifference, and ressentiment-filled academic politics.

There is a distinction to be made between the kind of loss that is the focus of racial melancholia from another kind of loss that is defined by trauma.[9] On the one hand, melancholia provides us with an apt tool for making sense of endemic forms of racial oppression, especially in the way such forms of oppression produce subjects. Trauma, on the other hand, comes into play only when racial oppression reaches a moment of crisis, such as during the riots. At such a moment, loss is not constitutive. Instead, it is felt overtly as a loss of the self. In trauma, one's psyche is literally a blank slate upon which oppression leaves its mark. Once this mark has been made, the mind circles around the moment of trauma, reenacting it; the mind is written by and has no ability to bear witness to what has happened but nevertheless has the capacity to speak of a loss that is perceived as no longer constituting oneself, in part because there no longer seems to exist a self in any ordinary sense of this term.[10] Trauma thus speaks out from an outer limit of audibility that tells us about a pain which by definition has no voice. We are required, then, to listen in new ways to such a cry without a voice. In part, we are immersed in its inarticulate crying out, and we must therefore take on the difficult task of bearing witness from this degree zero, an emptiness from which the social world has withdrawn.

To clarify, let me return for a moment to Claire Jean Kim, who tells us that she often teaches *Sa-I-Gu* in her undergraduate course on minority politics. When the class has finished watching the documentary, and has had time to reflect quietly on what they have seen, she makes it a point to ask,

> What are the other silent voices that we should listen for? Should we watch a companion film about Black perspectives on Black-Korean conflict? If we had to create one, what would it look like? I try, in other words, to take the class from the point where they do not notice the absence of such a companion film to the point where they are constructing it themselves. I try to broaden the focus so that they see not only the suffering of one group but the suffering of both groups involved and the daunting moral dilemmas raised by their confrontations. (2000, 222)[11]

The trauma embedded in *Sa-I-Gu* is not simply in the seldom-heard voices of its Korean American interviewees, but in the voices that are not heard but which beg to be listened to nonetheless, the outside of audibility. At one level, what Kim suggests here is the need to go beyond the simple confinement of our own identities, to listen in our own suffering for the pain of others who do not have the vehicles for expression that are available to us. In this way, she sounds similar to Kaja Silverman, who writes philosophically,

> We are not in the world merely by virtue of being born into it; indeed, most of us are not really in the world at all. Paradoxically as it may sound, we are only really in the world when it is in us—when we have made room without our psyches for it to dwell and expand. . . . The point here is not that the world does not exist in reality unless it exists for us subjectively. We do not possess the capacity to confer or withdraw being. Our power is both greater and lesser: we determine whether other creatures and things will continue to languish in the darkness of concealment, or whether they will enter in the light of Being. (2000, 29–30)

The voices of Korean American women, of course, are often muted and silent in the way Kim suggests the voices of African Americans have been in the aftermath of the riots, as somehow languishing "in the darkness of concealment," and we might with some validity argue that African Americans have had more opportunity than Korean Americans to express themselves in public. But in noting this disparity, we must remain open to what remains unspoken. Even as we insist that in listening to African Americans express their plaints, we must clear room to hear those voices that have not found expression and yet reverberate as echoes in the silence formed by their speech. In addition, there remains a third position created by the riots that Kim does not call our attention to and that suffers erasure in the imposition of a black-Korean interpretive frame upon the riots. Namely, we must seek out those Guatemalan and Salvadoran migrants who turned an expression of rage and hurt into a bread riot. As I already pointed out in the introduction, over 50 percent of all those arrested during the riots were of Mexican and Central American descent. There is, as well, anecdotal evidence that the Immigration and

Naturalization Service with the illegal complicity of the police used the cover of urban unrest to round up illegal immigrants for deportation (Davis 1993). Such experiences remain unheard within the frames that help us to interpret this event.[12]

Nevertheless, what is amazing to me about Claire Jean Kim's comments above, and also the work of many of her sociological peers writing about Korean Americans, is how capably they have cleared space in their psyches so that they might show us how to inhabit the world more fully. *Such* sociology might be an apt model for how to listen properly to the moment in *Sa-I-Gu* when the mother tells us her heartbreaking story of loss, so that we may make room for "other creatures and things." An essential starting place for this model, to judge from Kim's statement, is to engage in what Thomas Dumm calls "resignation." "A resignation can be understood," Dumm writes, "as the withdrawal of consent by someone who once entered into a compact with others, someone who had made a mutual agreement with others to be ruled in common. . . . People find their own voices in acts of resignation as a matter of learning to speak for themselves, against the idea that others can continue to speak for them, or even to them, about what matters most in a particular context" (1999, 58). By acknowledging, or being forced to acknowledge, our feelings of disaffection and loss (shared in the tortured moments created in *Sa-I-Gu* by others unable to give testimony to what they have lost), we commit an act of resignation from the founding compact of official race-neutrality, the belief that we live in a postracial society. Somehow, through the alchemy of neoconservative argument, we are supposed to be beyond race. We are told that race no longer divides us, breaks us up into antagonistic groups, or renders us with identities that are valued differently by one another.

Instead, we live in a society governed by neoliberal democracy, which, as Vijay Prashad reminds us, "pledges to stand for equality and to stand apart from the differences in civil society" (2000, 165). By standing apart, neoliberal democracy claims to provide all of its subjects equal treatment while forgetting the inequality that already exists and that liberal democracy's aloofness constitutionally prevents it from even acknowledging, much less addressing. "To stand apart from civil society," Prashad continues, "the state accepts its inequalities and therefore acts on behalf of those who have already secured power over society" (165). Or, as Claire Jean Kim puts it more directly, "Colorblind talk furthers racial power not through the direct articulation of racial differences but rather by obscuring the operations of racial power, protecting it from challenge, and permitting ongoing racializations via racially coded methods. In all of these ways, colorblind talk helps to maintain White dominance in an era of formal race neutrality" (2000, 18). To resign in this context by calling attention to the sadness inhabiting our emotional interiors means that we signal a break with the compact with neoliberalism and its self-serving professions of colorblindness and race-neutrality, and in the process clear space for the acknowledgment of a traumatic cry.

Resignation has another meaning that requires of us a less sanguine view of the metaphorical meaning of trauma than what has been suggested thus far. The second sense of resignation refers to a giving in to a moment defined by the acknowledgment of a break, and to the witnessing through such a break the ways in which care has left the world. When one *is not cared for*, which as I suggested at the start of this chapter was the condition in which the Korean American women represented by *Sa-I-Gu* found themselves, it is equally difficult to *care* for others. Perhaps we might then think of trauma as being in a state of carelessness, an exceptional state of removal from the social connections that make life worthwhile and that allow us to feel a part of the world that inhabits us. To be a person in such a state means a loss of selfhood, a being without Being, a resignation that withdraws so completely from the world that the world is suspended as an outside force, an extreme dissociative condition that empties one of a belief that care can ever again be given to oneself and that one can in turn provide care for others. Like the mother in *Sa-I-Gu* and the mood she creates throughout the documentary, this second sense of resignation is defined simply as waiting in a space that is somehow outside the flow of time and thus outside the spheres of social interaction.

As metaphor, trauma thus names a state of exception. Giorgio Agamben argues, "Here what is outside is included not simply by means of an interdiction or an internment, but rather by the juridical order's validity—by letting the juridical order, that is, withdraw from the exception and abandon it. The exception does not subtract itself from rule; rather, the rule, suspending itself, gives rise to exception and, maintaining itself in relation to the exception, first constitutes itself as a rule" (1998 [1995], 18). This definition of exception addresses the question, What does the exception do for the sovereign body that has withdrawn its care from the excepted? The metaphor of trauma asks us to consider a different question: What happens to the excepted when they are withdrawn care? One thing that occurs in the contemporary U.S. political context, I believe, is that the strong attachments to the fantasies of race neutrality, colorblind talk, and a Korean American dream that dovetailed with an older American dream of the immigrant are—as ideals and faiths about the world we live in—cruelly broken. The excepted, on being forced to recognize through acts of devastation and abandonment that these attachments are not as sure as once thought (trauma), are led to confusion and sadness—confusion because the excepted do not know what will replace what they now sense as missing, and sadness because they must say good-bye to an understanding of themselves that had once provided them with a place in the world. The excepted come face to face with a way of seeing the political that is a wild and nightmarish departure from the comforting banality afforded by neoliberal democracy. The state no longer appears benign, a lover the excepted might end up happily embracing or even accepting as a decent substitute. Instead, they confront a state founded on violence, that increasingly exists, or perhaps has always existed, to punish and accelerate death. State power, or sovereignty, appears simply as "the capacity to dictate who may live and who must die" (Mbembe 2003, 11).

Trauma as metaphor situates the excepted outside the limits of such power, giving witness in a state of carelessness to the blank horror of a world where such power is daily exercised in both the most spectacular manner, as in a state's military aggression against the peoples of another state, and in the most quotidian manner, as in the refusal to make available the basic social services that make life possible. Against such horror, trauma as metaphor confronts us with the enormity of the power that has withdrawn its care for us. We might therefore, understandably, shun such a metaphor, and cling to the belief that the state is after all more protective than arbitrarily death dealing.

If trauma as metaphor, then, pushes us to the limits of pessimism, in the sense that, in its light, the state appears to us as a nightmare gulag of irresponsible power, doesn't this potentially subvert the relationship between mourning as healthy and melancholia as pathology? Mourning might now be thought of as a reformer's attitude, the belief that without something positive to believe in, without in short the narrative of progress, we are left mired in a pessimism that fails to show us how we may move beyond loss and embrace a joy in, at the least, some future existence. Richard Rorty provides us with an impassioned reformer's plea for leaving open the possibility for mourning, rather than the descent into trauma:

> Readers of Foucault often come away believing that no shackles have been broken in the past two hundred years: the harsh old chains have merely been replaced with slightly more comfortable ones. Heidegger describes America's success in blanketing the world with modern technology as the spread of a wasteland. Those who find Foucault and Heidegger convincing often view the United States of America . . . as something we must hope will be replaced, as soon as possible, by something utterly different. . . . They begin to think of themselves as a saving remnant—as the happy few who have the insight to see through nationalist rhetoric to the ghastly reality of contemporary America. But this insight does not move them to formulate a legislative program, to join in a political movement, or to share in a national hope. (1998, 8)

If mourning thus leaves open the possibility for a reinvigorated faith in the United States as a nation of promise, after a long (and justifiable) period of doubt, and trauma points to a withdrawal so complete we are left only numbed by the enormity of the horror that contemporary life offers its subjects, perhaps melancholia might be rehabilitated as a middle term between these two extremes. Melancholia might henceforth be understood as the unresolvability of loss that leaves us radically uncertain about the future and unable to mourn because we have no way of knowing how deep the loss goes or, even, if the losing has come to an end. The melancholic is gifted neither with unusual perspicacity or with dumb optimism, but is rather only endowed with a mature respect for subjective limitations.

In *Sa-I-Gu*, many of its Korean American interviewees repeat the racism of a dream they cling to even as they are compelled to repudiate it, suggesting how loss does not sentimentally mean a greater openness to the pain of others. This dream is anchored to the emphasis on children, and reveals why the death of Edward Lee reverberates so traumatically alongside the other interviews. A son of one of the central women interviewed during the documentary claims that it was for him and his siblings that his parents came to the United States, so that they could have access to better education. Mrs. Lee also remembers this as an important reason for her family's decision to move to the United States: "We came to America to spread our young dreams. To raise our future children. We were young and our dreams small . . . but we came here with dreams." Children in *Sa-I-Gu* represent the future possibilities that motivate the merchants and blue-collar Korean American workers to continue along in their struggle to make a better life for themselves. Edward Lee's death represents in this documentary more than the tragic death of a single Korean American, but the figurative death as well of Korean American dreams about starting a new life in the United States. As we will see in the next chapter, the death of a child in *Native Speaker* (1995) occupies a similar figuration of lost hope and investment in a desirable future. Perhaps it almost goes without saying that for Asian Americans in general, who have endured a long history of de jure and de facto discrimination designed to prohibit reproduction (as the formation of nineteenth-century Chinese American bachelor societies and the passage of the 1875 Page Law, which prohibited most Chinese women from entering the United States on the grounds that they were prostitutes, might attest), children represent a willingness to remain in this country, and their loss, in turn, reverberates as the foiling of this determination.

Many of the interviewees are, in any case, explicit about their disappointment. Mrs. Han, a registered nurse, recalls, "I dreamed that America was a wonderful country. It was my dreamland." After her husband's sudden death, she took over her family's liquor store: "I got scared, because my husband took care of everything. After one year, I could do anything, but I cannot tell how difficult it was." These words are accompanied by pictures of a run-down storefront, with steel bars protecting the windows, and interior shots of a bullet-proof shield dividing mostly black customers from a Korean American cashier. At this point in her story, Mrs. Han begins to cry and cannot speak any further. Mrs. Song, a family-market owner, says, "I thought America was perfect, since she helped others abroad. After the riots, I feel there is a huge hole in America." Later in the documentary, she elaborates on this point: "We dreamed about America, just like we saw in the movies. There would be flower pots on windowsills . . . the streets would be clean. People in America would all have big noses. . . . Their faces would be white and their hair blond. It did not feel like America. I thought it was Mexico. It made more sense to call it Mexico. We hardly came into contact with white people. Even in schools . . . most teachers were second-generation Japanese and Mexican." Finally, Mrs. Song's husband says, "I regret coming to America in the first place. My friends in Korea are all millionaires. When I go to Korea, they say an American beggar has come. I want to live with money, but now I have none." For these interviewees, the riots represent more than simply the loss of their livelihoods. They represent the completion of a disillusionment with the immigrant narrative, which has as its terminus the picture of an affluent, white America made familiar through exported films. What buttressed this narrative was the interviewees' belief in their acceptance in American society that was indexed by their perceived position in a racial order.

Nancy Abelmann and John Lie provide us with an example of how this belief was shattered by the riots. They report that there was a story that circulated among Korean Americans in postriot Los Angeles concerning a survey supposedly conducted by a major but unnamed newspaper. The survey asked its respondents to rank fifty nations in order of favorable to least-favorable impressions. Korean Americans, according to this story, expected Korea to rank near the top, if not at the top, but were surprised to find it ranked near the bottom (1995, 34).[13] There is no verification that such a survey was ever conducted, but the story's popular retelling among Korean Americans in Los Angeles in the early 1990s highlights the degree to which their experiences during the riots—including the lack of police protection and the news media's unwillingness to solicit their opinions— may have led many to rethink their racial assumptions. No longer welcomed immigrants embraced by a country with a rich and uninterrupted history of rewarding the self-motivated, the Korean Americans interviewed by Abelmann and Lie began to think of themselves as disliked, shunned, and victimized.

Such a moment of trauma might have enabled these kyopo interviewees to reflect on the ways in which their suffering is mirrored by the unspoken suffering of blacks and Latinos, who have for years been the victim of this racial ordering. Suddenly made to see their place as at the bottom, they may have been able to acknowledge how much they have in common with those who have always been forced to see themselves in such an unflattering light. But racial melancholia untempered by the kind of public space Eng and Han advocate does not allow for reflection. As Mrs. Song's characterization of the America she found as more like Mexico suggests, disillusionment and suffering all too easily dissolve into racism, a lashing out against an Other without care for who is being targeted. One woman in particular is candid about her biases: "When I first went to South Central, I thought I must love black people. An old Korean saying goes, 'One cannot spit on a smiling face.' If they felt my love, I believe they would not come with guns. So I prayed a lot to help feel love. I tried hard. But when I saw how they behaved, I felt hatred, let alone love. . . . I am angry at blacks. Because we were hit by blacks." This woman's family-owned market was destroyed during the riots. With the help of extended family members, she and her husband opened a dry-cleaning store in the Pacific Palisades. The interview is filmed at the site of her new store, a shot of the storefront revealing a sign that reads, "Rickshaw Chinese Laundry" in chopstick lettering as affluent-looking white people enter with smiles and drive away in luxury sedans.

When she says these last words, "because we were hit by blacks," the documentary cuts to scenes of a less affluent neighborhood, where black children riding bicycles smile brightly into the camera and undermine the implicit appeal to a common sense that this explanation makes. Against her characterization of blacks as uniformly responsible for her misfortunes, the camera presents another image that attempts to show how misplaced this interviewee's rage is, and in doing so it allows us to hear what is unspoken in the traumas narrated by this documentary. To emphasize this point further, *Sa-I-Gu* alternates between footage of

PICTURE TAKEN BY KULING CHOY SIEGEL. COURTESY OF DAI SIL KIM-GIBSON

Beverly Hills and the burned-out landscape of Koreatown. The gap between the rich and the poor, between primarily white and nonwhite
neighborhoods, becomes the main topic in the spoken narratives. Mrs.
Han speaks next: "To me, it is unfair that African American people attack
Korean people at this time. From what I understand, they have accumulated all their problems and frustrations against white people, and now
they express their anger against Koreans. When I think about it, I am
most angry at white people. If the government had watched over the
blacks better, this would not have happened to us." While these comments still reveal a deep-seated paternalism toward African Americans,
they nevertheless also direct the blame for the speaker's misfortune at a
larger structure of inequality. This is taken up directly by another interviewee: "At first, I didn't notice, but I slowly realized . . . the looters were
poor. The riot happened because of the gap between the rich and the
poor. . . . Looking back, I realize that the police could have stopped the
riots. The media promoted a black/Korean conflict. . . . The media denies
that it is a black/white conflict. But no! We Koreans were sacrificial
lambs." These words of outrage against the police, the media, and a
general structure of inequality that seeks to make sense of the motivation
for black and Latino violence are made visually more pronounced by
footage of the peace rally that followed the days of rioting, when tens of
thousands of Korean Americans demonstrated in front of city hall, the
largest mass political protest of its kind in Asian American history. Two
policemen in uniform are shown looking down at the protesters from on
top of a building; one of them, who looks racially Asian (at least to me),
runs an arm over his eyes as if wiping away tears and is adamantly
explaining something to the other policeman. The sequence ends with
one woman holding up a placard that reads, "Apologize ABC for your bias
reporting."[14] The documentary thus asserts its own narrative frame over
the events it depicts. This frame tracks the evolution of political consciousness from sadness to anger to organization, and finally to more
sophisticated forms of political critique.

Despite these gestures toward redirecting the women's shared sense of
grievance beyond simply blaming blacks, there nevertheless remains the
sense of waiting in these scenes of protest. Partly this waiting comes from
the knowledge that these protests do not lead to redress; many Korean

American merchants have yet, more than a decade after the riots, to see any of the relief money that had been promised them. Abelmann and Lie explain why Korean American merchants have had so much trouble recuperating money from federal disaster relief funds: "The morass of forms, government letters, and edicts was an unfathomable onslaught. Suddenly they had been thrust into a sea of acronyms: SBA (Small Business Administration), FEMA (Federal Emergency Management Agency), and so on— empty letters for most immigrants. . . . For the well-established businesses with proper records, bookkeeping, and insurance coverage, the forms and red-tape byways were not insurmountable. Circumstances were different for those with informal arrangements, underreported incomes, and fly-by-night insurance policies that fizzled away after the riots" (1995, 44). In addition to the confusion of bureaucratic red tape and the emotional troubles many merchants suffered after the riots, many were also confronted by the problem of simply surviving: "Many of them were forced to borrow money at high interest rates in order to pay their living expenses and attempt to reopen their businesses. As a result, they could no longer pay their mortgages and many have already lost their homes or are now threatened with eviction" (Kim and Kim 1999, 26).

But more poignantly, this waiting comes from the fact that these scenes of protest must work against Mrs. Lee's framing narrative. As a preamble to her story about the two photographs, she tells us about the last conversation she had with her son. On the first day of the riots, KBLA, a Korean-language radio station in Los Angeles, broadcast the story of a famous Korean folktale. This tale is often told to children in Korea. It is about the protection of a castle (*san sung*) situated in the Korean province of *Hangju* against Japanese invaders in the sixteenth century. In the nationalist version of this tale, told by KBLA, the name of the province (Hangju) is confused with a similar-sounding Korean word for the apron women once wore (hengju). According to the nationalist version, the women used these aprons to carry rocks for the construction of a protective wall against the Japanese (M. Kim 1997, 377–378). Even before this story was broadcast, Edward Lee was agitated. Mrs. Lee recalls him saying "It has been twenty years since Koreans came here. Everything we have worked for is now in flames. . . . How can we sit here and watch it happen? We Koreans should go out and protect our own." After Mrs. Lee translates this version of the story broadcast on KBLA for her insistent son, he responds, "How can you sit still and tell such a story? Mother, you too must go out and fight." Thus inflamed, Edward Lee sneaked out of his family's apartment in a quixotic attempt to protect their small business and was accidentally shot by a Korean American merchant. Was it the loss of hope created by the belief that one was in a state of exception (an excess of pessimism) or was it too much hope created by the faith that blind action could automatically lead to better tomorrows (an excess of optimism) that led Lee to stumble into a public sphere that has left him a blank in memory instead of a person who should still be among the living?

AFTER ALL THESE YEARS, *Sa-I-Gu* remains both unique and raw. No other work of any kind has focused so insistently on the Korean American women who, in a few brief days of violence, lost their livelihoods, their dreams, and, in Mrs. Lee's case, a child. Thanks to the film's director, Dai Sil Kim-Gibson, we have a vivid account of how these women sought to make sense of what happened to them. Without a doubt, the viewpoints of these women found in the documentary are often limited. They say regrettable things, especially about African Americans, and, in their suffering, they seem to have precious little room for considering how others might also suffer. The candor with which they speak is what gives this documentary its rawness—its continued feeling of immediacy, relevance, and heartbreaking emotional impact. It is impossible to imagine how any act of kindness, care, or acknowledgment can alleviate the loss that a person such as Mrs. Lee has suffered, just as it is impossible to imagine how the fifty-plus other deaths that occurred during the riots could be compensated for, mourned over, and recognized fully as a devastating loss for those who were immediately left behind by the murdered.

In a recent conversation, Kim-Gibson recounted how, after a public screening of her documentary, an African American man asked her why she made such a big deal about the death of a single Korean American when a day does not go by without the death of an African American?[15] I am drawn to this question because it raises the stakes over how we view *Sa-I-Gu*. On the one hand, too much attention to Edward Lee's death threatens to crowd attention away from an already-crowded chorus of losses that clamor for mourning without any clear possibility for satisfaction. There is a limited supply of grief and an abundance of losses, and a viewer of this film cannot be expected to run through this supply for only one death when so many others remain unrecorded, unacknowledged, lost in the shrugs of too much indifference. On the other hand, this question leads to other questions. What would it take to think of Edward Lee's death as representing these other deaths? Is there any way to imagine Lee as symbolic of the many losses that fail to register in public as a loss worth grieving over? Can the emotional response that viewers have to *Sa-I-Gu* be understood through discussion and careful analysis as recognizing the inconsolableness of loss itself, the ways in which we must continue to make up for losses that can never fully be consoled without bringing the dead back to life? In trying to provide the care for ourselves that seems to have been withheld from us, can we learn to give care to others who have also been abandoned and thereby escape the weight of our too-numerous traumas? If we cannot respond "yes" to this last question, then we surely have good reason to worry about what may lie ahead.

A Diasporic Future?
Historical Trauma and *Native Speaker*

Nineteen ninety-five is a historical milestone for a number of reasons. A half century earlier, the U.S. military dropped an atomic bomb on Hiroshima and a few days later dropped another one on Nagasaki. On 15 August 1945, the Japanese formally surrendered to the United States and simultaneously declared its overseas possessions to be free. As a result, Koreans suddenly found themselves celebrating their independence from decades of formal colonial rule.[1] The celebrants were, of course, unaware that in just three short years their country would be politically divided into two and that in five years the resulting two states would be plunged into one of the bloodiest conflicts of the twentieth century. The Korean War lasted three years and left behind, conservatively, over 4.8 million Chinese, Korean, and U.S. dead, wounded, or missing (less conservative estimates put the number of total dead at over 5 million [Cumings 2004, 40]). Five million more Koreans became refugees. In the north, over three-fourths of all physical structures were leveled to the ground. The government headed by Kim Il Sung steered the devastated country back to an independent form of development and closed its borders to the West; these borders have remained closed ever since, while thousands of troops—many of them U.S.—remain stationed on the demilitarized zone separating north from south.[2]

In the south, a militant labor movement was crushed by a U.S.-installed Syngman Rhee and later, after a brief period of democratic efflorescence under *Chang* Myun's short-lived presidency (1960–1961), was crushed again by *Park* Chung Hee's seizure of state power (Koo 2001, 26–27). The subsequent and repeated evisceration of organized labor in South Korea, combined with U.S.-backed reforms that made primary and secondary education compulsory, led to the formation of a well-trained but frustrated working class (Liu and Cheng 1994, 83–85). Faced with almost no worker protection, little opportunity for economic advancement, political repression, and a universal military draft for their sons, and haunted by memories of colonization, foreign-backed civil war, crushing poverty, authoritarian rule, and mercenary military service during the Vietnam War, many in South Korea understandably decided to emigrate if they could.

One major opportunity for emigration opened up in 1965, when the U.S. legislature passed one of the most sweeping immigration reforms in its history. The Hart-Celler Immigration and Nationality Act abolished previous laws restricting immigration by race and ethnicity, creating in their place a yearly 20,000-person quota per country of emigration from the Eastern Hemisphere up to a total of 170,000 people and a first-come, first-serve system for immigrants from countries in the Western Hemisphere up to 120,000 people per year (Hing 1993, 40–41). The law also contained two provisions that unexpectedly favored immigration from Asia. First, it gave those who wished to reunify with family members already residing in the United States as citizens permission to immigrate exempt from any quotas. Second, it gave special preference to potential immigrants who possessed specialized skills that were in short supply in the U.S. labor market and that would not place them in competition with American workers (Reimers 1992 [1985], 92–99). Because of these two provisions, many Koreans found themselves eligible to leave their home country in large numbers for places such as Los Angeles, New York City, and, in lesser numbers, the regions in between. What lawmakers apparently had not realized was that these Koreans, like many of their other Asian counterparts, (1) were related to immigrants who had previously come to the United States, often—specifically in the Korean case—as the brides of American servicemen or as college students, and (2) were qualified to fill the jobs in medicine, engineering, and so forth left vacant by decades of expansive economic growth.[3]

During the height of Korean immigration, between the years 1985 and 1987, more than 15,000 people above the Korean national quota of 20,000 began to arrive annually, making Korea the third-largest sender nation after Mexico and the Philippines (Abelmann and Lie 1995, 67). Although these numbers have tapered off in more recent years, especially after the 1992 Los Angeles riots (Yu and Choe 2003/2004), there has been enough Korean immigration to the United States in the post-1965 period to produce an effect in which two generations of immigrants influence society in different ways.

If the first effect of large-scale, post-1965 Korean immigration to the United States has been to add substantially to the diversity of America's major metropolitan areas, especially in largely black neighborhoods where first-generation Korean Americans had become disproportionately visible as small business owners, then a second effect of this same wave of immigration might be found in their children's growth into adulthood. Unlike previous waves of Asian immigrants to the United States, the post-1965 wave was comprised mainly of families with small children or of couples of childbearing age. The oldest of these children were reaching adulthood in 1992, as the lawyer Angela Oh's appearance on *Nightline* in the week immediately following the riots signified for many Korean American observers (E. Park 2001b, 290). Since the riots, many (but by no means all) in the leading edge of this cohort—often referred to by their parents as the "knee-high" generation because so many of them were that tall during the early major wave of Korean immigration—found their way into some of the most prestigious universities and colleges in the country, and have since entered into the prime of their professional lives.[4] As they do so, this knee-high generation's coming adulthood is adding another layer to the popular, and delimiting, perception that all Asian Americans, regardless of ethnicity, are good students who are especially adept at math and science. Korean Americans, along with other Asian Americans of their cohort, are now becoming visible as cultural producers.

For those interested in Korean Americans specifically, then, 1995 is a milestone not only because it marks the fiftieth anniversary of Korean independence from Japanese rule and the thirtieth anniversary of the signing of the Hart-Celler Immigration and Nationality Act, but also because it witnessed the publication of Chang-rae Lee's novel *Native Speaker*, which was subsequently hailed as a major literary achievement for its then twenty-nine-year-old author. Novels by other young Korean Americans followed closely on its heels. In 1996, Heinz Insu Fenkl published *Memories of My Ghost Brother*; in 1997, Nora Okja Keller published *Comfort Woman*; and, in 1998, another unprecedented year for Korean American novelists, Patti Kim's *A Cab Called Reliable*, Mira Stout's *One Thousand Chestnut Trees: A Novel of Korea*, Susan Choi's *The Foreign Student*, and Mia Yun's *House of the Winds* began appearing in bookstores. Others have since been published to increasing critical acclaim.[5] These are not the first novels by authors of Korean ancestry ever produced, but they *are* the most numerous to be produced in such quick succession and under the sponsorship of corporate presses. Korean Americans of a certain age and educational background have gained access to a still-prestigious mode of expression that had been virtually closed off to previous generations.[6] Post-1965 second- and 1.5-generation (born in Korea but raised in the United States) Korean American writers, like many other post-1965 second- and 1.5-generation Asian American writers, are now publishing novels that are being reviewed in major newspapers and magazines and are, in the process, finding a wide readership.

The growing visibility of these authors raises the following question about interpretation. Should we approach their literary output as the product of individual and spontaneous creativity, as the product of a political sensibility that is markedly unique to an Asian American racial group, or as the product of a historical consciousness that remains alive to an extranational notion of group belonging, one that sees the past and present struggles of Koreans in Korea as somehow coterminous with the struggles of Koreans in a diaspora? In addressing this question, I focus specifically on *Native Speaker*. The narrator, Henry Park, fits the profile of the knee-high generation Korean American that I have been developing here. His character also foregrounds the stakes involved in being seen as a modernist creation, a member of a racial minority, or a harbinger of a diasporic future.

This chapter begins by considering the first two possibilities before turning its attention to the topic of diaspora. In reading *Native Speaker* for diaspora, the rest of this chapter argues that this concept has recently acquired a luster of newness, because it provides an alternative narrative to one provided by the disappointing performances of nation-states, and that Henry, after a personal tragedy, is faced with two competing notions of this social alternative to the nation-state, one of which is represented by his father and the other represented by a Korean American councilman he finds himself spooking. Neither of these last two options satisfies

Henry's longing for a sense of communality, a feeling of connection to other people, and peoples, made possible by the sense of sharing a common fate. The chapter concludes with general thoughts about the thorny political predicaments faced by Korean Americans of the knee-high generation, and by extension other knee-high generation Asian Americans, who are increasingly, though *not uniformly*, finding access to reserves of cultural capital that are out of proportion to their small numbers; this is occurring during a period of intense political reaction and pervasive pessimism about the nation's future. Can the emergence of this knee-high generation into adulthood offer us a third notion of diaspora?

··· **READING FOR MODERNISM, READING FOR RACE**

On the eve of Chang-rae Lee's novelistic debut, *New York Magazine* published a cover story about Korean immigrants in New York City that claims, wrongly, "*Native Speaker*—the first major novel by a Korean-American to be brought out by a major publisher—is an artful meditation on ethnic identity, fractured loyalties, and cultural confusion that is bundled inside a not-entirely-plausible spy thriller" (J. Goldberg 1995, 46).[7] This review seems to suggest that *Native Speaker* broaches important topics in a pleasing manner but is not a realistic portrayal of Korean Americans. This also suggests that *Native Speaker* must therefore be read as an allegory about larger, more abstract themes. It cannot, however, be read as a form of ethnography, because it does not correspond to the knowable reality about which it purportedly comments. Three months later, the *New York Times* reports, "The book has been acclaimed as a lyrical, edgy and perceptive tale of the second-generation foreigner, the child of immigrants stranded in a no-man's-land between the old culture and the new" (Belluck 1995, B1). In the same month as the *Times* article, the *New Yorker* argues, " 'Native Speaker' is driven by the silence of a Korean family, and its subtext is the tortured ethnicity of the immigrant. Park assumes that for Korean immigrant parents like his parents, class, ethnicity, and family are essentially subtle variations on the themes of identity and belonging" (Klinkenborg 1995, 77). Meanwhile, on the other side of the Atlantic, the *New Statesman and Society* makes explicit what these other reviews only hedge at: "It happens to be about being Korean in New York in the 1970s and 1980s. But what it says about acquiring dual identity could apply the world over" (Pavey 1995, 32). While *Native Speaker* might be about Korean Americans, this fact is incidental—what it merely "happens to be about" and perhaps gets wrong—to the much larger meaning of the novel. For these reviewers, it is ultimately a novel about deracinated themes that refer in equal proportion to everyone who might read it. *Native Speaker* is, to put it simply, a novel with universal appeal.

The habit of reading suggested by these reviews, according to Martin Kich, is shared by the author himself, who worries that "a novelist who chooses to focus on his ethnicity or region is too readily categorized as 'ethnic' or 'regional'—with both terms suggesting works with less than universal themes and less than lasting import" (2000, 176). Undoubtedly, this quickly accumulated critical opinion has a point. There may be something about *Native Speaker* that aspires to distance itself from the supposed ethnic ghetto of its subject matter. This, however, should not distract us from recognizing that the disproportionate popularity of this novel made it a de facto commentary on Korean American life for its many readers in the second half of the 1990s. What this novel suggests, intentionally or not, about Korean American subjectivity casts a long shadow over the interpretation of the other works mentioned at the start of this chapter. A divisive tension thus exists between the weight of its critical visibility as an achievement of Korean American, and by extension Asian American, literary production and a work that self-consciously seeks to transcend such supposedly narrowing labels. This tension between ethnic/racial specificity and universal thematic interest also runs throughout the breadth of *Native Speaker*'s narrative, as it shuttles back and forth between multiple plots.

But underlying this tension in the novel itself is the possibility that specificity slides easily into transcendental banality. This is so because the more we become acquainted with Henry as a character, the more the ethnic and racial markers that give him a social identity are sheered from him and the more he becomes an individual without a history or a visible place in a symbolic structure. As Tina Chen observes, "Henry Park is an invisible man. . . . That Lee's protagonist is a spy is no coincidence: Henry's vanishing acts, a professional opportunity to enact the spy's 'multiple roles,' are a logical extension of his personal history as a Korean American struggling to negotiate the divide that separates how others perceive him and how he sees himself" (2002, 638). In other words, the state of pure Being represented by Henry's "vanishing acts," while potentially inviting celebration as the modernist apotheosis of readerly acceptance, might alternatively be understood as an expression of muted dislocation, an anomie so profound that it leaves one feeling alone, unmoored to any place or network of associates, drifting in aimless discontent, pretending to be one thing and then another but never feeling at home in any single place or in any particular guise.

You-me Park and Gayle Wald call attention to how ghostly figures in the novel—who are identified primarily by gender, ethnicity, and race—cling to Henry and prevent his character from fully disappearing into the mainstream: "The shadowy figures of Korean American women disrupt Lee's narrative, which mostly concerns itself with the legitimation of a male immigrant subject in the public sphere. Tucked away in the hyperfeminized private sphere sanctioned by both traditional Korean ideals of domestic women and the U.S. belief in Asian American self-sufficiency ('they don't ask for social welfare'), these women are denied any meaningful access to the public sphere" (1998, 609). It seems important that such women remain in the shadows. As a novel about the maturation of a subject into an unmarked individual worthy and capable of participation in a functioning democratic society, *Native Speaker* needs at all costs to focus its attention on the lone character who is undergoing the pains of political adolescence. Read in this way, Chang-rae Lee's novel becomes an exercise in subject making that is a disciplining of the subject. In the process, the novel foregrounds the need served by such an act of disciplining in a public sphere that increasingly seems no longer a unitary place anchored by secure institutions and more and more, as we have seen in previous chapters, a place of wounding. What I am suggesting is that the public sphere itself is not a mechanism for granting and denying legitimacy for volunteering immigrants who wish to participate in the U.S. nation-state's democratic largesse, as Park and Wald seem to imply. Rather, the public sphere is a congregation of institutions racing belatedly to adjust to a changing political, economic, and social climate that upsets their smooth running. This might explain, then, the exuberance with which so many reviewers have publicly acclaimed Lee's novel. Henry, in his pursuit of individuality and political maturity, reinvigorates an image of a social order in need of ideological replenishment and affirmation by its subjects. By wishing so much to become a legitimate subject, one whose individuality grants him admittance into a rapidly fraying public sphere, Henry conversely grants legitimacy to an increasingly troubled nation-state.[8]

Of course, it would be premature to claim that nation-states, especially one as powerful and apparently viable as the United States, are somehow on their way to uniform dissolution in the midst of what, for lack of a better word, globalization has unleashed. Nevertheless, the constant need to produce a sense of stable locality, a political geography that matches a physical geography and thus guarantees the integrity of the nation-state as such, now seems more pressing than ever before. "This is a world where electronic media are transforming the relationships between information and mediation," Arjun Appadurai observes, "and where nation-states are struggling to retain control over their populations in the face of a host of subnational and transnational movements and organizations. . . . Put simply, the task of producing locality (as a structure of feeling, a property of social life, and an ideology of situated community) is increasingly a struggle" (1996, 189). Perhaps *Native Speaker* is so oddly anchored to the local because it is responding to this "struggle."

The novel concerns itself primarily with events taking place in New York City and its surrounding areas. This focus on a specific geography confined to a single nation's region does not invite us to think about events taking place elsewhere in the United States, much less outside its borders. Even when Henry's wife, Lelia, travels to Italy as part of a trial separation, we do not get to follow. We learn about what happened during her trip, as Henry does, from secondhand reports. Lelia herself adamantly refuses to tell Henry anything specific about her absence. "I take it back," she says. "I'm not saying anything" (125). The events of the novel also revolve around other kinds of local concerns: Henry's interrelated struggles with the memory of his father, the failing of his marriage, the death of his son, Mitt, and a career path that he finds morally questionable. There is little in these struggles that suggest thought concerning anything beyond the individual and the individual's desire to adapt to state ideological expectations, even as these struggles take place specifically in places that are in close proximity to all the other major events of the novel.

In its essentials, *Native Speaker* seems to conform to Lisa Lowe's characterization of the novel form as political bildungsroman: "The bildungsroman emerged as the primary form for narrating the development of the individual from youthful innocence to civilized maturity, the telos of which is the reconciliation of the individual with the social order" (1996, 98). We might wish to add one caveat to this definition of the political bildungsroman. The novel as political bildungsroman is a form that narrates individual development as reconciliation with social order; is subsequently contained by, and takes place as a result of, the individual's boundedness to a locality; and finally provides in the process *an anchor for the continued stability of the nation-state*. Reading *Native Speaker* as a work of Asian American literature, as Lowe's analysis leads us to consider, requires us to interpret it as an example of how this narrative breaks down, ruptures, loses its integrity in the face of the specificity of Asian American subjects. This is so because Asian Americans are defined in the nation's imaginary as a logical impossibility, a foreigner who can only ever be a suspect imitation of an original national subject, the citizen, that has historically and legally been defined as white (Lowe 1996, 6). Chang-rae Lee's focus on the local, then, might be understood as interrogating the ways in which the nation disciplines its raced subjects by binding them to the nation. By its perennial refusals to grant them full recognition as unquestionable citizens, the nation compels them to guard with paranoia against any intimation of disloyalty. Paradoxically, the more the nation refuses to recognize residents of Asian descent as full-fledged members of a national body, the more the nation can demand their loyalty and excuse its punishment of them when they dare to stray. As *Native Speaker*'s scrupulous preoccupation with the local demonstrates, for Asian Americans to look beyond the nation's borders is to engage in a potentially unpatriotic act fraught with dangerous personal consequences.[9]

Thus, even his career as a private-sector spy pits Henry, a lone subjectivity whose primary definer is the nation-state where he resides (a modernist creation), against ethnically charged and community-minded subjects such as Dr. Luzan, a Filipino American therapist who maintains transnational ties with the Philippines (a raced subject): "He was a primary organizer of a small New-York based Filipino American movement for Ferdinand Marcos's return to the homeland; he collected money for press notices, pro-Marcos picnics, and anti-Aquino rallies" (42–43). By maintaining these dubious ties to his "homeland," Luzan places himself in conflict with the political interests of various American government agencies, even though at another time, when the United States officially backed Marcos, his activities would have been considered patriotic. It is relevant that Luzan at this moment supports the deposed Marcos and not the more (at that time) politically acceptable Aquino. By transgressing temporary national interests, his activities place him at odds with then-current U.S. foreign policy, suggesting that all such transnational engagements and the kind of collective thinking underlying such engagements are suspect and will be restricted in the temporal realm of this novel. Asian Americans such as Luzan must work to become good Americans by only focusing their attention on life here, and concerning themselves only with the most practical matters of this life. Any straying of thought from the nation's dominant policies is a potential betrayal and a justifiable cause for severe disciplinary action. Luzan's "drowning in a boating accident off St. Thomas" is not accidental but related to the information Henry gleaned from their contact and supplied to his firm. As his boss explains in candid speech, "The doctor was veal, Harry, one huge medallion of sweet-ass veal. You were the wolf. You fed him cream, you fed him honey. You were holding the knife" (43). Asian Americans must not only regulate their own behavior to prove their worthiness to be accepted as honorary Americans, suppressing as best they can those ethnic or racial markers that make them stick out as unreliable citizens, they must also spy on one another to ensure that their cohorts do not endanger a fact that obdurately escapes proof.

··· **THE HISTORICAL TRAUMA OF DIASPORA**

If we can indeed read *Native Speaker* as revealing the disciplinary nature of the political bildungsroman, Henry himself seems to support such a reading in his profound unhappiness with the way his life is progressing.

He signals this discontent, for instance, when he responds to his boss's revelations about Luzan's death by saying, "No more knives . . . I swear I'll bolt" (44). This manifest discontent with work is also paralleled by disappointments in his private life. His marriage is failing and his father has just died, both of which preoccupy Henry more than the guilt over the doctor's death. In a way, these failures and deaths can be traced back to the son, whose premature end seems to be the main impetus behind Lelia's departure to Italy at the start of the novel, Henry's professional lapse with Luzan, and the suddenness of the father's death that occurs just after. Privately, Henry's personal maturation from immigrant's son to responsible American father—someone who is fully acculturated into the norms of his family's adopted culture, which partially entails immersion in the need for material wealth, professional advancement, and nuclear family reproduction—unravels when his son dies.

As the novel progresses, this death also takes on a more public meaning. Before his abrupt end, Mitt had attained the kind of acceptance Henry himself never found in his own childhood. When Henry and Lelia first began spending their summers with his father in an upscale New York suburb, their son experienced discrimination: "One afternoon Mitt tugged at my pants and called me innocently, in quick succession, a *chink*, a *jap*, a *gook*. . . . And after the same kids saw Lelia and me play with him in the front yard they started in with other things, teaching him words like mutt, mongrel, half-breed, banana, twinkie" (103). This discrimination, however, goes away with familiarity, until by "that last summer Mitt was thick with them all. Friends for life, or it seemed" (104). This is an accomplishment Henry partially envies, since he himself could not attain it in his own childhood. After the neighborhood children "pushed" Mitt "down to the ground and put dirt in his mouth," Henry recalls, "it seemed a repetition of a moment from many years before, when an older boy named Clay had taken away my cap pistol. I remembered how my father had spoken to Clay's mother in a halting, polite English and how he excused her son for taking advantage of my timidity and misunderstanding. . . . The woman hardly understood what he said, and Clay—grinning to himself behind her and looking more menacing than ever—only temporarily handed over my toy gun" (103–104). The sense of acceptance that Mitt's solidifying friendship with his former adversaries implies quickly collapses when Mitt dies of suffocation under a "stupid dog pile" (a game in which one boy jumps on top of another, yelling "dog pile," and is followed by many others into as big a mass of bodies as is possible) (105). As Hyungji Park has pointed out, Mitt can also be pronounced *mitt*, a possible Korean cognate that means bottom.[10] Thus, the death of their son seems to have been inevitable on a literal as well as a figurative level, the name of the son in one language inscribing in another his untimely demise. The tragedy of Mitt's death is not a random accident but something built into the logic of the narrative itself. This tragedy is symbolic of Henry's inability to translate his Korean ancestry into American assimilation for his son. This morbid cross-cultural linguistic pun expresses the impossibility of such translation. Race remains a staunch barrier to assimilation in *Native Speaker* and, in remaining, forces the normally passive Henry to challenge the confines of a political bildungsroman.

One reason for Henry's awakening from his passivity is John Kwang, the Korean American councilman Henry finds himself spying on with regrettable consequences. In one speech in particular, Kwang signals a preoccupation with serial historical traumas that might explain how Korean Americans are being constituted as such, suggesting in the process a very different way of thinking about one's self in the world that is not necessarily defined by the nation-state where one resides. According to Kaja Silverman, "historical trauma" refers specifically to male subjects who have suffered through a historical event, such as military service for American soldiers during the Second World War, that has brought them into an "intimate relation with lack" (1992, 55). Central to this concept, as Silverman defines it, is the widespread withdrawal of consent from a social order that such a new and often violent awareness of absence entails, so that the social order "finds itself without the mechanism for achieving social consensus" (55).

As we saw in the previous chapter's discussion on the concept of trauma as metaphor and its relationship to the state of exception, the Los Angeles riots served this function for the *kyopo* merchants interviewed in *Sa-I-Gu*, and, as I have been arguing throughout this book, the pervasive inability to imagine a desirable future also serves to undermine rule by consent and, by extension, the smooth running of the state. The lack of state protection and redress in the midst of civil unrest led many such merchants to question their faith in a social order that once seemed to promise stability, upward mobility, and material well-being. The possibility thus presented itself in the wake of such shaken faith for these merchants to withdraw their consent from the social order, and in doing so they potentially jeopardized the mechanisms for consensus building that the state relies on, at least in part, for its acts of nation maintenance. What Kwang's presence in *Native Speaker* suggests, then, is the way such a withdrawal of consent from one social order may enable the strengthening of other group loyalties. Korean Americans are not individuals removed from like subjectivities and slotted into the machinery of a homogenizing social order. Rather, they have a shared history of trauma that is potentially powerful enough to bond this ethnic group under the heading of diaspora.[11]

Kwang demonstrates the rhetorical efficacy of such a preoccupation when he makes the following speech before a predominantly black audience, referencing the same history with which this chapter began by reciting. This remarkable speech deserves lengthy quotation:

> We Koreans know something of this tragedy. Recall the days over fifty years ago, when Koreans were made servants and slaves in their own country by the Imperial Japanese Army. How our mothers and sisters were made the concubines of the very soldiers who enslaved us.
>
> I'm speaking of histories that all of us should know. Remember, or now know, how Koreans were cast as the dogs of Asia, remember the way our children could not speak their own language in school, remember how they called each other by the Japanese names forced upon them, remember the public executions of patriots and the shadowy murders of collaborators, remember our feelings of disgrace and penury and shame, remember most of all the struggles to survive with one's own identity still strong and alive. . . .
>
> Know that what we have in common, the sadness and the pain and injustice, will always be stronger than our differences. (153)

This passage is revelatory in a number of ways. What defines Koreans are traumatic events that afflict them at regular intervals. Such events provide Koreans—*minjung* (people plus masses) and kyopo (overseas Koreans) alike—with a sense of shared disaster, and, in their struggle to overcome such disaster, they become more aware of how they comprise a single people. The more traumatic events threaten Koreans as a group, the stronger the group becomes in response, conversely suggesting that there have been many historically traumatic events from which such a group *can* draw strength.

The burden created by the repeated occurrence of historical traumas provides Koreans with a way to sense in each other an affinity that is at once mutually beneficial and key to their survival. This sense is reinforced through the repeated experience of such traumas. This is so, according to Kwang, because the culture that holds Koreans and Korean Americans together as one definable group, and makes them unique, is not a culture of shared practices, habits, language, music, cuisine, or a host of other types of activities usually associated with a group's making of self-identity. All of these activities are decidedly unspoken in this passage. Rather, a culture of shared traumas, in the crucible of severe dislocation, violence, and widespread pain, produces these activities as a common possession. In this way, trauma becomes the paradoxical source of a group's identity that assumes a fraught, and often antagonistic, relationship to the states which juridically and coercively govern their lives. Perhaps this explains why Japanese imperialism figures so significantly in this speech: it literalizes the solidifying of a group identity during a period when this group had literally been forced to concede its geographical moorings and its apparent national sovereignty to a foreign power.

The logic of Kwang's speech also implies that this process of group maintenance is not exclusive to Koreans. African Americans, too, can be seen as similarly constituted, especially if we interpret slavery, post-Reconstruction betrayal, white rioting, Jim Crow, lynching, redlining, mass imprisonment, and the myriad other forms of oppression experienced by this group as examples of historical trauma. Hence, Kwang can argue that what blacks and Koreans have in common, "the sadness and the pain and injustice," makes them identifiable as discrete diasporas as well. But even while he makes this argument, Kwang suggests that Koreans have been luckier than blacks because the latter have not been able to maintain the kind of continuity that the salience of Korean traumas enables. As Kwang further explains in his speech, "And if they [African Americans] do not have the same strong community you share, the one you brought with you from Korea, which can pool money and efforts for its members—*it is because this community has been broken and dissolved through history*" (153; emphasis mine). This claim, I suspect, would surprise many African American readers currently living in vibrant communities with a strong sense of shared historical traumas, as well as many Korean American readers who, like the fictional Henry, have grown up in predominantly non-Korean neighborhoods with little connection to other Korean Americans, much less to a Korean history. There are acute differences in history and experiences, both between and within these heterogeneous groups, that make it conceptually difficult to collapse blacks and kyopos into a single narrative and, more important, to homogenize the diverse range of subjectivities contained in any one group designation.

Nevertheless, Kwang may still be making a valid point. As sociologists have discovered, "while 60 percent of whites believe that, by trying harder, blacks could be just as well off as whites, 60 percent of blacks feel the same. In fact, blacks so firmly believe in the American dream that they are nearly as convinced of its reality as whites" (Jennifer Lee 2002, 145). What is the difference between Korean Americans and African Americans that Kwang points to in this speech? Taking our cue from this kind of sociological observation, we might respond by saying that the difference lies in the length of immersion in an American culture that has been dominated over the last two or three decades by idealizations of individualism, ambition, and self-reliance. In other words, the longer groups remain in the United States, regardless of race or ethnicity, the more likely they are to accept the faith that personal freedom without any social obligations is an unassailable good, that upward economic mobility is the necessary bedrock of a vigorous society, that asking for help is an almost unpardonable sign of weakness, and that to question these values is to be anti-American. From the perspective of this faith, which is in fact a sharp departure from what many Americans believed about themselves even a few decades before and which is in any case discretely honored in the breech by its most vocal adherents, diaspora must appear a demonic deviance. The emphasis on community found in Kwang's speech points to a system of group reliance that violates what is currently held up in this country, especially in a period defined by the de facto dominance of neoconservative policies and neoliberal economics (in the sense that no other alternatives seem available), as nearly sacred. "The notion," Jennifer Lee points out, "that one must depend on and extend help to others to succeed stands in stark contrast to models that posit an atomistic person piloting his or her way with only human capital as the controlling feature" (2002, 135).

Kwang's argument thus belies a tension that seems to exist within each group. Are blacks and kyopos as cultural groups finding themselves shaped by the distrust of others like themselves, the prevalent belief in the United States that group identities are always coincidental with individual restrictiveness and exclusion of outsiders? Or, are they being shaped by a contrary creed that asserts intimate dependence is the only way in which they can survive, much less prosper, in a hostile environment? Advocates of diaspora supply a strong response. In an era of incredible migration and unprecedented technological connectedness over vast expanses of space—one in which profound dislocation, loss, and dreaming over commoditized ideals that are almost intentionally designed to be unattainable are increasingly the norm—diaspora as a social concept is in ascendance over other forms of identity manufacturing, such as the nation-state. For example, Appadurai writes with confidence: "Neither popular nor academic thought in this country has come to terms with the difference between being a land of immigrants and being one node in a postnational network of diasporas" (1996, 171). Diaspora is the primary signifier for the breakdown of nation-states that globalization apparently accelerates, and as such diaspora is also a central trope for the breakdown of the political bildungsroman's ability to narrate symbolically the supremacy of the nation-state over its subjects. Diaspora thus stands out as a possible alternative to the nation-state, supplying at the least some of the material and affective needs traditionally thought of as being served by the nation.

It is perhaps for this reason that *diaspora* as a term has found such wide usage in recent decades. As Khachig Tölölyan argues, the meaning of this term changed sometime around the mid-1960s, when many Western countries began to open their borders to new kinds of immigrants and when the term itself began to gain greater currency. "Where once were dispersion," he writes, "there is now diaspora" (1996, 3). Before, this little-known word used to refer to a tightly knit though geographically dispa-rate group of coethnics, forced away from their homelands for reasons beyond their control, who continued to maintain strong social con-nections with one another through frequent travel, exchange of letters, shared languages, clustered living, and common holidays and customs. They did this out of a felt sense of communality and also because their adopted lands did not fully accept them. Such groups often aspired to return to their homeland, or to reestablish it if destroyed. The term referred mainly to Jews and Armenians.

Currently, the term refers to any group, even nonethnic groups, whose members are spread out over distant geographies and who maintain ties with one another through the use of sophisticated electronic devices, frequent travel, and most important in shared imaginations of com-monality. For the well-off, these kinds of transnational linkages point to a life made possible through easy intellectual and physical mobility across heterogeneous "ethnoscapes" (Appadurai 1996, 33), a glamorous cos-mopolitan existence that transcends the confines of a territorially bound nation-state through the literal exchange of hard currencies and expendi-tures of accumulated wealth. In this context, diaspora points to the free-dom of travel, fast communication, and plentiful cross-cultural enter-tainment that are borne across continents and are made possible by accelerated technological sophistication. For the majority who are dras-tically less well-off, diaspora is the name of an unsettled identity that is forced upon them through compulsory travel across national boundaries and that places them in occasional coalition, or alternatively in conflict, with similar socioeconomically situated peoples. Such a dispersal of the dispossessed is made possible, is indeed made inevitable, by the need for cheap labor in overdeveloped countries, and by the systems of mobil-ity between the overdeveloped and underdeveloped countries—such as "coyotes" (smugglers who help people across the Mexican-U.S. border), "snakeheads" (smugglers who help Chinese enter the United States il-legally), temporary worker visas (like the one proposed by the President George W. Bush)—that have formed to meet this need.

Like goods and services, people are flowing across borders as cheap commodities, or they are halted at borders to prevent too much circula-tion from increasing the price of their labor. In either case, whole peoples now find themselves on the move or, just as important, dreaming over what it means to be on the move. For as Appadurai has persuasively argued,

> This is not to say that there are no relatively stable communities and networks of kinship, friendship, work, and leisure, as well as of birth, residence, and other filial forms. But it is to say that the warp of these stabilities is everywhere shot through with the woof of human motion, as more persons and groups deal with the realities of having to move or the fantasies of wanting to move. What is more, both these realities and fantasies now function on larger scales, as men and women from villages in India think not just of moving to Poona or Madras but of moving to Dubai and Houston, and refugees from Sri Lanka find themselves in South India as well as in Switzerland, just as the Hmong are driven to London as to Philadelphia. And as international capital shifts its needs, as production and technology generate different needs, as nation-states shift their policies on refugee populations, these moving groups can never afford to let their imaginations rest too long, even if they wish to. (1996, 33–34)

For the vast majority of people who are on the move in the contemporary moment, they have formed into diasporas in places that would have been unimaginable for their ancestors, who might have once lived in one geographical locality like their own ancestors had done for generations. In these unfamiliar lands—often concentrated at the world's meeting places of trade, industry, and transportation, which, crisscrossed by planes flying overhead, draw peoples like water from every conceivable rural district—fellow travelers meet, form into homogeneous communities, find themselves the neighbors of peoples from other faraway places, and commune in novel ways with these other displaced migrants. Displaced, migrants form diasporas. Relocated, diasporic peoples find themselves in close contact with other diasporic peoples. Collectively dreamy, they yearn for the same prizes of secure living, plentiful material goods, and a glamour that somehow will render their bodies whole and healthy, as can be found transmitted and popularized in the global flows of popular advertisements. In sharp contrast, the majority encounter lives that entail hostile states, unsafe working conditions, and the constant need to labor.

Such lives leave their bodies bent, aching, and tired. Diaspora thus names a process of displacement, relocation, and chance meetings; of the play of the imagination and the exigencies of global economics; of the defensive huddling together and the necessary contact with strangers from far-flung places—all of which vest this antique word with a sheen of an emergent modernity, a new "new world order" that is perhaps as old as the pre–Vasco da Gama Indian Ocean to which Vijay Prashad has recently directed our attention (2002). From its obscure etymological origins, diaspora has become a powerful signifier for futurity.

In similar ways, "Korean American discussions of the L.A. riots present a rich play of national memory and ethnic identity. . . . The riots are rendered as but another chapter in age-old stories. In the process, ethnic or national portraiture is posited as a reflection of this past" (Abelmann and Lie 1995, 19). Likewise, *Native Speaker* also uses the 1992 Los Angeles riots to connect Korean history with Korean American experiences of social trouble, resubstantiating the threads of ethnic connections thinned by travel and life far away from the places where one was born. John Kwang, again from his speech, becomes the spokesperson of the horror that resubstantiates: "A young black mother of two, Saranda Harlins, is dead. Shot in the back by a Korean shopkeeper. Charles Kim, a Korean-American college student, is also dead. He was overcome by fumes trying to save merchandise in the fire-bombed store of his family. . . . And I say that though they may lie beneath the earth, they are not buried" (151). It is important to notice that while these events are supposed to have taken place in Queens, they make specific reference to the Los Angeles riots. The name of the single Korean American fatality in the riots was, of course, Edward Lee, who died while trying to protect his family-owned store. Just as significant, however, is this passage's reference to Latasha Harlins (who is only barely disguised as a Saranda Harlins).

In 1991, Soon Ja Du shot and killed the fifteen-year-old Harlins over an argument about a $1.79 bottle of orange juice. Harlins had been on her way home after spending an evening with friends; there had apparently been disagreements at home between her and her guardian. There is no question that Harlins, herself a recent Los Angeles transplant from the Midwest, had lived a short and difficult life and that she had done so with great grace. Du, on the other hand, was a deeply troubled Korean American woman whose son had been robbed at gunpoint only a few months before. When the altercation between Du and Harlins occurred, Du was apparently unaware that the gun she had pulled on Harlins had been replaced with a hairpin trigger during the time it had been stolen in an earlier robbery and then returned to them by the police. Joyce Karlins, the presiding judge, landed this case because she had the least tenure (she had been on the bench for fewer than two weeks) and because the other judges were reluctant to preside over such a potentially explosive case. At the end of the trial, Karlins sentenced Du to a $500 fine, 400 hours of community service, and a commuted prison term. To make matters worse, she lectured the black attendees in the courtroom, including Harlins's family. The security videotape in which Du shot Harlins in the back of the head, then, is what was repeatedly shown in the local L.A. television news market during the days of the riots next to the tape that has the beating of Rodney King; this videotape did not show how Du grabbed Harlins first or how Harlins turned around and punched Du in the face several times. Unsurprisingly, the images from this recording and the trial's decision were reported to have fueled a great deal of black anger against Koreans in Los Angeles. During the middle of the riots, for example, Mike Davis was repeatedly told, "This is for our baby sister. This is for Latasha" (2002, 232).[12]

Clearly, the political tragedy Kwang speaks about is itself a metacommentary on the Los Angeles riots and how it helped forge a need for group consciousness among Korean Americans. His oblique reference to the riots is immediately followed by his speech on Korean history quoted earlier. It is as if the riots can only be understood by Kwang in the context of this history of sorrow. Kwang thus suggests in his speech that if Korean Americans are indeed diasporic, they are so for inescapable historical reasons, the historical trauma of the 1992 riots becoming the buried rationale for building a Korean American sense of collectivity, albeit one that remains open to coalition with others similarly traumatized by a tearful Benjaminian history.[13] The formulation of this rationale, as we have seen in Kwang's speech, is the continuation of a strategy for group definition that was originally conceived in the fierce heat of Korea's past. Korean Americans can turn to this past when they encounter group trauma in the United States and recover (or invent) an apparently old way of forging a sense of community founded on social upheaval. For Kwang, it is also important that such a recovery process bring Korean Americans into political cooperation with other diasporic groups.

··· COMPETING NOTIONS OF DIASPORA

Can we read Mitt's death, then, as a personal tragedy that allegorizes the need for a renewal of diaspora in Henry's life? This seems plausible, since this death forces Henry to reflect harder than he has perhaps ever done on what the legacy of his father's life has meant for his own life and also because after this death Henry turns to John Kwang, who seems, at least temporarily, to offer an alternative to the life choices Henry's father has made. What we see in this contrast between Henry's father and Kwang are competing notions of diaspora, one based on single-ethnic solidarity and transnational connectivity and the other on multiethnic coalition-building and confinement to the U.S. nation-state. If, as a novel, *Native Speaker* narrates the individual political maturation of Henry as a political bildungsroman, the plot complications represented by these two figures suggest that legitimation by the state is by no means guaranteed.

We encounter the first notion of diaspora, represented by the father, early in the novel. During his father's dying days, Henry finds himself thinking about him as a synecdoche for other Korean immigrants:

> For him [the father], the world . . . operated on a determined set of procedures, certain rules of engagement. These were the inalienable rights of the immigrant. I was to inherit them, the legacy unfurling before me this way: you worked from before sunrise to the dead of night. You were never unkind in your dealings, but then you were not generous. Your family was your life, though you rarely saw them. You kept close handsome sums of cash in small denominations. You were steadily cornering the market in self-pride. You drove a Chevy and then a Caddy and then a Benz. You never missed a mortgage payment or a day of church. You prayed furiously until you wept. You consider the only unseen forces to be those of capitalism and the love of Jesus Christ. (47)

If we read this passage as a commentary on post-1965 Korean immigrants, we might interpret it to mean the following: In their desire to make it in the United States, they enslave themselves to the ideal of upward economic mobility, and as a result they leave little room for sympathy with their nonwhite peers. At the same time, they consistently fail to take full advantage of the social opportunities life in the United States affords them: they focus too much on worldly gain and maintain an almost hereditary adherence to frozen traditions. In performing these tasks, the father's behavior suggests that the United States's ability to govern its subjects through widely shared ideologies based on individuality, material ambition, consumerism, and religion exists largely uncontested. As Henry concludes his soliloquy to his father, it becomes clear that this paternal monomaniacal quest for things has left the son with a mixed "legacy": "He had raised me in a foreign land, put me through college, witnessed my marriage for my long-buried mother, even left me enough money that I could do the same for my children without the expense of his kind of struggles; his duties, uncomplex, were by all accounts complete. And the single-minded determination that had propelled him through twenty-five years of green-grocering in a famous ghetto of America would serve him a few last days, and through any of my meagre execrations" (49).

This is not, however, a balanced reading of Chang-rae Lee's first novel. Even as Henry replicates a restrictive, and unflattering (as overly materialistic), view of Korean Americans through his representation of his father, we can find evidence of another interpretation of his father. This other interpretation does not reject the restrictive view of Korean Americans but, nevertheless, lends greater nuance to this view than a cursory examination may allow. We find such evidence in Henry's discussion of his father's "personal lore," which "said that he started with $200 in his pocket and a wife and baby and just a few words of English. Knowing what every native loves to hear, he would have offered the classic immigrant story, casting himself as the heroic newcomer, self-sufficient, resourceful" (40–50). This "lore," as Henry observes, has a clear ideological purpose, the reason why "natives love to hear" it. It reaffirms belief in America's inherently equitable social structure, and it makes other minorities incapable of such economic upward mobility appear, in comparison, personally responsible for their incapacity. This lore also bolsters the father's own desire to find a narrative that will make his past life in the

United States "heroic," and not simply the tale of toil and loss that his son reads into it. The bitterness with which Henry speaks about his alienation from his father, then, might be retroactively seen as a negative response to the belief that material success is the same as overall success in one's life, that even if the lore is correct in stressing individual gumption over structural barriers it is incorrect in believing such gumption will bring happiness. In doing so, his unflattering assessment of his father's life perhaps relieves some of Henry's repressed anger at being arbitrarily enjambed into his father's ameliorating self-romance.

Henry deflates his father's so-called personal lore in a way that is more sophisticated than an expression of popular sentiment. Not only does this kind of material success bring an attendant alienation, love as being more important than money, it is also based on a simple lie. Henry's father started with help: "The truth, though, is that my father got his first infusion of capital from a *ggeh*, a Korean 'money club' in which members contributed to a pool that was given out on a rotating basis. Each week you gave the specified amount; and then one week in the cycle, all the money was yours" (50). Henry goes on to describe this practice not only as a way to get an important start in business for those without the necessary capital but also as rooted in the social relationships that have developed amongst first-generation Korean Americans in strict defiance of the value of self-reliance. *Ggeh* is not the seamless continuation of a Korean cultural practice these immigrants have brought with them. It is a brought-over cultural practice that has been cleverly refashioned to meet the needs of their new situations. Foreigners in a foreign land—needing economic capital, fellowship, and an escape from uniform hostilities—pool their limited resources so they as a group can work together for financial gain while deriving some much-needed social interaction.[14]

Over time, as their needs change, as individuals eventually begin to make detectable gains, and as society with fellow migrants becomes less urgent, a refashioned cultural practice loses coherence. As its utility becomes less pressing, the community that formed around it begins to dissolve. As Henry remembers:

I know over the years my father and his friends got together less and less. . . . They all got busier and wealthier and lived farther and farther apart. . . . Some of them, too, were already dead, like Mr. Oh, who had a heart attack after being held up at his store in Hell's Kitchen. And in the end my father no longer belonged to any *ggeh*, he complained about all the disgraceful troubles that were now cropping up, people not paying on time or leaving too soon after their turn getting the money. *In America, he said, it's even hard to stay Korean.* (51; emphasis mine)

In providing a narrative to how ggeh came to exist, helped the father succeed like many of his peers, and eventually became obsolete by changing economic realities, *Native Speaker* reveals a keen awareness of temporality. Fortunes change, and along with them cultural practices also change or die out (which, it is worth pointing out, is as true for the dominant society as it is for the diasporic one). For Chang-rae Lee's narrator, the kind of diaspora implicit to the functioning of a ggeh does not decline simply because these lives have ceased to experience tragic events—the reference to Mr. Oh's death foregrounds the way all of their lives are punctuated by such tragedies—but because these tragedies have lost connection to a larger identity of shared pain. Material success and new social contacts have made it difficult to imagine such tragedies as contiguous with group-defining, historically traumatic events that span two countries an ocean apart and many decades, if not centuries.

In the passages that revolve around Henry's complex, and often contradictory, feelings about his father, we can observe how Henry fuses sentimentality (love is more important than money) with temporality (the waning of conditions that rendered diaspora meaningful) to make sense of what went wrong in his father's life:

I wonder if my father, if given the chance, would have wished to go back to the time before he made all that money, when he had just one store and we rented a tiny apartment in Queens. He worked hard and had worried but he had a joy then that he never seemed to regain once the money started coming in. He might turn on the radio and dance cheek to cheek with my mother. . . . They had lots of Korean friends that they met at church and then even in the street, and when they talked in public there was a shared sense of how lucky they were, to be in America but still have countrymen near. (51–52)

There is a sense of a common loss, a solace-providing community, and a spontaneous form of self-acknowledgment that is rendered sentimental, something that takes place on the plane of feeling and that moves one through pity to be better morally than what one already is, expressed by the narrator's regret that material success has meant for his father, and for himself, a failure of diaspora to sustain itself over time and through almost inescapable changes in their lives. The father's diaspora with his fellow immigrants has not been able to rejuvenate itself in the second generation and has thus weakened the bond between generations. In time, the quality of the father's life deteriorates, and the son is left stranded with the difficult task of establishing belonging in a country that continually isolates its subjects. What makes diaspora fail in this way is the lack of historically traumatic events. In historical trauma's stead, there are only personal tragedies not connected to the experiences of Korean Americans as a whole and thus lacking the affective potency required for diaspora's maintenance. The failure of the father's diaspora to renew itself over time is not, however, likely to happen to people who are not as materially successful and/or who continue to feel culturally isolated, as is probably the case with many Korean Americans whose families continue to be densely packed into "tiny" apartments "in Queens." Such people, I suspect, do not share the same kind of nostalgia expressed in this passage.

Almost as if in acknowledgment of such people, John Kwang refuses the privatization of tragedy that marks the end of life for Henry's father by specifically turning his attention toward the less fortunate, regardless of ethnicity or race, in need of the comfort and support that diaspora offers at its best. Kwang tries to help the disenfranchised through his desire to make "money clubs" available to constituents outside the Korean American community. Indeed, this desire for a supraethnic money club that will provide Kwang's electorate with the cash to pull themselves out of their limiting conditions and give them the necessary financial boost once only available to someone like Henry's father seems close to attainment, but even so Henry discovers, when he is given charge of the operation, it is based on a faulty assumption. "Small *ggeh*, like the one my father had," Henry observes, "worked because the members all know each other, trust one another not to run off or drop out after their turn comes up. Reputation is always worth more than money. In this sense we are all related. The larger *ggeh* depends solely on this notion, that the lessons of the culture will be stronger than a momentary lack, can subdue any individual weakness or want. . . . What John says about it" (279–280). For Henry, Kwang's project questions the foundation of a community formation that wishes to provide both a sense of belonging and material benefits to its members. It is almost as if Henry's reservations about Kwang's project is a direct rebuttal of Elaine Kim's postriot political vision of a "nationalism-in-internationalism," which can "call forth a culture of survival and recovery" (1993, 231). Such a concept of diaspora might work in limited situations, but can it work in a scope much larger and more diverse than anyone has tried?

As it turns out in *Native Speaker*, the answer is no. With Henry's help, the list of members of the money club eventually finds its way to the INS (Immigration and Naturalization Service, now folded into the Department of Homeland Security), whose agents use it to identify undocumented immigrants and deport them. Kwang himself begins to falter under the contradictions of his political position and, in the wake of the electorate's fury at his scheme's collapse, retires from public life completely. His attempt to fashion a narrative about diaspora that sees in the history of both Koreans and non-Koreans in Queens shared accumulated historical traumas ends in ruin when it comes into conflict with the machinations of powerful repressive state apparatuses that have not grown any weaker over the years. In his political demise, Kwang substantiates the father's pessimistic belief that diasporic cultural practices can only be built upon small, discrete groups of known people, whose face-to-face contact enables trust and stresses the importance of "reputation." He sees the difficulty of achieving these practices when the U.S. nation-state itself is so far from losing its eminence and its dominant political culture is so sternly set against interethnic cooperation. In the teeth of such hostility, the kind of diaspora envisioned by Kwang becomes the sport of charismatic individuals and the fabrication of hope that can be used against the very people the cooperation was supposed to help.

In a "sense," as Henry puts it, all must be "related." Otherwise, diaspora turns into tragedy. This is almost literally true in *Native Speaker*. Like Aristotelian notions of tragedy based on Greek drama, Kwang's fall, properly measurable by the grandeur of his aspirations, is accompanied by a scene of harrowing recrimination, mob justice, and a chorus who gives witness to his disgrace:

> The people who are angry with him are hollering and pointing at him, stretching the police tape as far as they can. . . . They are calling him every ugly Asian name I have ever heard. . . . I notice some others who are standing very still with their hands at their mouths. Most of these are Asian women. They look like the older woman you see working in the alley behind a restaurant, pouring out buckets of dirty dishwater. They are tired, expressionless. But now they gaze at him as if he were their son, one maybe gone bad though now finally home, and the numbed speech on their faces seems to say how sad he must be and hurt enough and how he should be forgiven. (342)

This passage suggests that Kwang's sin has been "hubris" (280)—not pride, as this word is often mistranslated to mean, but an offense of self-confidence, a belief in one's ability to do more than what the facts will bear. Or perhaps it would be more accurate to say, given the contemporary urban context of this scene and the kind of invectives being hurled at Kwang, that his belief was misplaced because he thought he could overcome the fractures and division created by race in attempting to forge a diaspora based simply on need and grassroots enterprises without state sanction. Although the ramifications of this tragedy are widespread, the focal point remains finally John Kwang. His downfall is again tragedy experienced individually, rather than historical trauma shared collectively.

The shortcomings of these two figures, Henry's father and John Kwang, critique opposing notions of diaspora. If Kwang's attempt to create a diaspora without ethnic restrictions fails, it is because Kwang does not see that the sentimental appeal of such a diaspora is overly dependent on one charismatic figure. There is no central narrative nor an enduring sense of commonality that will glue such disparate people to one another, except for Kwang's myth of benevolence, and that, therefore, can hold such a diaspora together during times of trouble. In focusing on the material benefits of ggeh, Kwang has not done enough to build mutual recognition of shared traumas to sustain political coalitions across a diverse population. If diaspora also fails Henry's father, it is because the main rationale for its existence has been lost in his and his peers' growing individual affluence. Without the narrative of historical traumas, the meaningfulness of ethnic affiliations weakens under the weight of material success and the accumulation of sui generis personal tragedies. In the former case (Kwang's viewpoint), historical traumas are not sentimental enough to hold a multiethnic diaspora together in the face of powerful state forces, while in the latter (his father's viewpoint), historical traumas are too absent to sustain the sentimental attachments capable of maintaining an ethnically defined diaspora.

· · · THE PERSISTENCE OF ESTRANGEMENT

By the end of the novel, the disillusioned Henry turns away from other Korean Americans altogether, preferring to seek refuge in a revitalized domestic space with his non-Korean wife. This is the only remaining alternative to both his father's and Kwang's opposing notions of diaspora that *Native Speaker* holds out to its readers. In considering this alternative, we need to keep in mind that the struggles Henry endures to define his sense of self are experienced primarily as a Korean American man. We might recall Park's and Wald's perceptive observation that in narrating "legitimation" for a "male immigrant subject," *Native Speaker* pushes its Korean American women into the shadows (1998, 609). But as we have seen, by the end of the novel, Henry's attempts at such legitimation fails. When its does, Henry retreats into the private sphere of his wife's domestic space; he becomes in a sense the "shadowy figures of Korean American women" who are at the margins of the novel. By the last page, it is Henry the narrator who is speechless. As an assistant to his wife's work as an ESL instructor, he dons a "green rubber hood" and cowers silently before the students "when anyone repeats the day's secret phrase" (348). As the couple says good-bye to these students, it is Lelia who is endowed with the Adamic power to name while it is Henry who observes silently: "Everybody, she says, has been a good citizen. . . . Now, she calls out each one as best as she can, taking care of every last pitch and accent, and I hear her speaking a dozen lovely and native languages, calling all the difficult names of who we are" (349). The shadowy Korean American women in the novel turn out not to be separate from Henry but to be his own shadows, doubles whose marginality adumbrates Henry's inability to speak in a classroom designed to manufacture "good citizens." The alternative to diaspora, either that of his father or of Kwang, is a focus on the proper acculturation of immigration children who will be trained to become functioning members of their newly, but still imperfectly, adopted nation.

In such a privatized space, diasporas of any kind lose their meaning and we are left contemplating how well, if at all, Henry as a lone subject is reconciled with his social order. In the last pages of *Native Speaker*, we are presented with an image in which Henry hides his foreign-looking face behind a grotesque rubber mask, taking refuge in his apartment from the tortured memories of his past experiences, and celebrating the bliss afforded by matrimonial union. There is a calm that settles over the loving and elegiac rendering of this image that can lead readers to feel optimistic that liberal pluralism is a happy solution to the problem of major demographic change, and of the many macroeconomic and political inequalities that have led so many people to reshuffle themselves over far-flung corners of the world in such large numbers in the latter part of the twentieth century. We might be tempted to read along the grain, and close the pages of the book with the reassuring belief that *Native Speaker* is, after all, a romance. Its ending reaffirms the reconciliation between a troubled male subject and the state that he has learned, resignedly, to accept. His wife stands in for the promise of that state as a liberal entity in whose embrace immigrants are still welcome, even if there are maverick forces within its institutions that from time to time to time lead the state to fail this promise. While such a state might succumb to such forces, it still holds out a vision of civil society worth struggling for, and defending. *Native Speaker* is, after all, yet another form of an intact political bildungsroman, one that proves ultimately resistant to a reading as an example of Asian American or diasporic literature.

To be satisfying, however, such a sanguine interpretation must overlook a couple of details. First, there is the large number of immigrant children whom Henry and Lelia are supposed to teach. The narrator admits that Lelia and her unpaid husband-aid are only freelance educators—in short, privatized teachers—taking on students who require more individualized and extended training than the city is willing to allocate funds for. "Lelia usually doesn't like this kind of work," Henry observes from behind his green mask, "even though it pays well, mostly because they are too many students in a class for her to make much of a difference" (348). The city saves money by paying one instructor well for a short period of time to teach many students than it would if it paid more instructors, perhaps at less pay, to teach longer hours and fewer students. Given the constraints of such *flexible* employment, Lelia must console herself simply with the alleviation of fear: "It doesn't matter what they understand. She wants them to know that there is nothing to fear, she wants to offer a pale white woman horsing with the language to show them it's fine to mess it all up" (349). This passage subtly suggests that these students will not go on to master their adopted language so long as the city lacks the political will to take on more of the responsibility to educate the nation's foreign-born children, undermining the rhetoric of "good citizenship" that the narrator adds to this scene.

All that can be hoped for is that the failure to master language, to mimic speech as it is spoken by a dominant class of natives, will not lead them to recede into silence and a habit of refusing to engage with others. Perhaps the most important lesson Lelia and her husband might teach their "kids," the narrator suggests, is the ability to avoid falling into the belief that expression is possible only for those who have been schooled in the conventions of standard language use. Rather than be preoccupied by the rigors of grammar or proper vocabulary, what Lelia stresses in her lessons is the need to take risks, make mistakes, and focus on the contents of what one wishes to say. Only by being comfortable in their strangeness, marking them both in face and in speech, can these economically and socially deprived children hope to communicate with others who are not like themselves and, in the future, carve out a habitable space in this unfriendly country.

Second, this focus on language as a communicative tool that does not have to be mastered to be used effectively clashes with the fact that Chang-rae Lee himself is such a fine writer. No discussion of *Native Speaker* would be complete without some attention to Lee's self-conscious skill in his craft. His flawless prose insists on the need to speak in a voice that can perfectly mimic the speech of the dominant classes. If we did not know the name of the author or anything about his racial background, we might be surprised to discover that the novel has been written by a Korean American. Like the children who peer into his face, we might find ourselves amazed by the fluency of the author's use of English—"some wonder in their looks as they check again that my voice moves in time with my mouth, truly belongs to my face" (349). In Lee's prose, there are no missing articles, no misplaced prepositions, no verbs in the wrong word order, no mistakes in agreement, and no other telltale signs of people who have had to spend their lives code-switching between imperfectly understood languages that operate by very different logics of grammar. Instead, what we find is a mimicry so thoroughly practiced that it at once hides the author's foreignness and calls attention to its flawless imitation as somehow forcefully acquired. We can never forget with Lee's prose that we are reading a work of literature, because it calls attention to itself through its self-consciously polished prose as a work of literature, and as such the prose seems to demonstrate the persistent need many Asian American authors feel to prove themselves masters of the tools of their profession and thus as fully interpellated members of their nation. Perennial foreigners, Asian Americans must prove that they can speak and write good English.

The danger is acute, of course, in insisting that because Chang-rae Lee is a nonwhite writer who belongs to an ethnic group whose members are largely seen as strangers to the United States, he must inevitably betray some sign of estrangement—either through subtle mistakes in language use or, paradoxically, through the lack of any such mistakes. This is tautology. It says that for nonwhite American writers of Asian ancestry, they will be judged, especially by their racial peers who are perhaps oversensitively attuned to such matters, by standards that for white and black writers who might write flawlessly, or not, will not apply. While I recognize the logical fallacy of this argument, I nevertheless insist that in the current historical moment this is a burden that Asian American (and possibly Latino) writers cannot fully evade. Lee's narrator admits as much when he has the children at the end of the novel examine his face to make sure that the spoken words are indeed being spoken by the foreign-looking person before them.

The narrator also calls attention to the imperfect perfection of fully acculturated Asian American speech-taking—a metacritical reflection on his own use of a flawless literary English?—when he remembers his first conversation with Lelia:

> "You speak perfectly, of course. I mean if we were talking on the phone I wouldn't think twice."
> "You mean it's my face."
> "No, that's not it. . . . Your face is part of the equation, but not in the way you're thinking. You look like someone listening to himself. You pay attention to what you're doing. If I had to guess, you're not a native speaker. . . . See? You say *Leel-ya* so deliberately. You tried not to but you were taking in the sound of the syllables. You're very careful." (12)

This passage brings us back to a critical problem explored in the previous chapters. When it comes to Asian Americans and others who somehow stick out as strange, is there ever a way in which they can melt into an American mainstream, or will they always appear as other, disruptive, poised to question the state's narratives of selfhood and consent, dumb to the neoconservatism that demands conformity to the ideal of a lonely individuality and the neoliberalism that favors the redistribution of wealth upward, their ears perked to the excruciating processes of their own speech-taking and their mouths ready to speak, carefully and self-consciously, a certain kind of truth to power that, despite their intentions, will wound public social spaces? Is the presence of so many foreigners and other nonconformists, in being strange, clouding our ability to envision a national future we might all care to claim? And, if so, isn't this a presence we should cherish?

NEW LITERARY WORKS by Asian American writers, Korean Americans not least among them, continue to be published at an astonishing rate. A year has not passed by in the last ten when the ranks of Asian American literature have not been added to by the appearance of significant, serious, and profound works of the imagination. Just in the year 2003 alone, for example, Susan Choi, Suki Kim, Jhumpa Lahiri, *lê* thi diem thúy, and Monique Truong have joined already well-known authors such as Jessica Hagedorn and Maxine Hong Kingston in releasing new novels published by major imprints (*American Woman, The Interpreter, The*

Namesake, The Gangster We Are All Looking For, The Book of Salt, Dream Jungle, and *The Fifth Book of Peace*). These novels are extraordinary in breadth of subject matter, in courageous willingness to engage with characters of diverse backgrounds, in fluid movement across nationally bounded geographies, and in an openness to the possibilities of social interaction that seem, at least to me, more pinched in many other sectors of contemporary American fiction. The growing maturity of these authors are in large part a product of the "knee-high" generation. The 1.5- and second-generation children of post-1965 Asian immigrants have spent the last few decades acculturating to their adopted lands, asking questions about who they are and where they come from, marveling (or being perplexed) by their incredible heterogeneity, and engaging in the slow, often painful, work of accumulating cultural capital (in the form of educational attainment, institutional position, and so forth). Implicitly, this generation's coming of age signals, in a quiet and little-remarked-upon way, another definition of diaspora only implicitly explored in this chapter. This third notion draws upon the literal meaning of *diaspora* as, in the Greek, a "casting of seeds." Mass movements of whole families away from a homeland, who were compelled by macrohistorical forces to settle in far-flung places, have led at this moment and time to the germination of a new generation of adults who, in entering the prime of their professional lives, seem ready to participate fully in the discussions, struggles, and movements now taking place on national and international stages.

That we are in the middle of an awe-inspiring literary flowering in Asian America watered by the knee-high generation's coming into maturity seems undeniable. This flowering is the first sign of what we might expect from this generation in the years ahead. The appearance of this sign must also, certainly, call for celebration. But why do so many Asian American literary critics show hesitation?[15] This chapter's discussion of *Native Speaker* suggests one reason why we might feel this way. Even in a novel such as this one, which is partially concerned with the prospect of extranational social formations that might question the repressive tendencies of the state and provide an alternative way of imagining ourselves in the world than the one offered by the nation, this prospect ultimately turns out to be little more than a chimera. Interethnic coalition-building is shown to be limited by the continued dominance of repressive state apparatuses and by the lack of a social glue that will bond peoples of disparate backgrounds to one another as if they share a common fate. Single ethnic groups, on the other hand, seem faced exactly with the problem that John Kwang argues plagues African American communities, group dissolution through overlong contact with the current dominant ideologies of the United States.

In the contemporary moment, neoconservatives have insisted with success that, no matter what our eyes might tell us, we must work shoulder against shoulder to maintain the faith that conditions will inevitably get better if we do what is best only for our individual selves, that group cooperation always leads to tribalism, and that asking for help only makes us into losers. Regardless of whether we call the process of acquiring these beliefs interpellation or assimilation, we literary critics are surely justified in wondering if the current flowering of Asian American literature can build a resistance to such a process. If not, there will be one less site for the imagination of more desirable futures than the futures that seem to be waiting for us now.

Epilogue
Bearers of Bad News

Everywhere we look, we are confronted by spectacles of human suffering. On television, in newspapers and magazines, in movies, in print fiction and memoirs, on the live stage, in video games, bodies are constantly and more vividly being beaten, cut open, dismembered, and murdered. Stories of the poor, of racial minorities, of new immigrants fill our lives with the most gruesome details of violence and death. Driven to extremes, people who seem to exist somewhere just outside the margins of respectability kill each other, kill their children, kill their lovers, kill themselves. The culpable stare lifelessly back at us when the news or movie camera (the distinction between the two has become harder and harder to define) captures the look on their faces as they are being taken to court handcuffed, or when they are being arraigned after what looks like a long night of sleeplessness in an unfamiliar jail cell. They—who are never well defined but often appear as menacingly foreign, racially other, poor, socially maladapted, or simply the person next door—are also dangerous, the cause of the suffering that is everywhere in evidence, and so we encounter stories too numerous to mention about how they must be kept in their places. Agents of the state routinely barge into their homes, beat them up in a back alley, yell at them to shut up, or chase after them in car-heavy traffic. The agents themselves are often abused, beaten, shot, and hurt severely in spectacular ways—often to the point of suffering injuries that would have killed them long before the credits start rolling. And when agents of the state refuse to behave in this way both at home and, *especially*, abroad, or when these agents turn out to be the villains they pretend to be fighting, lone vigilantes take it upon themselves to commit extreme and terrifying violence in the name of the very law their actions have already forsaken.

For the most part, we have responded to these spectacles with delight. I found this to be partially true, in a slightly different genre, when I began laughing a few years ago during a screening of the rereleased film *The*

Exorcist (1973). Part of my laughter came from the amusement of watching an old film, the way in which, for instance, the doctor walks into a hospital waiting room and lights a cigarette before talking to an anxious mother. I recall whispering to my friend, "We live in a very different country now." But we in the theater continued to laugh, even in the latter scenes when the daughter manages to rotate her head on the axis of her neck 180 degrees and performs unspeakable sexual acts upon herself. Someone in the audience yelled in disgust, "Stop laughing. This isn't funny." This voice in the dark seems to have assumed that we were laughing because we were incapable of being touched by profound demonstrations of evil. Our laughter was a sign of moral rot. It could be added to the many other signs pointing to a country that has become more lost since this film was first seen by audience members nearly three decades before.

I think this voice was wrong. We were laughing because the anachronism of the film allowed us to see the violence as it was, a fiction not anchored to any particular reality. The events of the movie were not happening to an actual person; it was entertainment. That we could tell the difference suggests that our laughter was a sign of health. No matter how tenuously, we in the audience were demonstrating our ability to differentiate between recordings of pain-inducing violence inflicted on human bodies (like the videotape of Rodney King's beating, like the news footage of Reginald Denny's attack, like the security camera's recording in which Latasha Harlins is shot in the back of the head by Soon Ja Du, like the twin newspaper photographs of Edward Lee's blood-soaked white shirt) and recordings of violence that only *seem* to inflict pain on human bodies. When viewing the former, we did so in shock. When viewing the latter, we laugh because we know the violence isn't physically hurting anyone.

Even still, while the dated nature of *The Exorcist* helped me to see through the mechanisms of its verisimilitude, my laughter was not completely without signs of unease. As the film progressed, and the priest was hurled by some unseen force through the window and down a tall, dark, narrow set of steps (or even earlier, in the hospital scenes, when the devil-afflicted child is subjected to a battery of medical examinations that compete with other scenes in the film for level of frightfulness), my laughter hid a mounting horror. I was afraid to find out what would happen next. I dreaded the next scene, and the scene after, as the film's narrative arc intimated that only more spectacles of incredible suffering were about to follow. As the automobile pulled away from the house, carrying a now seemingly recovered young girl away from the site of her torture, I still felt the lingering sensation that something bad was about to happen at any moment. It was a mood that remained with me deep into the night and long after the film had come to an end.

Laughter is one response to this dread. Another response is simply to get up and walk out of the theater. Turn our eyes away. Ban violence in movies, on television, in video games. But this doesn't seem like a viable option anymore, if there ever was a time when it was, as the body counts rise, as the spectacles of human suffering intensifies, as the horror fills our media-saturated world. We have already been exposed to the horror that is everywhere on display, and the sheer volume of what has been produced precludes the possibility of censorship. More important, arguing that we turn away from these spectacles might be a failure on our part to understand the cultural work that representations of horror do for most, if not all, of us. I like to believe—hardly an original idea—that the reason we surround ourselves with these representations is because they appeal to our profound sense of unease at the current historical moment. Like the laughter found at recent commercial screenings of *The Exorcist*, our apparently insatiable desire for violence and repression in popular media, regardless of whatever else it might signify, allows us to conquer our fears about an uncertain tomorrow.

If I am right and our laughter is a source of comfort, what happens when that laughter stops, when it edges so closely toward unease that it fails to conquer anything at all and dies in our throats before it can be heard? In light of this question, it becomes starkly clear that the works explored in this book allow precious little room for laughter. For the most part, these works are serious, meditative, gloomy, sobering, and, in short, pessimistic, almost as if the historical event that sparked their imaginativeness also dried them of humor and playfulness. Even the exploitative nature of Katherine Bigelow's *Strange Days*, which openly advertises its lust for the sensational, cannot blunt the edge of these qualities. The film is simply unpleasant to watch. Laughter is inappropriate to the spectacles of human suffering it contains. It could not completely divorce the suffering of its characters from the suffering of an actual body that is being beaten by the police, which Holliday had inadvertently filmed. Perhaps this is what led to its disappointing box-office results. And while Anna Deavere Smith is glorious in the way she seems to melt effortlessly into one character and then another, watching *Twilight* on the stage is hardly uplifting. We might laugh at times, but the laughter keeps lapsing into awkward silences. After a performance of this play, we do not leave uplifted, hopeful that great social change is around the corner. Instead, we find ourselves exiting the theater with a disheartening sigh of resignation.

This is the same for *Sa-I-Gu*, Dai Sil Kim-Gibson's reflections on a group of Korean American women stunned both by what has happened to them and by the fact that so few seem to care. The indifference to their suffering as suffering burdens the women in this documentary. What they have to report about their experiences makes me wonder if a major hidden cost of being uncared for is the withdrawal of care for others. Finally, even Chang-rae Lee's *Native Speaker*, which caught the leading edge of an Asian American wave that has still to crest, is doubtful that anything positive is waiting for its characters in the near future. We are only left with the image of a silent and deeply troubled man, face hidden behind a grotesque rubber mask, trying to maintain optimism at the sight of so many children wishing to make a home for themselves in a country that refuses to acknowledge them as its responsibility.

All of these works are bearers of bad news. Willingly or unwillingly, they take on the onerous task of telling us what we might need to hear but don't want to hear. These works—like other representations of human suffering that have found expression in such diverse forms throughout the past decade—speak to a present moment full of uncertainty, when many speak quietly and fearfully about what lies just ahead, when many more reply angrily that we live in the best of times (or, that we could if everyone were to do this or that), and when no one seems to expect much more than what he or she already has. The roundabout way in which these works must speak their meaning suggests how difficult it is to be a bearer of bad news; the accumulated weight of such works suggests that this bad news will not remain interred long. The spectacles of human suffering that literally hangs in the air all around us create—as the title of Anna Deavere Smith's play suggests—a "twilight" world, a world somewhere in between the everyday habitus of work, school, family, and so on and the habitus of the imagination, where extraordinary events are taking place, always elsewhere (in outer space, in another country, in the bad parts of town, in a rural place, in the past, in the future) but closer than is comfortable. In this twilight world, it becomes nearly impossible to separate the things we have good reason to fear from the hyperbole that ironically allows this fear to be spoken without being outright rejected as too horrible to consider. Thus, when the roundabout way in which pessimism must be spoken by bearers of bad news is not roundabout enough, this leads to a situation when reaction shuts conversation down, directs anger and fear at those who are often the most visibly in trouble, and exacerbates the very conditions that have given rise to this pessimism.

For instance, in the exaggerated twilight world of Octavia Butler's *Parable of the Sower* (1993), written when the fires from the riots were still smoldering, the precocious fourteen-year-old narrator observes to her friend what seems obvious. It is 2024; they live in a walled-in community of houses just outside of Los Angeles that is further guarded by razor-thin wires capable of cutting unsuspecting intruders in half; outside their walls are "the street poor—squatters, winos, junkies, homeless people in general. . . . They carry untreated diseases and festering wounds. They have no money to spend on water to wash with so even the unwounded have sores. They don't get enough to eat so they're malnourished—or they eat bad food and poison themselves" (9). These same people, despite the precautions taken against them, have found ways to break into their compound, stealing, raping, murdering, and hating those who seem to escape the desperate lives that they must endure. Inside this compound, nonetheless, the marginally better-off residents have found a way to settle into a routine, taking care of their children and their neighbor's children, working at jobs remotely through their computers, venturing out only when necessary and always armed to the teeth, and supplementing their meager incomes as best they can with garden vegetables and the like. This everyday habitus is what the narrator accidentally disturbs when she blurts out, "I'm talking about this place, Jo, this cul-de-sac with a wall around it. I'm talking about the day a big gang of those hungry, desperate, crazy people outside decide to come in" (48). In response, her friend says with a "nervous smile," shutting down all further conversation: "You've been reading too many adventure stories" (51).

Later, when the friend spreads word of their conversation to others in the compound, the father tells the narrator, "It's better to teach people than to scare them, Lauren. If you scare them and nothing happens, they lose their fear, and you lose some of your authority with them. It's harder to scare them a second time, harder to teach them, harder to win back their trust" (1993, 58). Perhaps, like the father in *Parable of the Sower*, this is what many critics had in mind when they exhorted their readers throughout the 1990s not to be too critical of the United States. If we cannot maintain the fiction that we live in an ever more egalitarian and fair society, we risk scaring ourselves into disengagement, inaction, and despair. No less an establishment figure than Nathan Glazer writes, reinforcing this point: "I know what is better for all of us to believe, from the standpoint of civic harmony. But others think that civic harmony should not be given primacy as an ideal: they believe in the slogan so prominently displayed in the disorders that broke out after the policemen who beat Rodney King were found innocent, 'No justice, no peace.' How will we convince those displaying this slogan that a substantial measure of justice already exists, and that the sphere of justice is constantly expanding?" (1997, 48).

This last question has reverberated throughout the previous decade. Not that we as a country have no problems. Not that we as a country do not unfairly treat its residents on the basis of race, immigrant status, sexual orientation, gender, and so forth. Not that we as a country have poor relations with other less well-off countries. Not that we as a country have not been leading the way in redistributing wealth upward, so that in the not-so-distant future the wealthy may well need to separate themselves with literal walls from the masses who have been left with nothing (that many suburban developments now do this, put up walls and place guards in the front entrance, is perhaps only an indication of what is still to come). Rather, Glazer's question asks us to consider how we can convince others and ourselves, often in the face of powerful evidence to the contrary, that progress is being made, that discrimination is quickly becoming a phenomenon of the past, that people in this country get along better with each other than ever before, that our politicians and civil officials and businesspeople have our best interests at heart if not in mind. How do we placate those who insist that injustices exist, that new inequalities are forming, that many people have been abandoned, and that many more are about to be hurt by our policies, so that in the ensuring social peace we might actually work toward what has already been asserted as a fait accompli? In short, Glazer proposes that we minimize all the horror-filled events that are taking place around us so that we do not become paralyzed. Just like Glazer, then, the father tells his daughter in *Parable of the Sower*: "It you can think of ways to entertain them and teach them at the same time, you'll get your information out. And all without making anyone look down. . . . You've just noticed the abyss. . . . The adults in this community have been balancing at the edge of it for more years than you've been alive" (1993, 58).

In the years since the riots, I believe an answer to Glazer's question has been forming, one that is allowing us to avoid looking down but that, in the process, is also discouraging concerted efforts to address the difficulties that are down there. In other words, at least three major policy arguments emerged in the last years of the twentieth century to convince all of us that there is, in actuality, nothing to worry about because social progress continues to be made, regardless of what the pessimists might have to say. These arguments, the policy equivalents of our uneasy laughter in the theater or the father's advice to his daughter in *Parable of the Sower*, have become more or less orthodoxy in the 1990s, and they were at least in part propelled into widespread acceptance by a will to contain the accumulated discontent unleashed during the 1992 Los Angeles riots. These changes might be tracked through the terms *official multiculturalism*, *post-civil-rights*, and *free-market ideology*—or, to be more blunt, *managed diversity*, *right-wing backlash*, and *neoliberalism*. All three of these policy arguments worked together with varying degrees of success, even when they were often in deep conflict with one another and even when they generated intense disagreement among neoconservatives themselves, to counteract the feelings of civic disharmony, economic uncertainty, and too-rapid social change stirred up in such a concentrated form by the riots. Less reform and more wishful thinking—the coming to dominance of these arguments in the 1990s suggests, in their inadequacy, how wrong Glazer has been in advising that we can only be granted justice *after* we have peace.

By official multiculturalism, I mean a vision of racial diversity that has been accepted, unwillingly and often angrily at times, as a new ideal of American society. Over the course of the last decade, this vision has been embraced rhetorically by various government agencies and corporations with the approval of many, but by no means all, educators and academics. Manifestations of this acceptance are visible everywhere in government posters and corporate advertisements, and have worked hard to conflate culture with race. These advertisements portray racially mixed faces interacting with one another with ease and bright smiles, even when the populations they are depicting are not nearly as diverse nor as cheerfully at ease with one another as these images suggest. This vision seeks, through the positing of racially and ethnically diverse faces, a happy coevality of social experiences that portrays a formal equality nonexistent in the lives of the faces depicted in this way, and in so doing it tries to manage a diversity that might call for a very different kind of social narrative.

At one level, official multiculturalism explicitly wishes to counteract the fears of national decline brought on by the media barrage of poor blacks spectacularly abandoned in America's inner-cities. At another level, it seeks to contain the disorienting effect of mass nonwhite immigration by reducing groups to culture, and culture into a ritual celebration of frozen differences that will brighten, but not substantially alter, the core identity of the nation. The ambivalence created by this kind of multiculturalism can be found dissected at the start of Paul Beatty's brilliantly funny novel *The White Boy Shuffle* (1996). In this contemporary satire, the students of "Mestizo Mulatto Mongrel Elementary, Santa Monica's all-white multicultural school" read the following story:

> I . . . opened my primer to the story about a war between a herd of black elephants and a herd of white elephants. I don't remember what the elephants were fighting about—something about hating each other for the color of their sponge-rubbery skins. It wasn't as if the black elephants had to use the mosquito-infested watering hole and rely on white elephant welfare for their quinine. After heavy casualties

on both sides, a cease-tusking was called. The elephants, as wounded and bedraggled as elephants could possibly be, headed off into the hills, only to return to the plains years later as a harmonious and homogeneous herd of gray elephants. (1996, 32)[1]

Official multiculturalism insists, as this fictitious children's story does, on the incomprehensibility of racial difference as a cause for social dissension, even as it dreams of race's disappearance as a hoped-for cure of racism. We are supposed to affirm our many cultural differences, which happily coincide with ingrained racial differences, as comprising a rich national mosaic, while simultaneously failing to notice the other kinds of differences—especially in terms of spatial mobility, residential options, educational opportunities, availability of jobs, and so forth—that might mediate our interactions with one another. We are supposed to look forward to a future moment, beyond multiculturalism, when racial and cultural differences (again conflated), and all the anxiety these unpleasant causative axes of differences necessarily entails, will have disappeared through intermarriage.[2] What official multiculturalism most values, in its positing of easy-to-read cultural differences and support for formal—but not substantive—equality, is distraction from the material inequities historically founded in large part on racial differences, even as it unsteadily seeks to affirm a heritage that will remain central despite the ongoing influx of nonwhite immigrants.[3]

By post–civil-rights, I refer to the backlash against affirmative action, AFDC, bilingual education, worker protections, environmental regulations, immigrants, and even Social Security that has characterized, but has not been limited to, the populism of the Right. Both major political parties in the United States in the 1990s, while paying homage to the language of racial equality, converged in their hostility to programs designed to facilitate access to higher education, better-paying jobs, adequate housing, and even clean food and water.[4] Such programs, in a game of rhetorical legerdemain, were widely characterized as unfairly benefiting nonwhites, fostering a culture of pathological dependence, and encouraging discrimination because they cause injury to a white middle class. In the name of advancing civil rights, many have worked assiduously to dismantle the most basic gains achieved by more than a century of struggle for greater economic and social parity. Indeed, it is worth noting that the emergence of this policy coincides with the rising tide of immigrants that took place in the last few decades of the twentieth century. As nonwhite immigrants, especially from Asia and Latin America, began to arrive in large numbers, programs designed to help the needy, the underserved, and the excluded began to shrink. Civil rights programs seemed to make less sense in the midst of an alien invasion. If these programs were mainly designed to help African Americans, as it was erroneously asserted, then they were now clearly serving the wrong communities.

During the campaign to end affirmative action in California through a voters' initiative known as Proposition 209, for instance, this advertisement could be heard on many radios:

> **Male Announcer:** The following actually happened January 19th, 1994.
>
> **Camarena:** The teacher said to me, "you have to leave."
>
> **Male Announcer:** Because you're white.
>
> **Camarena:** Yes. Then I left. (*door slams shut*—[there are] *sounds undercurrent*)
>
> **Male Announcer:** As she went out the door, students laughed. (*laughter fades*) But for this young, widowed mother trying to enroll in a class at a public college, racial quotas were no laughing matter.
>
> **Camarena:** I thought that discrimination was illegal.
>
> **Male Announcer:** But the law allows preferential treatment.
>
> **Camarena:** Another class was for Mexican American students only.
>
> **Male Announcer:** These programs are based *not* on merit, or even on need, but on race. Janice Camarena Ingraham is white. Her deceased husband was Mexican American.
>
> **Camarena:** Recently our public school asked the race of my children. I said the human race. (quoted in L. Chávez 1998, 217).[5]

What is perhaps most relevant about this advertisement, in addition to the reference to Camarena's deceased Mexican American husband, is the way it appropriates the language of civil rights to advocate policies that are much against the spirit of this popular movement. According to one exit poll, when voters were asked about their support for programs "designed to help women and minorities get better jobs and education,"

54 percent said they supported such programs and 46 percent said they didn't—"nearly the reverse of Proposition 209's vote" (L. Chávez 1998, 237). Meanwhile, law-and-order discourses that have propelled many politicians into public office in the past few decades have led directly to the massive construction of new prisons that housed by the late 1990s a population of almost 2 million men and women, the majority African American and Latino (Gilmore 1998/1999, 171). The incarceration of so many people might be reason enough for us to consider the ways in which the civil rights agenda has been destroyed by a backlash, the building of new prisons the form of welfare preferred by an ever-fearful, and growing, political Right. The proper role of government, and all of its ancillary arms, has increasingly been defined—in some cases with the unwitting help of voters—as the duty to police, punish, and fight wars abroad, not to provide social services nor to foster greater structural equity among the country's residents. No wonder, then, that so many people are manifestly suspicious of any form of big government or the state.

Finally, by free-market ideology, I am gesturing to the transnationalization of capital flows accelerated by the end of the Cold War, which has effectively drowned out ideological opposition to the invisible hand of capitalism, and by just-in-time manufacturing of most consumer items, where components for automobiles, electronics, and garments are subcontracted and subsubcontracted to producers all over the world. The latter does not mean that national borders have become irrelevant or that nation-states themselves have become somehow less important, just as the former does not mean that capitalism has proven itself to be evenly wealth producing, in the absence of its discredited twin, for all the countries now supposedly primed to enjoy its fruits. Rather, free-market ideology refers to the cozy relationship between postindustrialized national governments and multinational corporations, two entities who now see their interests as parallel in the maintenance of New York, Tokyo, and London as agglomerations of capital management in a nearly global system of production (Sassen 2000, 24–32).

Capital and the means of production thus seem to have become separated from one another in the name of flexible accumulation. As David Harvey argued at the start of the 1990s, in the midst of a terrible economic recession, the transition from a Keynesian mode of production (popularly defined) to a regime of flexible accumulation was facilitated by the founding of free-market ideology as the basis for an ideal subject who would be widely recognized, the entrepreneur: "Since the political success of neo-conservativism can hardly be attributed to its overall economic achievements (its strong negatives of high unemployment, weak growth, rapid dislocation, and spiraling indebtedness are offset by control of inflation), several commentators have attributed its rise to a general shift from the collective norms and values, that were hegemonic at least in working-class organizations and other social movements of the 1950s and 1960s, toward a much more competitive individualism as the central value in an entrepreneurial culture that has penetrated many walks of life" (1990, 171). Like finance, populations seem under the rule of free-market ideology to flow where they might be needed, to give up expectations of long-term investment for the requirements of liquidity, and to turn their backs on a commitment to place and community in the search for personal gain. Meanwhile, nation-states in an age of transnational capital, flexible accumulation, and unprecedented worker mobility act like Maxwell's devil to keep the whole system isomorphic. The kind of lives shaped by these macroeconomic and political forces is celebrated as the triumph of individuals over inefficient and heartless bureaucracies and is used, in part, to neutralize the sense of lost economic status among a capaciously defined white middle class. As a response to the growing hourglass contour of the U.S. economy, the figure of the lone entrepreneur promises that anyone who falls behind can not only catch up but vault ahead to the top of the hourglass—but only if one works hard and others play fair. Hence, if one fails to vault ahead, despite the long hours and tireless activity at one's places of work, it is because others are not playing fair.

As powerful as these policy arguments have become over the years, during which time their underlying assumptions have been incorporated into every stitch of American life, they have not fully shaken us free from the fears they overtly seek to allay. The white middle class continues to lose substantial economic ground, especially as the rate of manufacturing jobs fleeing the nation accelerates. Such job losses, especially as white-collar work is also apparently poised to follow industrial work overseas, have unfortunately been accompanied by the return of nativist labor arguments, one that would couple calls for protectionist legislation with demonizing portrayals of those third-world others whose crushing poverty compels them to trade their labor, now often very skilled, for little remuneration. The black urban poor continue to languish in daily misery, hounded by the police, disproportionately imprisoned, jobless, stuck in dilapidated school rooms from an early age, lacking meaningful social outlets, and mostly ignored by the nation's political establishments. Indeed, what might make the specter of their misery so menacing for many formerly middle-class whites is the possibility that this specter is a vision from their own future, as economic restructuring completes manufacturing capital's tripartite flight from (1) the rustbelt, to (2) the sunbelt, to (3) maquiladoras and other free-enterprise zones. At the same time that whole classes of jobs have bled out of the country, the large-scale immigration of peoples from all over the world continues. In turn, they are greeted, especially in a post–September 11 world, as even more of an alien invasion than before (if this is possible). Along with such greetings, there have been stepped-up deportations, differential judicial treatment of undocumented and documented immigrants alike, and a greater urgency within these communities that they must watch what they say.

What managed diversity, rightwing backlash, and neoliberalism help to produce is a domestic situation where the gap between the extravagantly well off and everyone else continues to widen perilously, where fear encourages passage of ever more draconian crime legislation (like the "three strikes" rule in California), where once impregnable categories of human difference are being shored up by bitter recriminations in the midst of turbulent reconfigurations of social relations in the places where they are most lived. Even the white-collar worker of specialized skill can no longer feel secure, since the sudden loss of his or her job can lead quickly to bankruptcy, foreclosure, and destitution. If this movement from high-paying job to poverty seems unlikely, one need only keep in mind that in the post–civil-rights era, where government programs of all kinds have fallen under siege, much of the social safety net has been dismantled. Given the ways in which animosity against programs designed to help racial minorities, women, and the poor has been mobilized to attack all federal and state programs except those that punish, it may not be long now before even Social Security, as beloved as it is, disappears.

For the many others in this country who have few marketable skills, who have been let down by a severely tiered educational system, who have fewer resources than those with accumulated economic and social wealth to draw upon, who may come from families and communities repeatedly abandoned and traumatized by the demands of market discipline, who may have ventured to new lands where they are actively not welcome, the ongoing disintegration of the social safety net has long ago created gaping holes through which they have been falling. For them, national decline is a long-lived reality, not a threat looming in the future that needs to be beaten back.

THE NEOCONSERVATIVES who first began the conversation about national decline did so to look back wistfully at a simpler time, when the country was predominantly white, when its rapidly expanding economy made well-paying jobs plentiful, and when blacks seemed to be making steady progress in their dignified fight against discrimination. How chagrined they must have felt to survey what had happened to their country by the early 1990s. Ungrateful blacks stuck in bombed-out inner-cities, non-white immigrants who couldn't count out change in comprehensible English, manufacturing jobs that once belonged exclusively to whites going to factories overseas. What would it take, once liberal and now very conservative intellectuals asked, to return to the country they remembered so fondly? The answer came to them easily. Let's do what we can to free our businesses from too many restrictions so that they can again make well-paying jobs more plentiful. Let's insist that those who come to the United States to live assimilate, so that if we can no longer be white we can at least be English speaking, God fearing, and respectful of this country's great heritage (we can call it multiculturalism, so long as it's understood what we mean by it). Let's stop feeling guilty about the problems of black people, since we as a country have already done more than is required by common decency to make up for the abuses they have suffered.

The neoconservative response to national decline was hence a denial of the many changes that this country, like many others, continues to endure. This response merely sought to turn back the clock to an imagined past, conveniently ignoring or minimizing its less attractive features.[6] And as it became clear that there is no turning back, neoconservatives became more insistent that their course was the only one that this nation, and perhaps other nations as well, could take. It is time, I believe, for us to redefine what we mean by national decline. This fear is not about the losses of a white middle class but about a process of economic restructuring founded on the principles of neoliberalism. This fear is not about a criminal class of black others abandoned in America's inner-cities but about growing inequality as the role of the state becomes only surveillance, policing, and punishment. This fear is not about alien invasion but about the breakup of communities, as ever more lonely individuals are forced to chase after ever increasingly mobile opportunities for a comfortable existence. The presence of the strange, I have been arguing, helps us redefine national decline in this way, and in doing so clears space for the hard intellectual work of thinking about how best to intervene in these changes, shaping them so we may all have futures that are not solely a disastrous looking back.

Notes

INTRODUCTION: WHEN THE STRANGE ERUPTS IN CULTURE

1   The first President George Bush picked up on this theme in his 1992 State of the Union Address: "And there's a mood among us. People are worried. There has been talk of decline. Someone even said our workers are lazy and uninspired" (1992). George Lipsitz traces the feeling of national decline named in this speech, and in Schlesinger's polemic, to a neoconservatism that gained momentum in the 1980s and that has continued to snowball ever since: "The narrative of national decline most frequently used by neoconservatives to justify their policies has a special anti-Asian edge to it, in part because decline is traced to the U.S. defeat in Vietnam, but also because of the rise of economic competition from Japan and newly industrialized countries in Asia, and the perceived threat to white privilege posed by immigrant Asian successes" (2001, 298). In addition, see Immanuel Wallerstein's *The Decline of American Power* (2003), which reiterates the "narrative of national decline" first put forward by Schlesinger and others: "The United States in decline? Few people today would believe this assertion. The only ones who do are the U.S. hawks, who argue vociferously for policies to reverse the decline. This belief that the end of U.S. hegemony has already begun does not follow from the vulnerability that became apparent to all on September 11, 2001. In fact, the United States has been fading as a global power since the 1970s, and the U.S. response to the terrorist attacks has merely accelerated this decline" (13). My account of this narrative differs from Lipsitz's and Wallerstein's in that I believe the feeling of decline to which the narrative gives form has been, especially at specific moments in the past decade, more pervasive than they argue. This narrative probably originated from neoconservatism's rise to ascendancy during the 1980s, but it lapped into and affected the mood of a wide cross-section of peoples who, in the early 1990s, felt let down by the U.S. nation-state in a variety of ways (as I will go on to argue throughout this book).

2   Mosley, who became famous after President Clinton declared him his favorite writer, retroactively traces from an early 1990s historical perch the fate of the post–Second World War black community in Los Angeles by following the adventures of Easy Rawlins, who creates a semblance of middle-class affluence for himself (in *Devil in a Blue Dress* [1990] and *A Red Death* [1991]) only to lose it all in the midst of uncontrollable forces (in *White Butterfly* [1992] and *Black Betty* [1994]). Interestingly, Rawlins's fortunes take a turn for the worse in the novels published after the riots. Yamashita has had less success as a popular writer, but her wonderfully quirky and surrealist tales have intrigued many readers and literary critics, especially her *Through the Arc of the Rain Forest* (1990). Yamashita's *Tropic of Orange* (1997), published only a few years after the riots, reflects on many topics of immediate relevance to the underlying causes of violence in 1992. Asian American literary critics have long held an understated but healthy respect for Kadohata's work: her first novel, *The Floating World* (1989), is a coming-of-age story that refuses simply to be a middle-class narrative about economic upward mobility; her second, *In the Heart of the Valley of Love* (1992), speaks directly to the pessimism surrounding the moment at which the riots took place (see the last part of chapter 1). Stephenson burst into popularity with *Snow Crash* (1992), a satirical novel about the rise of digital technologies in a postnational era that depicts Los Angeles as a place of homogenizing corporate franchises, privatized roads, walled-in suburbanites, and impoverished immigrants from around the world. Interestingly, Richard Rorty, in his patriotic jeremiad *Achieving Our Country: Leftist Thought in Twentieth-Century America* (1998), singles out this novel, and Leslie Marmon Silko's *Almanac of the Dead* (1991), as a sign of Left defeatism. Perhaps the most harrowing depiction of how bad national decline can become in a short period of time can be found in Butler's *Parable of the Sower* (1993)—briefly discussed in the epilogue—and its sequel, *Parable of the Talents* (2000), both of which imagine the future as a place of material scarcity, random violence, walled communities of only relatively well-off suburbanites besieged by crime, and responses to decline that are often more destructive than the symptoms of decline they are meant to repair.

3   See chapter 1 for further discussion of Davis's significance to the study of Los Angeles. Also, see Scott and Soja (1996), which provides an excellent panorama of the kind of work the Los Angeles school has come to be associated with; Fulton (1997), which is magisterial in its scope and detailed case-studies; Klein (1997); and Halle (2003).

4   As Michael Omi and Howard Winant observe, the first President Bush seized during his failed 1992 reelection campaign on the riots as a symbol of what was wrong with "liberal social welfare policies," articulating in the process what neoconservatives would argue in the remainder of the decade with caustic anger. "Not only had they consumed billions of federal dollars," Omi and Winant write, "but even worse, they had fostered state dependency, nurtured irresponsible personal behavior, and facilitated the overall deterioration of inner city communities. In place of such programs, Bush called for 'policies that foster personal responsibility'" (1994, 146). These ideas, given new life by the spectacles that comprised our collective experiences of the riots, could have been lifted almost word-for-word from Schlesinger's *The Disuniting of America* (1992), Bloom's *The Closing of the American Mind: How Higher Education Has Failed Democracy and Impoverished the Souls of Today's Students* (1987), and Murray's *Losing Ground:*

American Social Policy, 1950–1980 (1994 [1984]). By *neoconservative*, I refer to Winant's definition:

> former liberals who have been affiliated with the moderate wing of the civil rights movement, but were disaffected by its post-1965 nationalist and class-based radicalisms. Marked by their white ethnicity, by their experiences as the children of immigrants, and in particular by their youthful leftism and their struggle against anti-Semitism . . . neoconservative thinkers and politicians have made visceral commitments to what they saw as the core political culture of the United States: pluralism, consensus, gradualism, and centrism. . . . Thus they sought to confine the egalitarian upsurge, to reinterpret movement ideas more narrowly and individualistically, and to channel them in more conservative politics and a sense of "optional" ethnicity. (1994, 46–47)

From these historical beginnings, neoconservatism has grown in the 1990s to become a dominant principle of government: fewer social services, greater punitive laws, upward redistribution of wealth, cultural allegiance to an Anglo-Christian heritage, and support for an individualistic, colorblind, and formal (but not substantive) equality. As Lisa Duggan points out, a neoconservative-inspired "third-way" politics—depending on neoliberal economic ideas—emerged as an alternative to "old" liberalism and "paleoconservativism" to advocate for "a leaner, meaner government (fewer social services, more 'law and order'), a state-supported but 'privatized' economy, an invigorated and socially responsible civil society, and a moralized family with gendered marriage at its center" (2003, 10).

5 Perhaps one of the most startling findings in *Bowling Alone: The Collapse and Revival of American Community* (2000), Robert Putnam's groundbreaking study on the waning of social capital in the United States, is that Americans are socializing less with one another on a day-to-day basis. When compared to an earlier generation, they are on average less likely to eat out, go to bars or nightclubs, share evening meals with one another, and entertain friends at home. Two empirical findings starkly substantiate this claim: first, "the frequency with which Americans, both married and single, went out to bars, nightclubs, discos, taverns, and the like declined by about 40–50 percent over the last decade or two" (101); and, second, "Between 1970 and 1998 the number of full-service restaurants per one hundred thousand fell by one-quarter, and the numbers of bars and luncheonettes were cut in half. Meanwhile the per capita number of fast-food outlets . . . doubled" (102).

6 In comparison to what occurred in 1992, the violence that washed over Watts in August 1965 left 34 people dead, 1,000 injured, and 4,000 arrested, and left about $200 million in property damage, unadjusted for inflation (Horne 1997, 3). Many observers end the actual dates of rioting in 1992 two days before Mayor

Bradley lifted the curfew, because the violence and looting had largely subsided by the end of the third day. For detailed journalistic accounts of the riots, see Los Angeles Times (1992), which contains articles from the newspaper; Dan Hazen (1992), comprised of articles by journalists writing for the alternative press; and an exhaustive study of the riots by the *Washington Post*'s former Los Angeles bureau chief, Lou Cannon (1999). In the latter, Cannon seeks—unpersuasively in my opinion—to exonerate the four officers directly involved in the beating, placing the full blame of what happened in 1992 on city government and the adversarial culture of the Los Angeles Police Department. In addition to these accounts, I have found the following rich sources of information and reflection about the riots. The Independent Commission on the Los Angeles Police Department (1991; also known as the Christopher Commission report, after its chair, Warren Christopher) provides a thorough assessment of the King arrest and the endemic problems within the Los Angeles Police Department that led up to it. In the two years after the riots, the following collection of essays and symposium papers appeared in print (and because of the rushed nature of their publication, are of mixed quality): Mark Baldassare (1993); Haki Mabhubati (1993); Robert Gooding-Williams (1993); George Totten and Eric Schockman (1994); and Eui-Young Yu (1994). Finally, more recent publications have added a historical perspective to these works, and are important additions to the scholarship dedicated to understanding the riots. Among these are Abelmann and Lie (1995); K. Kim (1999); and the last chapter of Davis (1998).

7 According to William Julius Wilson, "By manipulating market incentives, the federal government drew middle-class whites to the suburbs and, in effect, trapped blacks in the inner cities. Beginning in the 1950s, the suburbanization of the middle class was also facilitated by a federal transportation and highway policy, including the building of freeway networks through the hearts of many cities, mortgages for veterans, mortgage-interest tax exemptions, and the quick, cheap production of massive amounts of tract housing" (1996, 46). Thomas Sugrue tells a similar story, but also insists that economic growth in the 1940s and 1950s masked the loss of "hundreds of thousands of entry-level manufacturing jobs" during the same decades. "The manufacturing industries that formed the bedrock of the American economy," Sugrue writes, "automated production and relocated plants in suburban and rural areas, and increasingly in the low-wage labor markets of underdeveloped regions like the American South and the Caribbean. The restructuring of the economy proceeded with the full support and encouragement of the American government. Federal highway construction and military spending facilitated and fueled industrial growth in non-urban areas" (1996, 6). Michael Yates (2003, 119–158) provides an unusually clear explanation of the competing economic theories that informed the policies that tolerated these changes; according to his analysis, liberal neoclassical theories informed by the writings of John Maynard Keynes eclipsed libertarian neoclassical theories that had been dominant before the start of the Great Depression. Since the early 1970s, libertarian neoclassicism, also known as neoliberalism, has experienced a resurgence and is quickly becoming dominant once more. The *liberal* in neoliberalism refers specifically to nineteenth-century notions of liberalism associated with the work of Adam Smith, David Ricardo, and John Stuart Mills.

8   "In the 1980s," Saskia Sassen writes, "there was intense debate in the U.S. around the preliminary evidence on increased inequality with many analysts disputing the findings. Today the debate centers on the causes" (2000, 224). Also, see Paul Krugman: "The 13,000 richest families in America had almost as much income as the 20 million poorest households; those 13,000 families had incomes 300 times that of average families" (2002, 62); and David Howell: "The U.S. appears . . . with the highest earnings inequality and the highest unemployment inequality" for male workers when compared to countries such as Canada, France, the United Kingdom, Germany, Australia, and Italy between the years 1973 and 1993 (2002, 9). On the difficulties faced by earners of minimum wage in the era following welfare reform, see Barbara Ehrenreich (2001); on the same difficulties from a broader perspective, see David Shipler (2004); on the importance of taking wealth into account as a further measure of economic inequality, especially as it manifests itself between black and white households, see Melvin Oliver and Thomas Shapiro (1995). Certainly, there is no getting around the fact that inequality in income and wealth disproportionately places black groups at the bottom, though it should be noted that black groups found in depopulated districts of previously manufacturing-centered cities have faired comparatively worse than those black groups found in more affluent regions of the United States, where these groups are able to share in the growth of nonmanufacturing jobs (Sassen 2000, 247).

9   In a groundbreaking study on the 1995 heat wave that took over 700 lives in Chicago, many of whom were poor, elderly, black, and alone, Eric Klinenberg dramatically illustrates the often invisible social costs of those left behind in such urban districts when he observes: "A key reason that African Americans had the highest death rates in the Chicago heat wave is that they are the only group in the city segregated and ghettoized in community areas with high levels of abandoned housing stock, empty lots, depleted commercial infrastructure, population decline, degraded sidewalks, parks and streets, and impoverished institutions" (2002, 127). Just as manufacturing capital fled from the traditional industrial cities of the Midwest and Northeast in search of cheaper labor and fewer restrictions starting in the late 1940s—leaving behind environmental damage, racial animosity, and deep inequalities in income—manufacturing capital at the end of the 1980s was already well along in the process of fleeing the Sunbelt for even cheaper labor and even fewer restrictions south of the border and over-

seas. For instance, Los Angeles saw its "share of manufacturing employment" go down "from just over 31 percent of all employment in 1977 to under 18 percent in 1997" (Gladstone and Fainstein 2003, 88). Indeed, when this kind of manufacturing capital remained, or returned, to Los Angeles during the 1980s and 1990s, it often did so to exploit vulnerable, and often immigrant and women, laborers (Scott 1996; Su and Martorell 2001). While Los Angeles's economy in the 1980s and 1990s remained relatively robust due to its more diverse base, unlike Detroit with its heavy reliance on manufacturing, it has certainly not escaped recession and rising income inequality, nor a concomitant racial-economic gap, especially as measured by foreign-born versus native-white households (Gladstone and Fainstein 2003; Pastor 2001; and see chapter 1). The rippling effects of such disturbing macroeconomic trends on race relations in places hard hit by the loss of manufacturing jobs and a decrease in revenues from corporate, homeowner, and industrial employee taxes in the late 1980s seem, in hindsight, predictable. "Faced with rising unemployment and declining wages," economist Rhonda Williams reflected in the immediate wake of the 1992 riots, "white workers seeking simply to hold their own, could gain relatively, if not absolutely, from exercising their agency to impose the costs of recessions and income stagnation on workers of color. For profit-conscious capitalists, discrimination facilitates workplace control and costs minimization" (1993, 93).

10 The popularity of "hood" films such as *Colors* (1988), *Boyz n the Hood* (1991), and *Menace II Society* (1993) in the early 1990s comes especially to mind here as a symbol of this increased economic inequality and racial division (Gormley 2003)—though these films routinely failed to take into account the greater complexity of economic stratification caused by increased immigration to cities such as Los Angeles and New York. For an especially rich and approachable discussion on the spotlighting of African Americans as markers of violence, drug use, criminality, social disorder, and hence as premier threats to the nation's well-being, see Jacqueline Jones (1992, 269–292).

11 The term *interpellated* comes from Louis Althusser, who writes in his famous essay "Idelology and Ideological State Apparatuses" (originally published in 1969), "Ideology 'acts' or 'functions' in such a way that it 'recruits' subjects among the individuals (it recruits them all), or 'transforms' the individuals into subjects (it transforms them all) by the very precise operation which I have called *interpellation* or hailing, and which can be imagined along the lines of the most commonplace everyday police (or other) hailing: 'Hey, you there!' " (1971, 174; emphasis in original). I also take this adjective *scabrous* slightly out of context. It appears during a moment in the narrative when Henry, the narrator of *Native Speaker*, recalls the difficulty he had learning to speak English as a child: "I thought English would be simply a version of our Korean. Like another kind of coat you could wear. I didn't know what a difference in language meant then. Or how my tongue would tie in the initial attempts, stiffen so, struggle like an animal booby-trapped and dying inside my head. Native speakers may not fully know this, but English is a *scabrous* mouthful" (1995, 233; emphasis mine). This passage speaks profoundly to a pervasive feeling among Korean Americans, and perhaps other immigrant groups whose first language is orthographically and phonically far apart from the conventions that rule the language of English, that if they could speak English better they could navigate the difficulties of everyday life in the United States better, dominated as this life is by the demand for Anglo-language fluency. The feeling of inadequacy suggested by a lack of language fluency points, as well, toward the material differences that bar full participation in the public spheres of American society for those who come from elsewhere and have little besides their labor to exchange for their physical survival. The word *scabrous* punctures the narrative because it raises the larger sociopolitical import of an immigrant child struggling to learn English: it is a struggle not only with language, but also with a history that has led him or her into this position of pedagogical catch-up, hinting subtly at the injured nature of this history. If English is a language defined by scabs, to pull it apart (to master its codes and conventions, to try to pass as a native speaker) risks as well the possibility that scabs will come off, that painful wounds will be exposed and are, in any case, not fully healed. The act of pulling it apart subtends an array of potential conflicts emerging from the convergence of different histories on the site of America's multiracial cities that makes the patching over of gaps in the realm of the symbolic with surface encrustations necessary.

12   *Kyopo* is a Korean term used to refer to overseas ethnic Koreans. This term usually has a descriptive valence, but is also tinged with the secondary meaning of Koreans who in traveling away from their home country have lost touch with their roots and have in some way become inferior replicas of an original self. To counteract such negative meanings, some will replace *kyopo* with *dongpo*, which might be roughly translated as "brotherhood" and "comrade." The latter has a much more positive meaning than the former, but cannot at the same time be separated from the tradition of militant Marxist movements that gives this word its meaningful context. This is why *dongpo* would be inappropriate in describing Korean American merchants, who by virtue of their social position do not belong to such a tradition. In Gary Phillips's novel *Violent Spring* (1994), however, it might be appropriate to refer to at least one of his Korean American characters with the term *dongpo*. The fictional murdered body found at the corner of Florence and Normandie in the days following the riots, which sets the novel's plot into motion, turns out to have belonged to a former Korean student-activist who came to the United States to escape dictatorial repression at home.

13   Sassen succinctly states the reasons why we might find this received wisdom unsatisfactory: "While changes in the United States immigration legislation in

1965 and the existence of prior immigrant communities are important factors explaining immigration over the subsequent decades, they are not sufficient to explain the continuation of this flow at ever-higher levels, even in the late 1970s and early 1980s, a time of growing unemployment in the United States and rather high employment growth in the immigrants' country of origin. Nor are they sufficient to explain the disproportionate concentration of immigrants in major urban areas, a trend that continued in the 1990s" (2000, 322). Nor, finally, does this focus on changes to U.S. laws and the country's local history of receiving immigrants take into account the incredible flows of immigrants to other places in Europe and Asia during the same period, many of which have no history of receiving immigrants. As Sassen continues to point out, Japan—which we normally associate with populational homogeneity—has witnessed a great deal of undocumented immigration in the last two decades, especially from South Asia (2000, 314–321). Also see David Reimers (1992 [1985], 61–90), who argues that the 1965 law was not intended by lawmakers to alter the racial composition of the United States; and Ethne Luibhéid (1997, 2002).

14 As Leo Chavez points out, one significant contributor to popular moods—commercial magazines such as *Time*, *Newsweek*, the *New Republic*, *National Review*, the *Nation*, and the *Atlantic Monthly*—demonstrated an increased propensity over the last two decades of the twentieth century to express alarm about immigrants and immigration. "The metaphor of the 'browning of America' captured the idea," Chavez writes, "that changes were occurring as a result of immigration and high birth rates (compared to whites) among Latinos and Asian Americans. Demographic change raised further questions about an America that would no longer be predominantly white. Would America still be America?" (2001, 300).

15 As Edward Park reports, Korean Americans in Los Angeles have divided their efforts to enter the political mainstream of the United States after the riots along exactly these two vectors of "social egalitarianism" and "individual liberty": "Liberals have argued that Korean Americans are an oppressed racial minority group and that their rights and interests can be best protected by joining the civil rights coalition and the Democratic Party. By contrast, conservatives have insisted that Korean Americans have fundamental economic and political differences with key members of the civil rights coalition and that they can better meet their interests with the Republican Party and its commitment to fiscal conservatism, law and order, and the dismantling of the welfare state" (2001b, 303).

16 Proposition 187 was a California voter initiative designed to deprive undocumented immigrants of essential social services and was mainly targeted at Mexican immigration (Ancheta 1998, 38). The fear that Mexican, and by extension Latino, immigration to the United States has generated since the Los Angeles riots can also be found articulated in numerous policy journals and books. One of the most striking examples appears in *The Clash of Civilizations: Remaking of*

Word Order (1996), a definitive neoconservative statement on U.S. foreign policy by the much-respected Samuel Huntington (he is routinely described as the most influential political scientist in the United States): "Western culture is challenged by groups within Western societies. One such challenge comes from immigrants from other civilizations who reject assimilation and continue to adhere to and to propagate the values, customs, and cultures of their home societies. This phenomenon is most notable among Muslims in Europe, who are, however, a small minority. It is also manifest, in lesser degree, among Hispanics in the United States, who are a large minority. If assimilation fails in this case, the United States will become a cleft country, with all the potentials for internal strife and disunion that entails" (305). Huntington cites Schlesinger in making this argument.

17 In an early essay that would later be published unchanged as the first chapter of his monumental *Postmodernism, or the Cultural Logic of Late Capitalism* (1991), Fredric Jameson writes: "The last few years have been marked by an inverted millenarianism in which premonitions of the future, catastrophic or redemptive, have been replaced by senses of the end of this or that (the end of ideology, art, or social class; the 'crisis' of Leninism, social democracy, or the welfare state, etc., etc.)" (1984, 13). This "inverted millenarianism," which is emblematic of what Jameson calls postmodern, unfolded in works of architecture, visual arts, belles lettres, and serious-minded theoretical conversations. As such, it can be said to gauge the start, rather than the "end," of a cultural malaise that would, in the early 1990s, expand in scope to encompass more and more levels of social life in the United States.

1 RACIAL GEOGRAPHY

1 I borrow the term *orthodoxy* from Pierre Bourdieu. Anyone familiar with his work, especially his attempt at clarifying for an American audience some of the operative terms in his critical repertoire in *Practical Reason: On the Theory of Action* (1998), might be surprised by this, for Bourdieu seems explicit that domination takes place through what he calls "doxa": "Doxa is a particular point of view, the point of view of the dominant, which presents and imposes itself as a universal point of view—the point of view of those who dominate by dominating the state and who have constituted their point of view as universal by constituting the state" (57). But for Bourdieu, even in this passage, doxa is always a matter of asserting as universal what is much more contingent, a naked aggressivity of the powerful whose competing interests struggle to make commonsensical what is in their best interest. Because interests conflict, doxa is never stable, and whatever its pretensions to universal acceptance, it must always fall into the contingency of a less widely embraced view of the world that I believe is better called orthodoxy. "The state does not necessarily have to give orders or to exercise physical coercion in order to produce an ordered social world, as long as it is capable of producing embodied cognitive structures that accord with objective structures and thus of ensuring the belief of which Hume spoke—namely, doxic submission of the established order," Bourdieu observes, again in *Practical Reason*, only to revise this statement quickly by writing, "This being said, it should not be forgotten that such primordial political belief, this doxa, is an orthodoxy, a right, correct, dominant vision which has more often than not been imposed through struggles against competing visions. This means that the 'natural attitude' mentioned by the phenomenologists, that is, the primary experience of the world as common sense, is a politically produced relation, as are the categories of perception that sustain it" (56).

2   In his interview with Anna Deavere Smith, which appears in the print version of *Twilight: Los Angeles, 1992* (1994; discussed at greater length in chapter 3), Davis further expounds on what has been lost as technology and the state turned against its population, in part as a response to racial fears (please also see chapter 3 for further description of the format of quotations from *Twilight*):

> I mean, there was a core of freedoms / and opportunities and pleasures that have been established / again like, you know, / working-class white kids in my generation. / My parents hitchhiked out here from Ohio. / You know, I grew up with, with, with, / you know, Okies and Dust Bowl refugees / and we got free junior college education. / There were plenty— / there were more jobs than / you could imagine out there. / *We* could go to the beach, / *we* could race our cars. I'm not saying that, you know, it was utopia or / happiness / but it was . . . / it was incredibly important. / And the whole ethos of the civil rights struggle and movement / for equality in California's history / was to make this available to everyone. / The irony now is that even white privileged kids / are losing these things. (30–31)

It is exactly this lost feeling of ease and bright futurity that Davis mourns throughout his works, from his first book, *Prisoners of the American Dream: Politics and Economy in the History of the U.S. Working Class* (1986), to *City of Quartz: Excavating the Future in Los Angeles* (1992b [1990]), to *Ecology of Fear: Los Angeles and the Imagination of Disaster* (1998), and it is the contrast between plenty and evisceration that makes life in the United States (and, in his more recent books *Late Victorian Holocaust: El Niño Famines and the Making of the Third World* [2001] and *Dead Cities and Other Tales* [2002], the whole planet) an unbearable place of enduring social contradiction.

3   Indeed, the dreamy quality engendered by a mix of science fiction and memoir in Davis's sociocultural reporting may help to explain the factual errors that critics of *Ecology of Fear* have discovered. The discussions about these errors have

often been denunciatory and ideologically driven. The ideological motivation for the criticism that *Ecology of Fear* has had to endure is made particularly troublesome when we consider that the originator of this criticism, Brady West-water, is a pseudonym for Ross Ernest Shockley, a Malibu real estate agent, an amateur historian, and an aspiring screenwriter, and that Davis singles out Malibu real estate development for special scorn in *Ecology of Fear*. For more discussion of this controversy, see Robert Jones (1999) and Ted Rohrlich (1999). Why these criticisms have been so vitriolic, and extended, might in part be explained by the fact that Davis's work has captured the attention of a wide readership and, at least in cultural criticism, become a model for the study of urban forms. While Davis's influence stretches far beyond the study of the built-up environments of Los Angeles and into academic disciplines as far-flung as geography, urban studies, history, literature, anthropology, and so forth, his most important contribution has arguably been to the region in which he spent his childhood. One cannot go into a bookstore in Southern California without finding his books prominently adorning its shelves.

Ironically, I suspect that the popularity of Davis's excavation of a history in which corruption, neglect, social inequity, and carceral logic exert their influence in the lived environments of Los Angeles has had the effect of making this city a more glamorous destination for critics and for lay readers alike than the image of it as a land of sunshine, ease, and vacuity that boosters would like to purvey. His critics have failed to recognize how much Davis's brew of criticism and nostalgia has helped to make Los Angeles a more attractive, and certainly more interesting, place to live and visit than the sugary concoctions its boosters wish to sell. At the same time, one cannot help but wish *Ecology of Fear* had been more scrupulously documented as proof against criticism that distracts from the main thrust of its argument. It is, in any case, exactly because of the probable causes of these errors that I am most interested in this book here, and not the more well-known *City of Quartz* (1992b [1990]). Through the progression of *Ecology of Fear*'s chapters, we can follow an internally logical movement of thought about disasters in Los Angeles from the familiar to the fantastical— from, that is, earthquakes, droughts, and riots, to floods, firestorms, tornadoes, and wild animal attacks, until we arrive at a chapter dedicated to apocalyptic fictions. This progression belies a mixing of fact and fiction that is a constant throughout, which compels us to consider why such scenes of destruction visited upon Los Angeles, realistic seeming or extravagantly fanciful, fascinate us so much. It is almost as if we want to see the city of Los Angeles destroyed, to the point where we embellish on the all-too-actual inequalities, crises, and social pain that people suffer every day there. In part, Davis seems to believe, we turn against the city because it has so repeatedly failed to fulfill its potential, with the ambition of its utopian planning matched only by its repeated historic betrayals.

Its promises of free mobility and spacious living made possible by technological advancements have not been met, compelling us to look back at what went wrong and dream of how to start over again.

4   The pleasure of nostalgia in either its restorative or reflective manifestation, however, is in the work of fantasy itself. This fantasy is a "romance" with a home that lives mainly in our imagination and that can, as a result, be ardently wished for, missed, and mourned without any chance of our being contradicted. As Susan Stewart observes, "The nostalgic is enamored of distance, not of the referent itself. Nostalgia cannot be sustained without loss" (1993, 145). Nostalgia is a commentary on the present, an expression of dissatisfaction with the feelings of displacement that seem to characterize a contemporary moment more fraught through its comparison with something that probably never existed.

5   Davis is not the only prominent figure in criticism about Los Angeles who has turned to Ray Bradbury as an important touchstone in representations of this city. Reyner Banham, for instance, peppers his well-known, incredibly influential, and surprisingly playful book *Los Angeles: The Architecture of the Four Ecologies* (2001 [1971]) with references to Bradbury, writing in the conclusion, "There is even the unspeakable Sam Pakhill, patented title-holder to half the land of Mars, for all the world like a Yankee 'Don' newly possessed of some vast Spanish rancho; there are the canals by which the crystal pavilions stand, as they were meant to stand in the dream-fulfillment city of Venice; above all, there are the dry preserved remains of the cities of an earlier Martian culture, like abandoned Indian pueblos or the forgotten sets of famous movies long ago. . . . Angeleno Bradbury, sensibilities turned to the verge of sentimentality, touches the quintessential dream in every other paragraph of his Martian chronicles" (222–223).

6   In the first of Wingrove's seven novels in this series, *Chung Kuo: The Middle Kingdom* (1990), we are introduced to an unpleasant future Earth dominated by Chinese overlords who are dedicated to stasis as a chief social virtue and who resist a movement led by decidedly Nordic men, with names such as Soren Berdichev and Pietr Lehmann, to bring about cataclysmic, but invigorating, changes.

7   It is no mistake, for example, that one of the greatest jump cuts in film history, found at the start of Stanley Kubrick's *2001: A Space Odyssey* (1968), begins with a caveman learning to use a weapon for the first time (he finds a long bone, which he uses to hit a fellow caveman on the head) and ends with a man traveling to Earth's orbit as if he were taking a trip on a jet airliner. This man is of course white. Indeed, only white people are to be found in the outer space of this movie, all others having chosen to remain on Earth. I do not bring this example up to somehow excoriate Kubrick for his lack of vision, but to point out how much this vision of futurity—an unbroken line of human development figured by a

bone used as a weapon tossed into the air turning into an orbiting nuclear silo—
is informed by the times in which it was made, when space travel was conceivable only for white people, who stood as the unquestioned inheritors of scientific
and technological innovations (mainly because they were understood as being
largely responsible for it) and when, not incidentally, the only women who are to
be found in the film take decidedly subordinated roles, as stewardesses who
bring the film's bored space traveler coffee in his uneventful trip to space. It is,
finally, a tribute to Kubrick's brilliance as a filmmaker that the development
figured by one weapon turning into another suggests little has actually changed
in the millennia spanned by this great temporal cinematic cut. In *2001: A Space
Odyssey*, the triumphalism of a humanist diachrony led by and for white domination is undermined by a destructive synchrony it figures as essential to such
linear human development.

8   In her study on American suburban fiction, Catherine Jurca points out how this
fiction expresses an enduring complaint among the most affluent segments of
America's societies. She argues, white, middle- and upper middle-class home
owners claim for themselves the position of dislocation, dispossession, and affliction exactly because they are too materially comfortable in an overly com-
modified way. Jurca observes: "[George Follanbee] *Babbit*'s appeal to the home
is marshaled in the service of representing suburban house owners as emotional
casualties of the proliferating comforts and conveniences achieved and represented by standardization. To possess these commodities is to be dispossessed by
them" (2001, 56). Such an argument can make sense only when we make a
distinction between the house, which provides material comfort and shelter that
foregrounds too plainly its status as a collection of objects that have been mar-
keted, sold, and readied for resale, and the home, which is a more intangible site
of affective belonging and acceptance. Thus, while some of us might be comfort-
ably ensconced in luxurious suburban houses, the very luxury afforded by these
houses is rhetorically converted into a source of oppressive homelessness that
troubles us with, in short, nostalgia. The suburb is a landscape defined explicitly
by the kind of cleft nostalgia Boym points toward, discussed earlier in this
chapter. The postwar process of suburbanization I am concerned with here can
be said to be plagued by the problem of home, as something that developers wish
to re-create for their clients and, at the same time, cannot.

9   Garreau somewhat arbitrarily defines an edge city as containing 5 million square
feet or more of office space, 600,000 square feet or more of retail space, and more
jobs than bedrooms. An edge city must also be perceived as a definable place by
the surrounding population, and, most important of all, it must not have existed
before the 1960s (1991, 6–7). The last qualification is important because, "Edge
City's problem is history. It has none. . . . Who *knows* what these things look like

when they grow up? These critters are likely only in their nymphal, if not larval, forms. We've probably never *seen* an adult one" (9).

10   The planned nature of Irvine was largely made possible by the Irvine Company, founded and operated for most of its history by a single family who had originally purchased the land the city sits on as a ranch. For an excellent discussion of this company, see Martin Schiesl (1991). I wish to stress that while the ambitions of such planning were great, its ability to follow through on its vision was often subject to various local controls, from emerging city councils, environmentalists, and increasingly in the 1980s and beyond the rise of NIMBY (Not In My Backyard) organizations, whose resistance to fast growth is partially a response to the congestion of highways and local roads exacerbated by the zoning of work, shopping, and homes found in suburbia and the resulting dependence on collector roads. The rise of NIMBYism suggests the failure of builders to create the kind of utopian spaces they had once promised their customers. See Andres Duany, Elizabeth Plater-Zyberk, and Jeff Speck (2000) for a cogent discussion of zoning, NIMBYism, and alternative community developments. What is to be criticized, according to Duany et al. is not a lack of planning, but a lack of good planning: "Somewhere along the way, through a series of small and well-intentioned steps, traditional towns became a crime in America. . . . It is these practices, and the laws that encourage them, which must be overcome if good growth is to become a viable alternative" (xi). This alternative, however, seems driven by a form of restorative nostalgia, and is therefore likely only to result in islands of well-planned but artificial-feeling communities, like Disney's Celebration in central Florida, in a sea of Irvine-like developments. Also see Fulton (1997), an impressive study on the local politics and activism that have frustrated developers throughout Southern California in the past two decades.

11   As Richard Weinstein succinctly puts it, "The spatial porosity of the system [Southern California], its void/positive character, together with the blockages represented by parking structures and the emptiness of parking lots, effectively preclude the hierarchical, linear, narrative ordering of traditional urban space with its organized public realms that depend on either consensual or authoritarian politics and the traditionally clear separation of public and private space" (1996, 30).

12   In *The Martian Chronicles*, the most ancient inhabitants of Mars are mystical, helpful spheres that float mysteriously in the air above the hills and only show themselves on rare occasions. See the story "Fire Balloons" (120–143). The most common aliens occupy the plains and, while clearly alien, still maintain humanoid appearances: "They had fair, brownish skin of the true Martian, the yellow coin eyes, the soft musical voices" (3). Unlike the ancients, the second class of aliens are belligerent toward the Earthmen who in the book begin to arrive on their planet.

13 As Fulton reports,

> Faced with a massive influx of immigrants from the Midwest [in the 1880s], the city's fledgling growth merchants had to choose between growing up or growing out. Eager to market land in outlying areas, they chose to grow outward, using the then-new technology of street railways to achieve this goal. . . . The city did not have much of a settled urban form prior to the arrival of the street railway and the real estate speculators who thrived on it. Though downtown Los Angeles was the region's crucial hub up through the 1920s, it had nothing like the cachet of Manhattan or close-in areas like Boston or Philadelphia, which had been centers of commerce and culture for hundreds of years. . . . Unlike other American cities, Los Angeles began decentralizing before it had been able to centralize. (1997, 128)

14 *LA 2000* has become an important historical document of this period, and it has also been seen as a major turning point in the rhetoric city boosters endorsed as the increasing racial diversity of Los Angeles became harder to ignore. For alternative discussions on this document, see David Rieff (1991); Davis (1998, 357–422); and Cannon (1999, 5–19).

15 See especially Davis (1992b [1990], 264–322). Operation Hammer was a program devised by then chief of police Daryl Gates, which involved the summary arrest of young Latino and African American men who might have membership in a gang. Most of the arrestees were released quickly, the point of the sweep being to create a vast database of information about these men so that future arrests would be easier to facilitate. This program gained popular support after a gang-related shooting in Westwood Village resulted in the death of a young Japanese American woman named Karen Toshima, who was uninvolved with any gangs. See John Glionna (1998). It is interesting, particularly in the context of this chapter, that Toshima's race has occasionally been misremembered in critical discussions about this event. For instance, Thomas Dumm writes, "Indeed, one of the terrifying visions of white suburbanites is that of the migration of drive-by shootings of gang-bangers in South Central to the more prosperous (white) peripheral neighborhoods. This nightmare came true in December of 1987 when a *young white woman* was caught in the cross fire of a gang drive-by shooting in the posh neighborhood of Westwood" (1993, 185; emphasis mine). It is also interesting to note that after this shooting, Westwood Village became less "posh," experiencing a significant downturn in foot traffic, as shoppers, diners, and other spenders of disposable income migrated to newer places of entertainment, which are presumably more safe and certainly less accessible to the historic downtown area: Old Towne in Pasadena, Third Street Promenade in Santa Monica, and City Walk inside the Universal Studios (which seeks to simulate the experience of being in a traditional downtown shopping district without any of the perceived risks). In recent years, Westwood Village has recaptured some of its luster.

16 I am, of course, borrowing from the toolbox of concepts developed by George Lipsitz. In *The Possessive Investment in Whiteness: How White People Profit from Identity Politics* (1998), Lipsitz explains the central concept named by his title: "Whiteness is invested in, like property, but it is also a means of accumulating property and keeping it from others" (viii). Whiteness, in other words, needs to be understood as a structure that distributes wealth and relative privileges according to racial demarcations. It does not mean, however, that all whites are wealthy or enjoy absolute privileges; nor does it mean that all nonwhites are poor and lack any kind of privileges for participating in the maintenance of such a structure. Rather, whiteness distributes wealth and privilege to those who willingly participate in a political economy that disproportionately grants a better life for those who are white and who aspire to enjoy the benefits of a white-dominant society.

17 In a famous essay entitled "Mr. Bennet and Mrs. Brown" (1924), Woolf writes of James Joyce: "Mr. Joyce's indecency in *Ulysses* seems to me the conscious and calculated indecency of a desperate man who feels that in order to breathe he must break the windows. At moments, when the window is broken, he is magnificent. But what a waste of energy!" (Woolf 1978 [1950], 116).

2 THE BLACK BODY IN PAIN

1 According to Regina Lawrence, "News icons arise when dramatic, unexpected events prove irresistible to news organizations both because their image is so compelling and because the cultural and political tensions they raise are profound and troubling" (2000, 140). Examples include the shooting of an alleged Vietcong guerilla by a South Vietnamese Army officer during the Tet offensive, the grounding of the *Exxon Valdez*, and the 1987 spectacle of the garbage barge *Mobro* unable to find a port to unload its refuse. "Similarly," Lawrence continues, "when George Holliday's video camera captured the images of LAPD officers raining kicks and blows on a prone African American man, a news icon was born. The event challenged Americans' beliefs about police, the war on crime, the protection offered by due process rights, and the prevalence of racism in contemporary American society" (141).

2 *Strange Days* cost $42 million to produce, and it earned only $7.919 million in box office sales. After its box-office failure, Bigelow stopped directing Hollywood films until recently. As a result, all the most well-known producers and directors associated with the incredibly lucrative action genre for the rest of the decade became again exclusively male (the only exception would be Mimi Leder, who directed *The Peacemaker* [1997] and *Deep Impact* [1998]). Partly because of her

unique status as a woman director of such films, and also because she has not shied away from inflammatory subjects, Bigelow's career has long been shadowed by controversy. Bigelow's first breakthrough picture was arguably *Near Dark* (1987), a low-budget vampire action movie that remains, to this day, one of the most accomplished examples of its kind. She followed this film in 1990 with *Blue Steel*, perhaps her first controversial film with its loving filmic fascination with a .45 handgun, and in 1991 with *Point Break*, an action-packed cop-and-robber thriller that involved the actor Keanu Reeves as an undercover detective who infiltrates a band of criminally minded surfers. After the release of *Strange Days* in 1995, Bigelow took a long hiatus. She did not direct another film until *The Weight of Water* (2002) and *K-19: The Widow Maker* (2002).

Starting with her first films, then, Bigelow has made a career out of making violent and, after *Blue Steel*, controversial films, until this strategy seemed to backfire with *Strange Days*. For a review of the opinions and controversy that sprang up around *Strange Days*, see Jamie Portman (1995). Controversy continued to stalk Bigelow in one recent project: *K-19* is based on the real-life disasters afflicting a Soviet nuclear submarine on its maiden voyage in the late 1960s, and many of its survivors have taken offense at its depiction of the crew as heavily alcohol dependent. See Anna Badkhen (2001). Cost and revenue figures are from the Internet Movie Database (IMDb.com). In general, film critics have not paid much attention to *Strange Days* until recently. For the most extended treatments of this film, see the issue of *Camera Obscura* that contains Brian Carr (2002), Despina Kadoudaki (2002), and Mark Berretinni (2002).

3   In the revealingly titled essay " 'Slanging' Rocks . . . Palestinian Style': Dispatches from the Occupied Zones of North America" (2000), Robin Kelley reminds us that there is an international context against which such scenes of racial, and ritualistic, violence might be interpreted. After recalling a personal confrontation with the police in Southern California, in 1981, when he was hit over the head with a police baton after being surrounded by officers for running (he was trying to catch a bus), Kelley discovered himself powerless to make any formal complaints: "My own efforts to file a complaint with the Lakewood Sheriff failed miserably. I had no badge numbers and was told that the department had no record of the incident. I might as well have been in Johannesburg in the days of apartheid or, for that matter, any ex-colonial metropole where the color line keeps the world's darker people under an omnipotent heel. Whether we are speaking of North Africans in Paris, West Indians in London, indigenous peoples in Sydney, Australia, Black people in Birmingham (Alabama or England), or Palestinians in the West Bank, relations between the police and people of color have been historically rooted in a colonial encounter" (23–24). Unlike Alexander, who sees the King beating explicitly as part of a national history rooted in the founding sin of slavery, Kelley explicitly eschews the limits of nationalism in

4 Alexander is not alone in making this kind of argument. In *Police Brutality: An Anthology* (2000), a collection of timely essays, the editor Jill Nelson provides a litany of gory police shootings of people of color in the introduction—Amadou Diallo, Abner Louima, Anthony Baez, Tyisha Miller, Gidone Busch, Margaret Laverne Mitchell, Daniel García Zarraga, and Yong Xin Huang. Nelson observes, repeating Alexander's analysis of the King beating: "The notion of the 'Black male predator' is so historically rooted in the American consciousness that we have come to accept the brutalization and murder of citizens by the police as an acceptable method of law enforcement. The assumption is that Black men are the bad guys, the police are the good guys, and if the police killed someone it must have been for good reason. They must have done *something*. This attitude, ingrained since slavery, is nurtured and manipulated by the police" (13). Notice how the actual victims of police abuse do not have to be either "black" nor "men" to become another iteration of the black body in pain, which again forms an "American consciousness." It is also worth noting that the title page of *Police Brutality* reproduces an enhanced still from the Holliday video of King lying on the ground.

5 At a conference, I mentioned to another attendee this fact, that Briseno's father is of Mexican descent. The other person's response was almost instantaneous. She claimed this fact did not matter, because once Briseno put on the uniform of the Los Angeles Police Department he had become racially white. I offer this as one vivid, albeit anecdotal, example of how the racial complexity of this event can be overridden by a narrative overly fixated on the power of the black body in pain as national trope.

6 *Cultural Left* is a term that Richard Rorty has helped to make popular. In his jeremiad against what he perceives as the un-American activities of Left-leaning academics, Rorty writes,

> One of the good things which happened in the Sixties was that the American Left began to realize that its economic determinism had been too simplistic. Sadism was recognized as having deeper roots than economic insecurity. The delicious pleasure to be had from creating a class of putative inferiors was seen as Freud saw it—as something which would be relished even if everybody were rich. . . . The heirs of the New Left of the Sixties have created, within the academy, a cultural Left. . . This cultural Left thinks more about stigma than about money, more about deep and hidden psychosexual motivations than about shallow and evident greed. (1998, 76–77)

Gitlin is clearly influenced by this account of how a "cultural Left" came into existence. See Bruce Robbins (1999) for a rich discussion about Rorty's claims, especially Rorty's rejection of identity politics—that is, ethnic nationalism—that seems, paradoxically, to be founded on another form of identity politics—national patriotism (137).

7 An extensive body of critical literature exists in Asian American studies that takes up the theoretical question at the heart of Gitlin's complaint about the term *Asian American*. See, for instance, Lavina Dhangra Shankar and Rajini Srikanth (1998) on South Asians; David Eng and Alice Hom (1998) on the role of sexuality; Kandice Chuh and Karen Shimakawa (2001) on the problem of nation, disciplinarity, and the Asian diaspora; Rachel Lee (1999) on gender; and Chuh (2003) on the critical function of an apparently self-contradictory racial term such as *Asian American*. Kandice Chuh is interesting to quote in this context:

> "Asian American" . . . connotes the violence, exclusion, dislocation, and disenfranchisement that has attended the codification of certain bodies as, variously, Oriental, yellow, sometimes brown, inscrutable, devious, always alien. It speaks to the active denial of personhood to the individuals inhabiting those bodies. At the same time, it insists on acknowledging the enormous capacity for life that has triumphed repeatedly over racism's attempts to dehumanize, over the United States' juridical attempts to regulate life and culture. "Asian American" provides entry into these histories of resistance and racism. It transfers the properties of the racialized and gendered nation onto bodies—of people, of literatures, of fields of study. Far from being a transparent, objective description of a knowable identity, the term may be conceived as a mediating presence that links bodies to knowledge regimes of the U.S. nation. "Asian American" is in this sense a *metaphor* for resistance and racism. (27)

As Chuh suggests here, perhaps the fact that a term such as Asian American may seem like nonsense to many observers is reason enough for the term's wide adoption and incorporation into our racial lexicon. Rather than name a knowable subject, as the terms *white* and *black* can easily be confused as naming, the term *Asian American* can best be understood as a metaphorical relationship between certain kinds of marked bodies and a history of U.S. nation making.

8 Nathan Glazer insists, "as Hispanics and Asians become less different from whites from the point of view of residence, income, occupation, and political attitudes, the two nations become the black and the others. The change that has shaken our expectations for the future of American society is not the rise of women or gays and lesbians. It is rather the change in our expectation as to how and when the full incorporation of African Americans into American life will take place" (1997, 149). According to this passage, white identity has not been substantially affected by the tumultuous events of the last four decades—as immigration to the United States returned to levels not seen since the start of the twentieth century, as gender roles grew more confused (in large part because, for economic reasons, many women have had to enter the workforce), as sexual mores did their tango of relaxation and reaction, and as working-class ethnic whites found themselves losing financial ground to their more Anglo professional peers. Rather, white identity has simply absorbed the influx of new immigrants, the rise of women's rights movements, and the acknowledgment of gay and lesbian issues, while simultaneously remaining perplexed by its inability to absorb a little over 20 million blacks. And, yet, the vehemence with which Glazer argues that blacks remain at the center of the "American dilemma" (148) points away from the facetiousness of his argument toward the fear that if blacks should no longer hold center stage in our discussions on race, then white identity can no longer remain somehow coeval with Americanness. Without this appeal to the centrality of blacks in our racial history, Glazer would undoubtedly have a harder time selling us on the idea that "Hispanics and Asians" have somehow uniformly "become less different from whites," as if these terms—*Hispanics, Asians,* and *whites*—name something real and homogenous (and are not, as Glazer himself points out, severe reductions of very heterogeneous populations).

9　According to Kaja Silverman, the term *screen* derives from Jacques Lacan, for whom "the subject relies for his or her visual identity on an external representation," which

> he refers to . . . as a "screen." . . . Moreover, rather than simply misrecognize him- or herself within the screen, the subject is now assumed to rely for his or her structuring access to it on an "unapprehensible" and unlocalizable gaze, which for over 150 years now has found its most influential metaphor in the camera. In order to emerge in the field of vision, the subject must not only align him- or herself identificatorily with the screen, but must also be apprehended in that guise by the gaze. . . . If it is to be even momentarily "captating," identification must be a three-way rather than a two-way transaction, requiring a symbolic "ratification." (1996, 18)

What I find useful about Silverman's understanding of the "screen" is the way it triangulates a subject's recognition, or misrecognition, of him- or herself with a projection external to him- or herself that must also, simultaneously, be in accordance with a returning affirmation, the "gaze." Put a slightly different way, the spectacle of the black body in pain is itself a screen upon which recognitions or misrecognitions can be made via an affirming, and perhaps regulating, gaze. The degree to which a subject holds onto this process, even in the presence of the strange that imposes itself in the camera's—and thus the gaze's—line of sight, suggests a strong unwillingness to give up the kind of explanatory clarity and grounding this process enables. Even when the force of a gaze is gone, or changes in direction, will the memory of a screen that once seemed to give delight in the comprehensibility of a whole self endure as an external representation worthy of identificatory alignment?

10 The image of belligerent Korean American merchants has become a common trope in post–Los Angeles riots cinema, found in such films as *Menace II Society* (1993), *Falling Down* (1993), *Bad Lieutenant* (1992), *Kids* (1995), and in many more films that have New York or Los Angeles as their primary location.

11 Cannon points out how both the prosecution and the defense asked the jurors to identify with their clients' predicament. The prosecution asked the jurors to place themselves in Rodney King's position, to feel what it was like to be the victim of police brutality. By insisting on the racial dimension of the arrest, the prosecution also asked the jurors to feel what it was like to be racially profiled, to be singled out for extraordinarily abusive treatment primarily because of one's blackness. As one of the prosecuting attorneys put it during his closing argument, "When you look at this video, what you see is a man feeling the pain of these batons. This was a man in pain. You can clearly see it on the video. They continued to hit him and hit him and hit him" (quoted in Cannon 1999, 243). To buttress this appeal, the prosecution relied heavily on the videotape and the recorded events that followed. The videotape, of course, showed a black man's beating by four white police officers with steel batons while a ring of other officers watched. There were a total of twenty-one Los Angeles Police Department officers on the scene along with two Unified School District officers and two California Highway Patrol officers who had originally spotted King speeding. A police helicopter hovered overhead and beamed down a cone of light on the beating, as if to provide extra lighting for Holliday's camcorder. What the prosecution added to this image was a litany of the injuries King had suffered. Even after being severely beaten, however, King was trussed with his legs and arms tied behind his back, "hog-tied" in the vernacular of the LAPD, and dragged along the roadway toward a waiting patrol car until another officer insisted he be lifted off the ground.

The defense's lawyers made a similar appeal to the jurors' empathy. They screened the videotape over and over again during the trial, at times stopping it frame by frame. They played, and made much of, an early few seconds of the tape that had apparently been cut out of the version aired on television (partly because of its low quality). The deleted clip shows King upright and approaching the officers. These seconds allowed the defense to argue that, to the officers involved in the incident, this approach appeared to be a life-threatening attack, especially since King made this approach after being hit by a stun gun and after having thrown off several officers who had tried to tackle him to the ground. Expert witnesses testified about each moment in the beating. What the officers were perceiving, the defense asserted, was a reasonable threat emanating from King's body. No matter how often he was beaten, King remained in control of the scene and could have stopped the violence if he had only complied with the officers' demands. The length and severity of the beating were something wholly determined by King's actions. The officers themselves only responded accordingly and acted within the guidelines set down by the police department governing the use of force. In order to substantiate these claims, the defense put the jurors in the officers' position, to feel what it was like to be the victimizer, to feel their fear and relentless need to strike out against an implacable foe.

There was one moment in the trial that seemed to encapsulate the competing demands for empathy made on the jurors by the defense and the prosecution. Against the characterization that the four officers were brutish and unfeeling, Sergeant Stacey Koon, the officer in charge of the arrest, revealed a depth of feeling unbeknownst to anyone in the courtroom. Cannon describes this moment at length:

> Fighting back unbidden tears and struggling to keep his voice from breaking, Koon said, "They show a picture when you are in the Academy [taken] at the morgue, and it is four [highway patrol] officers in full uniform that are on a slab and are dead, and it is the Newhall shooting." . . . This *human moment* had come upon the courtroom unsuspected, revealing the intensity of the emotions that had guided Koon and had been disguised, even to himself, as cool and professional judgment. Against the revelations of Koon's true feelings, which demolished with equal force the prosecution's portrayal of Koon as a brute and his own contrived defense of managed and controlled use of force, even the violent videotape seemed pale and unconvincing. (1999, 213–214; emphasis mine)

12 Mace says melodramatically about this recording, keeping pace with the general tone of the film: "This tape is a lightning bolt from God. . . . It can change things, things that need changing before we all go off the end of the road." Interestingly, she and the other characters refer to the recording as a "tape," though it is clearly a minidisk. Such references to this technology with an anachronistic label suggest how much the recording of Jeriko One's murder is meant to stand in for the videotape recording of Rodney King's beating. Taken out of context, the above quotation sounds as if Mace is referring not to the minidisk containing a recording of Jeriko One's murder but, rather, the "tape" of King's beating.

13 In *Talk to Me: Travels in Media and Politics* (2000), Anna Deavere Smith makes a shrewd observation that comments directly on this paragraph:

> When I turned on the television, except for Amos and Andy, everything I saw was white. I *identified* with white people, but I didn't know very many. . . . I was brought up with a false intimacy with people who had nothing to do

with me. I was brought up identifying with their world, the problems and joys they had, and the products that they were selling. . . . The fact is, we didn't have any trouble identifying with the other in the first place. My grandmother, a devout Christian woman, had no trouble identifying with the people on her "story" as she called it, her "soap opera." (71)

Lately, as the *New York Times* recently reported, the demand that all moviegoers identify with a white lead star in films has started to give way a little to the demands that all moviegoers identify with a racially and ethnically ambiguous actor, such as Keanu Reeves, The Rock, Vin Diesel, and Jessica Alba. See Ruth La Ferla (2003). It is impossible, of course, to know how long this trend (if it is indeed a trend) will continue, and there is certainly no shortage of white film stars that remain clearly at the center of audience attention.

3 CULTURE OF WOUNDING

1 *Fires in the Mirror: Crown Heights, Brooklyn and Other Identities* (1993) focuses on the rioting that occurred in the Brooklyn neighborhood of Crown Heights in August 1991. Largely remembered as a Jewish-black conflict, Smith's careful selection of interviews with numerous people directly and peripherally involved calls attention to the specificity of this event. The Jews in this neighborhood largely belong to "an orthodox Hasidic sect known as Lubavitchers" (A. Smith 1993, xxxv), and the blacks who are their neighbors are largely immigrants from the West Indies. In Smith's theatrical interpretation of the events that led to what happened in Crown Heights, one is not allowed to forget the complexity of a neighborhood where disagreement, accident, and long-held resentments led to ever increasing acts of public violence.

2 For a detailed discussion of the riots' destructiveness, see introduction.

3 The adaptation appeared on pbs as part of the "Stage on Screen" series on 29 April 2001. Directed by Marc Levin.

4 This excerpt is also quoted in the published version of *Twilight* (1994, 106–107).

5 I am only assuming, of course, that these are black Muslims Denny comes into contact with in this passage. This assumption could easily be wrong. They could be Muslims from the Middle East or from Southeast Asia, rather than one of Elijah Muhammad's followers. Given the demographic diversity of Southern California, Denny could just as easily have come into contact with Muslim immigrants on this street as he could have with members of the Nation of Islam.

6 Here is another example of the kind of performative prose found throughout Seltzer's book: "The most popular current television series, *ER*, is pure wound culture: the world, half-meat and half-machinery, in a perpetual state of emergency. *ER* is an endless series of torn and open bodies and an endless series of emotionally torn and exposed bio-technicians. There are the routine hook-ups of bodies and appliances; trauma and techno-speak; cardiac arrest and broken hearts" (1998, 22).

7   More than a decade after he became the center of such attention, his personal fate has become only an afterthought for those who saw in him a symbol of white innocence suffering or reactive black blaming. Both of these responses to Denny's sudden media visibility could not see how Denny himself would end up another victim of a culture of wounding against which naïveté—an inchoate yearning for a sense of community beyond his bodily isolation and the pained surprise of violent rejection—is only the flimsiest of protection. Although Smith's play can record the way in which he retreats into this naïveté, regardless of his motivation for doing so, it cannot convey the future disappointments that awaited his earlier optimism. According to a brief *People Magazine* profile, "He tends to avoid crowds and unnecessary risks and describes himself as 'withdrawn.' . . . Money has also been a concern. As a result of the beating, Denny is susceptible to seizures, so he can no longer drive a truck, and despite having graduated at the top of his class from a marine-mechanics course in 1997, he has so far been unable to find steady work. He scrapes by on the $120 a week he receives in disability. Unable to afford rent, he bunks in the home of his former in-laws or with friends" (Sanz 1999, 233; originally cited in Cannon 1999). Ironically, the only people who seemed to show Denny any care in the long run were wealthy African Americans. According to Cochran, he enabled Denny to receive worker's compensation after the lawsuit was dismissed and he also acted as a go-between for Denny and Bill Cosby, whose sympathy for Denny's plight led him to establish an educational trust fund for Denny's daughter (Cochran 2002, 98).

8   Rather than trace my use of the term *abjection* to its often-cited definition in Julia Kristeva's writings (especially her works *Black Sun* [1992], *Strangers to Ourselves* [1991], and *The Powers of Horror: An Essay on Abjection* [1982]), I wish to point more directly to recent critical work that has applied this concept directly to the U.S. context. Most notably, see Shimakawa:

> For U.S. Americanness to maintain its symbolic coherence, the national abject continually must be both made present and jettisoned. . . . In employing the lexicon of abjection I do not intend to import the entire apparatus of psychoanalytic theory with respect to the formation of the subject nor to suggest that a uniform, linear process takes place in psyches of all (white? Non-Asian?) "Americans" who experience and process the "difference" posed by Asian Americans in order to arrive at a determination of Asian American abjection. . . . I utilize *abjection* as a descriptive paradigm in order to posit a way of understanding the relationship linking the psychic,

symbolic, legal, and aesthetic dimensions of national identity as they are performed (theatrically and otherwise) by Asian Americans. (2002, 3–4)

Although this passage suggests that Asian Americans somehow occupy a special relationship to the U.S. nation-state that renders them especially abject, Shimakawa is careful at the end of her study to clarify that while abjection can take different forms, there nevertheless remain multiple variants of abjection that affect numerous other U.S. groups, including Native Americans, Chicanos/as, Latinos/as, and African Americans (160–161). In addition, Shimakawa insists that abjection is not only linked to race in the United States: "Gender and sexuality are not merely stereotyping side effects of race-based national abjection; for lesbian, gay, bisexual, and transgender Asian Americans heterosexism is often the primary, and most virulent, form of national abjection" (162). Also on abjection and Asian Americans, see David Leiwei Li (1998).

9 This passage can be confusing, since Salas speaks a few lines earlier about his frustrations with "cholos" as well as whites. But he dismisses his thoughts on cholos as "something else." Presumably, then, when he goes on to talk about "masks," he is speaking in particular about whites: "We, they put on the mask—you ever notice that?— / it's sort of a mask / it's, uh . . . / You know how they stand in your face with the ugly faces" (5). These are the people whose "dads" he fantasizes about killing. Nevertheless, the confusion of antecedents in this passage suggests as well how racial aggression that is directed outward at another group can often reflect an inwardly directed aggression against one's own group, a self-dissatisfaction that cannot be fully divorced from a hatred of others.

10 Even Parker, who is the most unapologetic among these four interviewees about the kind of anger he feels, betrays this sadness when he stumbles over his own rhetoric:

> You either be black
> or you die
> and (*exhale*),
> you know, with No Justice No Peace
> it . . . it's,
> you know, um. (178)

The confident exhortation to stay true to one's persecuted identity gives way in this passage to a moment when his speech stops, stumbles over a parenthetical exhalation that denotes a pause in thought, a moment of recollection and doubt. He changes directions after this exhalation, tries to continue along the same line of thought on a parallel track, but stumbles again, first with another pause suggested by ellipses and then a stutter in speech, an "um," that points to an unspoken uncertainty about what to say next. These moments of hesitation speak about a sadness that is as articulately expressed as the sadness that pervades Salas's more overt struggle to think about the sources of his angry feelings.

11 Bourdieu, from whom I am borrowing generously in making these claims, observes, "Domination is not the direct and simple action exercised by a set of agents ('the dominant class') invested with powers of coercion. Rather, it is the indirect effect of a complex set of actions engendered within the network of intersecting constraints which each of the dominants, thus dominated by the structure of the field through which domination is exerted, endures on behalf of all the others" (1998, 34). What this passage suggests is that power is produced in relation to numerous sets of agents who together comprise a "dominant class" in a society. Individual agents within such a network are not free simply to produce ideas, policies, and initiatives as they might happen to see fit. Rather, they are constrained by the network that grants them the power to produce ideas, politics, and initiatives, but of course only within certain well-defined limits. As mayor of Los Angeles, for instance, Bradley could not simply call out the national guard when the police failed to stop the riots at their inception. He could, however, make a public call for the national guard to be mobilized, and he could hope that others in another position of relatively greater power, such as the governor of California, would respond to this call. The governor, in turn, cannot simply call out the national guard without reason, and without a series of consultations with experts who might be able to inform him (in this case, Governor Pete Wilson) of its legality, precedence, and ramifications for his career as a politician.

12 As Chandler himself highlights at the start of his interview, "I think / if you think about America and you think about the families / that have had the opportunities / by accumulating wealth, whether it be newspapers or mining / or / whatever, and you think about / who . . . what families / have really made a contribution over many generations, there aren't / many. / I can think of the / (*He counts his fingers*) / Kennedys, / the Rockefellers, / maybe the Mellons in Pittsburgh, / hopefully / immodestly, the Chandlers / in Los Angeles, / but there aren't very many" (218–219).

13 Later on, however, Duke does register some social protest when he complains to a higher-ranking officer that batons are not as efficient as the "upper-body control hold," a maneuver he favors for its quick results despite its history of causing deaths. The response he receives is "We're gonna beat people into submission / and we're gonna break bones" (65). Ever the consummate professional, Duke does not pursue this officer further; nor does he seek to advertise his worries elsewhere that "you gonna get some policeman indicted, / you gonna get some policemen sent to jail, / and they're gonna hurt somebody and it's gonna be perceived to be / other than a proper use of force" (64).

1   The title is transliterated Korean for 4-2-9 (29 April), the first day of the riots. In Korea, important historical events, especially those with large political significance, are often remembered by the numerical dates on which they occurred. All translated quotations from *Sa-I-Gu* are copied from the English subtitles that appear on the bottom of the screen and therefore have no page numbers accompanying them.

2   Elaine Kim, one of the producers of the documentary, recounted in an interview with me how such a lack of care exacerbated the shock these women were experiencing:

> I met another woman who talked about how frustrated she had been because she could not tell other Americans how she felt about the situation, since she could not speak English. She said she was so excited when a PBS reporter asked her to talk to the camera. Her daughter was there and could translate for her. They had been at a small demonstration in front of City Hall a few days after the peace march, asking for help because their store had been burned down and they were no longer able to make their living. Some people inside the building were throwing things from the windows at the group. She had gotten hit with an ink bottle or some white-out, so she had some ink on her face, but she really wanted to have her say at last. That night, when she saw her interview on television, all they had was the image of her dirty face. They didn't translate what she said. Maybe it was too much trouble or too expensive to bother with a voice-over or subtitles. So she never had her say. She wept when she related what had happened.

The interview took place on 22 May 2000 in Elaine Kim's office at the University of California, Berkeley. For text of interview, see Song (2004).

3   When I talked with her about the making of *Sa-I-Gu* (phone conversation, 21 March 2004), Dai Sil Kim-Gibson recalled the hurdles she faced in making her directorial debut. Few people were willing to give her the financial support she needed. Therefore, she was forced to rely on the limited resources that were at her disposal. She also wanted to maintain a high level of filmmaking independence so that she could give a group of women, who otherwise would not have been given this opportunity, a chance to be heard simply as people, with their losses—especially Mrs. Lee's, the mother of Edward Lee—registering as nothing less than a story of "universal mourning." To reiterate this position, Kim-Gibson later wrote to me regarding my contention, later in this chapter, that the loss Mrs. Lee suffers is full of racial meanings: "Whatever interpretations you might like to put forth about that, I would say that Mrs. Lee's narrative is not racial or particular—it is universal—DEPTH OF MOTHER'S DEATH! Mothers in different cultures might express their sorrow and pain differently but the sorrow is universal" (personal correspondence, 22 March 2004). While I appreciate the conviction with which Kim-Gibson insists on this point, I am disturbed by her suggestion that recognizing Mrs. Lee's racial specificity robs Mrs. Lee's suffering of its universality. This sounds to me much like the neoconservative argument that we must choose between an attention to race or an attention to humanity. In order to humanize Mrs. Lee, in other words, we must insist that the universality of her grief is not tainted by the fact that she is Korean American; and, ipso facto, to be Korean American means we cannot be representative of more than just ourselves. Although this might not have been the intent of her comments to me, her account of making and promoting *Sa-I-Gu* often pulls alongside the grain of this kind of either-or logic. For instance: according to Kim-Gibson (again in our phone conversation), when mainstream media tries to represent racial minorities, it always does so by presenting them as a problem that needs to be handled in some way. In response, she argued, *Sa-I-Gu* represents the Korean American women who were directly victimized by the riots in unqualified human terms. She said that *only* someone like herself, another Korean American woman, could—or would—have made a film like this, which takes such care to let these women speak about what they had lost with such candor. Put another way, she as a Korean American woman was the only one who could have shown such empathy toward these Korean American women, but we shouldn't forget that the plight of these women should not be understood as having anything to do with the fact that they are Korean Americans.

I would gently like to suggest, with all due respect, that indeed Kim-Gibson's racial identity inevitably influenced the making of this film (as she insists), though it is at least theoretically possible for a person of another racial background to make a film that is just as thoughtful, *and* that to recognize her Korean American interviewees as Korean Americans does not, or at least should not, demean the wider meaningfulness of their experiences. In any case, I do not want to draw attention away from the important point that projects such as *Sa-I-Gu* have a very difficult time getting made and finding viewers when they do get made—in large part because commercial broadcasters are reluctant to fund and show programs that do not seem to have immediate universal appeal. Thus, it is worth mentioning that PBS, which is one of the few television outlets that might even consider broadcasting this kind of film, was initially reluctant to broadcast *Sa-I-Gu*. Eventually, PBS did air it after a prolonged debate, which was in part about its use of subtitles rather than voice-overs. The difference between the two, Kim-Gibson observed, is that voice-overs literally drown out the voices of the women in her film, while subtitles allow their actual voices to be heard even as their words are made understandable to an English-speaking viewer.

4   See E. Park (2001a and 2001b) for admirably succinct discussions about the ways

in which Korean Americans in Los Angeles after the riots have sought to enter mainstream electoral politics.

5   Claire Jean Kim is especially adamant about the pernicious effects of this argument. She writes, "Conventional accounts of Black-Korean conflict tell a story that is comfortable for us to hear. The story involves a group of aspiring newcomers caught in the crossfire of ancient feuding, a group of malcontents acting out of malice and rage, and a group of colorblind observers noting events from a distance. . . . The story cheers us because it fixes the problem on a renegade minority, lets most of us off the hook, and reinforces our moral certainty in the face of racial conflict" (2000, 221–222).

6   Rather than use the term *state*, Honig (2001) prefers to use the term *regime* to refer to the government and its apparatuses, both bureaucratic and ideological, that govern a people. She does so to foreground the ways in which such a government is always suspect in the eyes of those governed, who cannot be sure if their interests are being represented or if they are being compelled to behave in a certain way for someone else's interests. I have decided not to pick up her terminology, because *regime* seems to decide in one direction the ambivalence she refers to in the people's relationship to the law, thus not leaving room to explore the ambivalence that a less connotatively loaded term such as *state* allows.

7   The following is a list of the most pertinent works I consulted for this chapter. On psychic trauma, Judith Herman (1992) is important for helping to popularize its concepts for a larger audience outside the academy. Inside the academy, no one has done more to bring our attention to trauma's potential significance to diverse fields of inquiry concerned with historical reclamation and interpretation than Cathy Caruth; see especially her short monograph *Unclaimed Experience: Trauma, Narrative, and History* (1996) and the edited collection of essays *Trauma: Explorations in Memory* (1995). In literary criticism, Kirby Farrell (1998) and Kalí Tal (1996) productively mine the possibilities enabled by Caruth. In history, Dominick LaCapra has worked along similar lines for a long time in his work on the Holocaust; see especially *Writing History, Writing Trauma* (2001). Several recent works have also cast doubt on the coherence and utility of this concept. See Allan Young (1995); Ruth Leys (2000); and especially Patrick Bracken and Celia Petty (1998), which I found to contain the most illuminating critiques. For widely available psychological accounts of grief in general, see Elizabeth Kübler-Ross (1969). Also, for a good overview of developmental approaches to this topic, see Catherine Sanders (1999). Kay Redfield Jamison (1999) is perhaps the most important popular and academically respected work on depression and suicide, and it should be consulted by lay readers interested in psychological, but not psychoanalytic, approaches to these topics. In the field of psychoanalysis, the works I found most engaging were Cheng (2001); Eng and

Han (2000); and Butler (1997). I discuss the former two at some length in this chapter. In addition, the following have been influential to my thinking on these topics in this chapter: Chungmoo Choi (2001); Behar (1996); Abelmann and Lie (1995); and Renato Rosaldo (1993 [1989]).

8 This does not mean that I eschew academic work, but like Claire Jean Kim I have my doubts about the presumption that academics by virtue of their privilege always have something to teach activists; indeed, I think the reverse is often more true. And, of course, being an academic and being active in community organizations are not mutually exclusive. There are abundant examples of doing so. The recent celebration of the academic public intellectual, finally, requires more interrogation than it has received, in part because it assumes that intellectual work directly addressed to a specialized audience of academics cannot have its own value. This position, it seems to me, is simply another form of anti-intellectualism.

9 Cheng is emphatic on this point: "Segregation and colonialism are internally fraught institutions not because they have eliminated the other but because they need the very thing they hate or fear. (This is why trauma, so often associated with discussions of racial denigration, in focusing on a structure of crisis on the part of the victim, misses the violators' own dynamic process at stake in such denigration. Melancholia gets more potently at the notion of constitutive loss that expresses itself in both violent and muted ways, producing confirmation as well as crisis, knowledge as well as aporia.)" (2001, 12). Indeed, in discussions about historically traumatic events such as the Holocaust (and unlike the melancholia created by endemic forms of institutional racism), there is a strong strand of argumentation that holds it is worthless, if not simply offensive, to try to understand the "violators' own dynamic process." Claude Lanzmann, the director of *Shoah* (1985), is famous for taking this position. See Lanzmann (1995).

10 Cathy Caruth, in her groundbreaking study on the subject of trauma and critical theory, develops this sense of being stuck in an impossible expressive aporia when she writes, trauma "is always the story of a wound that cries out, that addresses us in the attempt to tell us of a reality or truth that is not otherwise available. This truth, in its delayed appearance and its belated address, cannot be linked only to what is known, but also to what remains unknown in our very actions and our language" (1996, 4). On the other hand, for Ruth Leys, one of Caruth's toughest critics, trauma is a problematic concept because it focuses too much on the victim, and as such has no third-party way to verify its claims to victimhood: "In short, from the beginning trauma was understood as an experience that immersed the victim in the traumatic scene so profoundly that it precluded the kind of specular distance necessary for cognitive knowledge of what had happened" (2000, 9). Although this charge is certainly a pressing one, it does not quite address the slipperiness of Caruth's claim. For Caruth, the concept of trauma is valuable exactly because it is not a coherent concept and does not allow "specular distance."

11 Finished more than ten years after the riots, Dai Sil Kim-Gibson's *Wet Sand: Voices from L.A. Ten Years Later* (2003) seems to address the question that Claire Jean Kim asks of her students. "In the past, my life was kind of easy," Mrs. Han, one of the women who appeared in *Sa-I-Gu* (discussed later in this chapter), says in the newer documentary, "I was a really happy person. I didn't feel like to consider other people. But then, when I was in trouble, I tried to look around, how other people live, and think, and manage their lives. And then I had a lot of contact with other peoples. I learned a lot about life. For some people, how hard the life is. I did not know before. By listening to their problems, strangely, I became encouraged to develop new life." According to Kim-Gibson, this interviewee, "a registered nurse who had to take over the family liquor store after her husband died of cancer, was evicted from her house, unable to pay her mortgage. She had opened a sandwich shop after her liquor store burned to ashes but, invaded by a huge deli across the street, she had to close it. Now nearing sixty, she cannot find a job that would sustain her daily needs. She is barely surviving with help from her sister in Germany" (personal correspondence, 22 March 2004). Given all that she has endured, it is extraordinary to hear Mrs. Han speak about an openness to how "hard the life is" for some people. One might reasonably expect that hardship would leave her preoccupied with her own troubles; instead, hardship seems to have led her outside an exclusive concern for herself.

12 There is a certain irony in using Claire Jean Kim's work to illustrate a point concerning a psychological explanation for racial conflict. For instance, she writes, "Once Black-Korean conflict is depicted as an essentially psychological phenomenon bereft of political significance, it is easily dismissed as irrational or pathological or even evil" (2000, 6). I believe, however, that I am working within the spirit of her argument, in that I am trying not to pathologize the psychological phenomenon I am writing about. At the same time, it does seem difficult to avoid a certain trend toward pathologization in psychological explanations of social phenomenon, partially because I believe Seltzer (1998) is observant in insisting on the pathological nature in toto of the public sphere insofar as it remains possible to say that there is something called a public sphere in the United States in its current attenuated form. Take for example Eng and Han, again, who write, "We are dissatisfied with the assumption that minoritarian subjectivities are permanently damaged—forever injured and incapable of being 'whole'" (2000, 693). While this is a strong disclaimer, it does nevertheless leave open the possibility that at least *temporarily* minoritarian subjectivities do become pathologized. We walk a tightrope here between the desire to claim the

special vulnerability of Asian Americans qua other racial minorities and the equally strong desire to acknowledge the agency, especially the political agency, of the people we write about.

13 Also, see Bruce Cumings (1997, 448) on this survey. Compare as well with the essays in K. Kim (1999), many of which challenge the assumptions underlying the belief in deep-rooted animosity between blacks and Koreans.

14 The bluntness of this placard speaks powerfully of how politicized the riots made Korean Americans. During the Red Apple boycotts, Korean American groups in New York had organized what was until then the largest gathering of Korean Americans in a public display. In the days before this prior rally, an intense debate broke out between the organizers about the tone their rhetoric should take. Many were afraid of reprisals and loss of sympathy. The organizers ultimately decided to invite then mayor David Dinkins to speak at the rally! This was despite the fact that the main impetus for the rally itself had been Dinkins's refusal to enforce a police ordinance against the boycotters (C. Kim 2000, 177). The timidity suggested by these debates seems to have disappeared in the aftermath of the 1992 Los Angles riots, at least for a time.

15 Conversation took place by phone on 21 March 2004. After this conversation, Kim-Gibson elaborated further on this incident:

> At a screening of *Sa-I-Gu* at the Human Rights Festival in New York City in 1993, a young African American with two small boys was in the audience. During the Q&A period, he asked, "Do you have any idea how many young African American men die a day? Why do you make such a big deal about one death (he meant Mrs. Lee's son)?" His eyes were ablaze with anger. My legs went weak, with my head spinning, confronted with a totally unexpected question. I closed my eyes a second and then these words came out of my mouth. "You know, I am a child of the Korean War. As a child, I stepped over dead bodies, some of them those of my friends. The first corpse sent an electric shock through my body but as I saw more corpses, I became numb— no feelings. Day in and day out, people watch dead bodies on the tube and think nothing of it; people see too many of them too often. I want to humanize victims of Sa-I-Gu, dead as well as living. I wanted people to know that the dead body has a mother who will carry him in her chest as long as she lives. It is not that one death I am glorifying—I am saying that for each dead body, there is a mother mourning." (personal correspondence, 22 March 2004)

5 A DIASPORIC FUTURE?

1 The commemoration of 15 August 1945 as a day of liberation is necessarily tinged by the memory of Hiroshima and Nagasaki. This day is further tinged by the fact that there were many Koreans, along with others from different parts of Asia, who worked in these two cities when the United States military dropped its atomic bombs; many of these Koreans who survived were no longer considered Japan's responsibility after the signing of the surrender and were as a result ineligible for any medical treatment for radiation sickness. For an especially sensitive discussion of this largely unremembered chapter from the end of the Second World War, see Toyonaga Keisaburô (2001).

2 Don Oberdorfer reports,

> a widely accepted estimate is that 900,000 Chinese and 520,000 North Korean soldiers were killed or wounded, as were about 400,000 UN Command troops, nearly two-thirds of them South Korean troops. U.S. casualties were 54,000 dead and another 105 wounded. In Korea the war devastated both halves of a country that had only just begun to recover from four decades of Japanese occupation and the sudden shock of division. Around 3 million people, roughly a tenth of the entire population of both sides at the time, were killed, wounded, or missing as a result of the war. Another 5 million became refugees. (1997, 10)

Bruce Cumings also comments on the U.S. destruction of the north: "By 1952 just about everything in northern and central Korea was completely leveled. What was left of the population survived in caves, the North Koreans creating an entire life underground, in complexes of dwellings, schools, hospitals, and factories" (1997, 296). John Feffer helps to enumerate the damage of such aerial bombardment: "The United States used massive bombardments in an attempt to erase North Korea from the map, destroying 75 percent of all physical facilities (by comparison, half of South Korean facilities were destroyed)" (2003, 32–33).

Of course, reliable information about what has happened in North Korea since the end of the war has been hard to come by, as U.S. hostility toward the continued existence of this nation has further made attempts to portray North Korea in any light other than caricature both difficult and dangerous. Two attempts that stand out as especially worthy of attention are J. T. Takagi's *Homes Apart* (1991) and Dan Gordon's *The Game of Their Lives* (2003).

3 Twenty-eight thousand Korean women married American men between 1950 and 1972; they were the largest group to immigrate to the United States in the years between 1945 and 1965; and their numbers had probably swelled to over 50,000 by 1980 (Ablemann and Lie 1995, 58). Before 1965, more than 10,000 Koreans studied abroad in Japan and, in increasing numbers, in the United States; many of those who studied in the United States decided to stay or returned as the elites of their country; and by the start of the most recent Los Angeles riots, there were 25,720 Korean students in the United States (59–60). Thus, "military brides and students constituted a two-tiered immigration for the

1950s and the 1960s, representing the lower and upper reaches of South Korean society" (60). It bears keeping in mind that, like all immigration between countries, this one is a highly complicated phenomenon that cannot, and should not, be reduced to a number of simple determinants. At the same time, Korean immigration to the United States did experience a major wave in the 1970s and 1980s that allows for some generalization.

4   This has led to the popular perception that Korean Americans, like many other Asian Americans, are somehow culturally hardwired to excel in school, even when more precise evidence reveals inconsistencies in the popular perception. As Hing notes, statistics provided a strong prima facie case for the popular perception: "while Asian Americans are less than 3 percent of the population, they are 9 to 25 percent of the entering classes at Harvard, Stanford, MIT, the University of California at Berkeley, Princeton, and Cal Tech" (1993, 142). Hing also goes on to explain that this perception and the cultural explanations that often accompany it turn out to be deeply flawed. This is so because Asian Americans are an extremely heterogeneous group, with individual ethnicities proving difficult to generalize about. One particular example stands out as indicative of the complexity of this phenomenon as it plays out across ethnicities, generations, class, gender, and region: "Just as the popular image downplays differences between groups, it pays little attention to variations in academic performance within each community. A Chicago cohort analysis revealed that third-generation Asian American students have lower grades than immigrant children. But researchers reported in a similar San Francisco Bay Area study that only grades for Filipinos decreased from the first to the second generation, while those for Koreans and Chinese remained the same. And grades for Japanese American students actually increased across generations" (146).

5   More recent Korean American novels published by major imprints include Chang-rae Lee's *A Gesture Life* (1999) and *Aloft* (2004), Frances Park's *When My Sister Was Cleopatra Moon* (2000), Alexander Chee's *Edinburgh* (2001), Nora Okja Keller's *Fox Girl* (2002), Susan Choi's *American Woman* (2003), Suki Kim's *The Interpreter* (2003), and Don Lee's *Country of Origin* (2004). To this list, one might add Gary Pak's *A Ricepaper Airplane* (1998), which was not included in the list above because it was printed by a university press, and Don Lee's *Yellow* (2001), a prizewinning collection of short stories. One might want to put Leonard Chang into his own category, since he started by publishing with a small independent press and has since begun to make a name for himself as a writer of mysteries: see his, *The Fruit N' Food* (1996), *Dispatches from the Cold* (1998), *Over the Shoulder* (2001), *Underkill* (2003), and *Fade to Kill* (2004). For a selection of short writings by new Korean American authors, see Elaine Kim and Laura Hyun Yi Kang (2003). There have also been simultaneous and subsequent publications of plays, memoirs, and poetry (indeed, there has been an equally im-

pressive explosion of memoirs) that undoubtedly require exploration elsewhere. For a thoughtful introduction to Korean American literature as a whole, see E. Kim (1997).

6   I have focused on the works mentioned at the start of the chapter to foreground the significance of the novel as a mode of personal self-fashioning that speaks directly to this book's central concern with identity, expression, and politics. While doing so, I want to stress even further in this note how much the success of these authors in getting their books published and finding a wider audience may reflect not only their ethnicity but also their socioeconomic class status. For instance, if college reputations in the United States mark class gradations that are normally more subtly at work, then it is certainly worth noting what colleges the authors I refer to here attended: Chang-rae Lee went to Yale, as did Susan Choi; Mira Stout attended Brown; Heinz Insu Fenkl attended Vassar; Patti Kim attended the University of Maryland, College Park; Nora Okja Keller received a BA from the University of Hawai'i, Manoa, and an MA from the University of California, Santa Cruz; Mia Yun attended the fairly prestigious Hankuk University of Foreign Studies, Seoul, and received an MFA in creative writing from City College, New York; Don Lee is a graduate of UCLA This is an impressive, and predominantly upper middle-class, curriculum vitae by any standard.

7   Usually, the honor of being called the first novel by a Korean American is awarded to Younghill Kang, for the publication of *East Goes West* (1997 [1937]). His previous work, *The Grass Roof* (1931), is a memoir about his childhood in Korea, and so would not apply. See Seiwoong Oh (2003/2004), for discussion about the earliest Korean American writers.

8   Alan Wolfe, working in Arthur Schlesinger Jr.'s shadow, is candid about how useful, perhaps even necessary, immigrant desire for national belonging is to shoring up an eroding sense of vigor and largesse in the adopted nation at a time of troubled boundaries, when "conceptions of citizenship are changing as the more or less ethnically homogeneous welfare states of North America and Western Europe face ever higher levels of immigrants within their borders" (2003, 11). Even worse, "Minority groups that once tried to live quietly now demand recognition, if not autonomy" (11). "Still, for all its associated pain and even violence," Wolfe writes, "immigration underscores the value of citizenship, for the native-born and the immigrant alike. By risking life and limb to obtain this dispensation, immigrants remind the native-born why what they take for granted is priceless. And by granting citizenship to people from cultures radically different from their own, the native-born acknowledge that citizenship is too precious to be distributed solely on the basis of luck" (11). These observations lend weight to Bonnie Honig's contention that "in the contemporary United States, a variety of American institutions and values, from capitalism to community to family to consenting liberal individual, are seen to be periodically reinvigorated by that

country's newest comers, its idealized citizens: naturalizing immigrants. Again and again, the cure for corruption, withdrawal, and alienation is . . . aliens" (2001, 4). Or, as Vijay Prashad asks of Asian Americans in particular, "How does it feel to be a solution?" (2000, viii).

9   For this argument to work, however, Asian Americans must be understood as incompatible with a unitary and more-or-less stable national identity. This may, of course, not be the case, or at the least this situation might be experiencing a period of flux, especially since many Asian Americans have made substantial gains in economic terms and in social acceptance, to the point, perhaps, that they may eventually be accepted as culturally white. Patricia P. Chu leads us to consider this possibility with the question, "when will Asian Americans write as assimilated subjects, and when we do, what will it mean to write as an Asian American?" (2000, 189). Also see Glenn Omatsu (2000 [1993]); Tomo Hattori (1999); and Nguyen (2002). In any case, as the recent difficulties faced by the Taiwanese American nuclear scientist Wen Ho Lee and the campaign finance scandal that plagued Clinton's second term in office remind us, Asian American neoconservatives have a long way to go before they can stop proving to a disbelieving public their undiluted patriotism to the United States (Chuh and Shimakawa 2001, 1–5).

10   Personal discussion. I thank Hyungji Park for allowing me to use her insight in my essay. It also seems worthwhile for me to recall that when I was a gradeschool student in a white suburb of Detroit during the early 1980s, we boys used to call dog piles by a less benign name. We called them "nigger piles." On the significance of such racist terms for everyday practices, see David Roediger (1991), who recalls, "Even in an all-white town, race was never absent. I learned absolutely no lore of my German ancestry and no more than a few meaningless snatches of Irish songs, but missed little of racist folklore. Kids came to know the exigencies of change by chanting 'Eeny, meany, miney, mo/Catch the nigger by the toe' to decide teams and first batters in sport. We learned that life—and fights—were not always fair: 'Two against one, nigger's fun.' We learned not to loaf: 'Las one in is a nigger baby.' " (3).

11   Such people making, of course, is not an original concept. As Dominick LaCapra points out, "Moreover, on a somewhat different level, there has been an important tendency in modern culture and thought to convert trauma into the occasion for sublimity. . . . Even extremely destructive and disorienting events, such as the Holocaust or the dropping of the atomic bomb on Hiroshima and Nagasaki, may become occasions for negative sublimity or displaced sublimity. They may also give rise to what may be termed founding traumas—traumas that paradoxically become the valorized or intensely cathected basis of identity for an individual or a group rather than events that pose the problematic question of identity" (2001, 23). Traumatic historical events, in other words, entail two possi-

bilities. The first is the unraveling of identity, which we explored at some length in the previous chapter and which has been emphasized repeatedly in the critical literature (especially by figures such as Caruth 1996). The second is the formation of an identity, one that takes advantage of whatever unraveling might have occurred as the occasion for the founding of an alterier sense of selfhood. These two possibilities suggest that a person or a people who have been afflicted by a traumatic event may either remain psychically stuck in the wake of such an event, exhibiting the classic signs of post-traumatic stress disorder (see Herman 1992, 33–50) or, in seeking relief from such oppressive symptomology, construct (or reclaim) an identity that will allow a person or persons to reenter social existence.

12 For more information about the Harlins-Du case, see Cannon (1999, 108–120, 148–173) and Neil Gotanda (1996). Also see the documentary *Wet Sand: Voices from L.A. Ten Years Later* (2003) and *Twilight* (1994), both of which contain significant interviews regarding this case.

13 Kwang's speech echoes Elaine Kim's insistence made at the end of the riots that "Self-determination does not mean living alone. At least for now, that may mean mining the rich and haunted lode of Korean national consciousness while we struggle to understand how our fate is entwined with the fate of others lying prostrate before the triumphal procession of the winners of History" (1993, 230–231). Kim is clearly referring here to Walter Benjamin, when he writes, "Whoever has emerged victorious participates to this day in the triumphal procession in which the present rulers step over those who are lying prostrate. According to traditional practice, the spoils are carried along in the procession. They are called cultural treasures, and a historical materialist views them with caustic detachment, for without exception the cultural treasures he surveys have an origin which he cannot contemplate without horror. They owe their existence not only to the efforts of the great minds and talents who have created them, but also to the anonymous toil of their contemporaries" (1969, 256). This is also what I mean by a Benjaminian history; please see, as well, the introduction for another discussion on Benjamin's ideas about history. As Kim further makes clear in her essay, a notion of diaspora-as-nationalism is founded upon a series of disasters that has a specific name: "*Han* is a Korean word that means, loosely translated, the sorrow and anger that grow from the accumulated experiences of oppression" (1993, 215). This word *han*, then, is constitutive of the ontological state of being Korean. It refers to the way being Korean has been defined over a long period of time by the kinds of "sorrow and anger" the group has shared collectively, revealing that Kwang is not the only one to mark this kind of narrative. Also, see the introduction for my slightly idiosyncratic use of this term. In Kim's introduction to a groundbreaking collection of Korean-Angeleno oral histories, cowritten and coedited by Eui-young Yu, we find the link between a nationalism founded upon "accumulated experiences of oppression" and diaspora made firm: "Our purpose, in any case, is not to render Korean Americans transparent and knowable, but to open up spaces for engaging heterogeneities of many kinds, without losing sight of shared pain and common struggles. For us, bringing together many different narratives is not simply a call for Korean American visibility, but also a bid for Korean American participation in establishing the terms of that visibility" (1996, xxii).

14   According to Jennifer Lee:

> Although the use of rotating credit associations may not be as prevalent as the start-up phase, this resource is highly utilized in later stages of business. Rotating credit associations range in both membership size and value, with participation extending from only a few people to more than thirty, and the value of loans ranging from $100 to over $100,000 or more. Korean merchants report that the average *gae* [another transliteration of *ggeh*] includes ten to twenty people, with each member contributing $1,000 to $2,000 monthly into a pot totaling $10,000 to $40,000. Every member contributes to the fund, and each receives his or her share according to a predetermined schedule. (2002, 35)

As Lee goes on to point out, the availability of such capital for Korean American small business owners allows them to avoid the use of commercial lending agencies, which tend to require too much documentation and have a poor record of loaning money to minorities. Also, the association grants them access to money quickly during times of economic hardship, such as after a robbery. For African American small business owners, who have no access to such pools of money, any kind of economic hardship may easily lead to delinquency of bill payment, lack of funds to buy new merchandise, and a poorer credit rating.

15   At a panel convened at the Annual Meeting of the Modern Language Association held in San Diego, Calif., on 26–30 December 2003 (the panel was entitled "The Future of Asian American Literary Studies"), in which I was lucky enough to participate, James Kyung-Jin Lee and Yoonmee Chang made a compelling case for recognizing the incongruity between such a literary flowering and the social ground from which it springs. Lee asked us to consider the hard to consider: might such a literary flowering legitimize the unquestioned buildup of an "economy of death," one evinced in the imprisonment of so many people in the United States, the withdrawal of crucial social services by the state, the widening gap between poor and rich that is taking place globally, and the military mobilization of bombs and surveillance cameras and new fences that seem the logical extension of the President George H. W. Bush's "new world order"? What responsibilities do writers and critics have to explore connections that we might understandably prefer to deny?

Chang argued that when we acknowledge the apparent successes of Asian Americans, not only in literary but also in economic terms, we often find ourselves having to define success narrowly according to quantitative measures (as I did earlier in this chapter)—rates of college attendance, degree of family income and wealth, and prestige of commercial presses who print our works. Do such successes entail being mute about political and social matters, lest we be accused of being ingrates? Can we talk about culture, which many neoconservatives have demanded is more important than economics, without casting a suspicious glance at this often overused euphemism for racial difference and at the history of unequal access to the apparatuses of the state that make all of our lives possible? What these questions point to is the irony of our timing. Just at the moment when Asian Americans seem ready to claim a little of the ground that has for so long been denied us, in terms of shaping public discourse, we have gained this position exactly when entering public discourse makes us vulnerable, perhaps even complicit, with a state that increasingly exists to accelerate death rather than to encourage life.

EPILOGUE: BEARERS OF BAD NEWS

1   On the surface, the existence of *The White Boy Shuffle* seems to disprove my claim that the creative works inspired by the 1992 riots have almost uniformly been solemn in tone. Without a doubt, this is a hilarious novel and offers some of the most wonderfully utopian images of where interethnic cooperation can lead. The best example of this takes place about two-thirds of the way in, when Ms. Kim, the owner of a local small grocery store, is passing out Molotov cocktails and yelling, "Look, goddam it. You saw the video. Remember Latasha Harlins. Burn my fucking store down. I feel better. Rod-ney King! Rod-ney King! Rod-ney King!" The narrator continues:

> The crowd refused. Ms. Kim was too well liked. Maybe if she had been one hundred percent Korean they'd have busted a few windows just for appearance's sake. Holding one of her makeshift grenades, Ms. Kim lit the oil-rag fuse and strode to the front of the store. The crowd surged to stop her, and she held them at bay by waving the torch in their stunned faces. Then she wheeled and sent the bomb hurling through the glass doors. The flames slowly crawled across the floor, whipping through the aisles, then scaling the counter. Ms. Kim silently hook-shot another cocktail onto the roof and watched her store burn with a satisfied smile. A few folks tried to douse the flames with garden hoses, but Ms. Kim cut their hoses in half with a Swiss Army knife, then went looking for the police to place herself under arrest. (133)

By the end of the novel, however, the narrator has turned himself into an unwilling social messiah who preaches mass suicide as the only effective response to a repressive state power. The novel concludes with the narrator surrounded by many of his black followers encamped in a fictitious neighborhood of Los Angeles while the federal government threatens to kill them all if they don't quit threatening to kill themselves: "Congress passed a motion to quell our insurrection by issuing an ultimatum: rejoin the rest of America or celebrate Kwanzaa in hell. The response was to paint white concentric circles on the roofs of the neighborhood, so that from the air Hillside looks like one big target" (224). Such absurdity makes the reader laugh until it hurts.

2 Glazer worries: "If intermarriage is taken as key evidence for powerful assimilatory forces, then blacks are not subject to these forces to the same degree as others. Hispanic groups and Asian groups, despite the recency of immigration of so many of them, and thus the greater power of family and group attachment, show rates of intermarriage approaching the levels of Europeans. Blacks stand apart, with very low rates of intermarriage, rising slowly" (1997, 120). Arthur Schlesinger Jr., however, finds cheer in intermarriage rates in an otherwise bleak cultural climate: "Whatever their self-appointed spokesmen may claim, most American-born members of minority groups, white or nonwhite, while they may cherish particular heritages, still see themselves primarily as Americans and not primarily as Irish or Hungarian or Jews or Africans or Asians. A telling indicator is the rising rate of intermarriage across ethnic, religious, even (increasingly) racial lines. The belief in a unique American identity is far from dead" (1992, 19). Todd Gitlin provides figures that support this claim: "For all of America's racial antagonisms, the number of interracial couples rose by 535 percent between 1960 and 1980 to nearly 2 percent of all married couples; whereupon, in the following decade, according to preliminary analysis of the 1990 census, it rose again, to 2.7 percent. . . . Astonishingly, in 1986, outside the South, more than 10 percent of black men who married were marrying white women, up from 3.9 percent in 1968" (1995, 109).

David Hollinger similarly feels uplifted by the same figures, going so far as to claim, "Mixed race people are performing a historic role at the present moment: they are reanimating a traditional American emphasis on the freedom of affiliation, and they are confronting the American nation with its own continued reluctance to apply this principle to ethno-racial affiliations" (1995, 166). At the same time, as Halter observes, increased rates of intermarriage across all racial boundaries are leading to "a greater acceptance of the choice to claim more than one racial ancestry. People are beginning to feel less boxed in by the color line, since even on official documentation, it is no longer necessary to select only one racial designation" (2000, 171). There can be no doubting that all of these critics are pointing to an irrefutable social trend: the rate of intermarriage has increased dramatically in this country in the last two decades. But even as this has occurred, race continues to be a source of conflict. Perhaps what needs to be refuted here is the assumption that intermarriage automatically means the diminishment of racial prejudice. For to offer just one possibility, it should be obvious that someone married to a person of a different race can still remain a racist.

3 For more discussion on this understanding of multiculturalism as managed diversity, see especially Manning Marable (1995); Lisa Lowe (1996); George Sánchez (2000); and Avery Gordon and Christopher Newfield (1996). I thank James Kyung-Jin Lee for allowing me to read *Urban Triage: Race and the Fictions of Multiculturalism* (2004) before its publication. His brilliant analyses have helped me immensely to think about the rise of official multiculturalism during the Reagan years, its transformations into dominant policy in the 1990s, and its mixed legacies (greater minority representations at a time when whole urban communities in this country were being eviscerated). Also worth examining is Viajay Prashad (2002), who presents us with the notion of "polyculturalism" as an interesting alternative to notions of discrete, static, and autonomous multicultures.

4 Often, the end of the civil rights era is dated as corresponding to the shift from Martin Luther King Jr.'s activism on behalf of southern blacks in rural areas, to his activism on behalf of northern blacks in urban ghettoes. For instance, see Michael Dyson (2000). This shift was accompanied—so it is argued—by a white backlash, as more and more people perceived blacks through negative stereotypes, and as the intransigence of poverty, spatial segregation, and police misconduct gave rise to rioting and militant identity-based groups such as the Black Panthers. As Doris Kearns Goodwin observes,

> Nearly one-third of the whites interviewed [in a 1964 study] said they thought differently about Negroes now than before—they felt less regard and respect; the Negroes were demanding too much, going too far. This was not, the media said, a temporary downturn. It was, instead, "the end of the civil rights era." Initiative had passed from the leaders who had brought about the Civil Rights Act of '64 and the Voting Rights Act of '65—LBJ, Martin Luther King, Roy Wilkins, Whitney Young, Clarence Mitchell—to a new group of militants, young and angry blacks whose primary experience had been in the ghettoes of the North, where the gains of the sixties had barely penetrated. Or so the media claimed as it crowned the militant kings of the civil rights movement, summarily rejecting the old leaders as men of a forgotten age. From a later perspective, the media's image turns out to have been more myth than reality—studies indicate that even at the height of the radical activity, the old leaders still retained the overwhelming support of the Negro community. (1991 [1976], 304)

What was perhaps not overstated, however, was the turning tide of white opinion, never very charitable to begin with, against black attempts to find greater parity in access to housing, education, and jobs.

5   Lydia Chávez also reports in *The Color Bind: California's Battle to End Affirmative Action* (1998), a thorough journalistic account of the different political campaigns surrounding Proposition 209, that Camarena claimed she was denied admission into a remedial English class at San Bernardino Community College designed for African American students and could not get into a similar class designed for Latino students. College officials claim that these courses do not exclude students on the basis of race. Camarena was denied admission, according to the latter source, because she had not preregistered and because she had not taken a prerequisite; a similar course open to all students without prerequisites was also available at the same time block (216). Also worth noting in this context, black and Latino enrollment at colleges and universities actually witnessed a decline during the years when an end to affirmative action were first debated: "Black and Hispanic enrollments on college campuses, measured against high school graduation rates, declined by about 15 percent between 1976 and 1988, and then began to rise again, though by 1991 they had still not returned to the levels of 1976" (Gitlin 1995, 118).

6   Bruce Cumings provides a vivid example of this process at work: "As the intimation of American decline multiplied in the 1980s and early 1990s, so did nostalgia for the 1950s. Reagan was the first two-term president since Eisenhower. His smiling persona drew on Ike's public mastery, and Reganites made frank comparisons with that quintessentially Republican era. . . . Subsequently Newt Gingrich nominated 1955 as the year when the American Dream hit its apogee. The Korean War is errant counterpoint to these rosy memories, and so it vanishes" (2004, 5).

Works Cited

Abelmann, Nancy, and John Lie. 1995. *Blue Dreams: Korean Americans and the Los Angeles Riots*. Cambridge, Mass.: Harvard University Press.

Agamben, Giorgio. 1998 [1995]. *Homo Sacer: Sovereign Power and Bare Life*. Trans. Daniel Heller-Roazen. Stanford, Calif.: Stanford University Press.

Alexander, Elizabeth. 1994. " 'Can you be BLACK and look at this?': Reading the Rodney King Video(s)." In *Black Male: Representations of Masculinity in Contemporary American Art*, ed. Thelma Goldman. New York: Whitney Museum of American Art, 91–110.

Althusser, Louis. 1977. *For Marx*. Trans. Ben Brewster. London: New Left Review.

——. 1971. *Lenin and Philosophy and Other Essays*. Trans. Ben Brewster. New York: Monthly Review Press.

Ancheta, Angelo. 1998. *Race, Rights, and the Asian American Experience*. New Brunswick: Rutgers University Press.

Appadurai, Arjun. 1996. *Modernity at Large: Cultural Dimensions of Globalization*. Minneapolis: University of Minnesota Press.

Badkhen, Anna. 2001. "Russian Thumbs Are Down on U.S. Film: A Sub's Saviors Assail Hollywood Liberties." *Boston Globe*, 29 April, A11.

Baker, Houston. 1993. "Scene . . . Not Heard." In *Reading Rodney King, Reading Urban Uprising*, ed. Robert Gooding-Williams. New York: Routledge, 38–50.

Baldassare, Mark, ed. 1993. *The Los Angeles Riots: Lessons from the Urban Future*. Boulder, Colo.: Westview Press.

Ball, Kathryn. 2000. "Introduction: Trauma and Its Institutional Destinies." Special Issue: Trauma and Its Aftereffects. Guest ed. Kathryn Ball. *Cultural Critique* 46:1–44.

Ballard, J. G. 1973. *Crash*. New York: Farrar, Straus, and Giroux.

Banham, Reyner. 2001 [1971]. *Los Angeles: The Architecture of the Four Ecologies*. Berkeley: University of California Press.

Beatty, Paul. 1996. *The White Boy Shuffle*. Boston: Houghton-Mifflin.

Behar, Ruth. 1996. *The Vulnerable Observer: Anthropology That Breaks Your Heart*. Boston: Beacon Press.

Belluck, Pam. 1995. "Being of Two Cultures and Belonging to Neither: After an Acclaimed Novel, a Korean-American Writer Searches for His Roots." *New York Times*, 10 July, B1+.

Benjamin, Walter. 1969. *Illuminations: Essays and Reflections*. Trans. Harry Zohn. New York: Schocken.

Berlant, Lauren. 1997. *The Queen of America Goes to Washington: Essays on Sex and Citizenship*. Durham, N.C.: Duke University Press.

Berretinni, Mark. 2002. "Can 'We All' Get Along? Social Difference, the Future, and *Strange Days*." *Camera Obscura* 17:155–188.

Bloom, Allan. 1987. *The Closing of the American Mind: How Higher Education Has Failed Democracy and Impoverished the Souls of Today's Students*. New York: Simon and Schuster.

Bourdieu, Pierre. 1998. *Practical Reason: On the Theory of Action*. Trans. Randal Johnson. Stanford, Calif.: Stanford University Press.

——. 1993. *The Field of Cultural Production: Essays on Art and Literature*. Ed and Intro. Randal Johnson. New York: Columbia University Press.

Boym, Svetlana. 2001. *The Future of Nostalgia*. New York: Basic Books.

Bracken, Patrick, and Celia Petty, eds. 1998. *Rethinking the Trauma of War*. London: Free Association Books.

Bradbury, Ray. 1997 [1946]. *The Martian Chronicles*. New York: William Morrow.

Brown, Wendy. 2001. *Politics Out of History*. Princeton, N.J.: Princeton University Press.

——. 1995. *States of Injury: Power and Freedom in Late Modernity*. Princeton, N.J.: Princeton University Press.

Bukatman, Scott. 1993. *Terminal Identity: The Virtual Subject in Postmodern Science Fiction*. Durham, N.C.: Duke University Press.

Bush, George H. W. 1992. Presidential State of the Union Address. Web page visited 24 March 2004, printout on file with author.

Butler, Judith. 1997. *The Psychic Life of Power: Theories in Subjection*. Stanford, Calif.: Stanford University Press.

——. 1993. "Endangered/Endangering: Schematic Racism and White Paranoia." In *Reading Rodney King, Reading Urban Uprising*, ed. Robert Gooding-Williams. New York: Routledge, 15–22.

Butler, Octavia. 2000. *Parable of the Talents*. New York: Time Warner.

——. 1993. *Parable of the Sower*. New York: Time Warner.

Cannon, Lou. 1999. *Official Negligence: How Rodney King and the Riots Changed Los Angeles and the LAPD*. Boulder, Colo.: Westview Press.

Carr, Brian. 2002. "*Strange Days* and the Subject of Mobility." *Camera Obscura* 17:191–216.

Caruth, Cathy. 1996. *Unclaimed Experience: Trauma, Narrative, and History*. Baltimore: Johns Hopkins University Press.

——, ed. 1995. *Trauma: Explorations in Memory*. Baltimore: Johns Hopkins University Press.

Chang, Edward. 1999. "New Urban Crisis: Korean-African American Relations." In *Koreans in the Hood: Conflict with African Americans*, ed. Kwang Chun Kim. Baltimore: Johns Hopkins University Press, 39–59.

Chang, Edward, and Jeannette Diaz-Veizades. 1999. *Ethnic Peace in the American City: Building Community in Los Angeles and Beyond*. New York: New York University Press.

Chang, Leonard. 2004. *Fade to Kill*. New York: St. Martin's Press.

——. 2003. *Underkill*. New York: Thomas Dunne Books.

——. 2001. *Over the Shoulder*. New York: Ecco.

——. 1998. *Dispatches from the Cold*. New York: Black Heron Press.

——. 1996. *The Fruit N' Food*. New York: Black Heron Press.

Chavez, Leo. 2001. *Covering Immigration: Popular Images and the Politics of the Nation*. Berkeley: University of California Press.

Chávez, Lydia. 1998. *The Color Bind: California's Battle to End Affirmative Action*. Berkeley: University of California Press.

Chee, Alexander. 2001. *Edinburgh*. New York: Picador USA.

Chen, Tina. 2002. "Impersonation and Other Disappearing Acts in *Native Speaker* by Chang-rae Lee." *Modern Fiction Studies* 48:637–667.

Cheng, Anne Anlin. 2001. *The Melancholy of Race: Psychoanalysis, Assimilation, and Hidden Grief*. Oxford: Oxford University Press.

Choi, Chungmoo. 2001. "The Politics of War Memories toward Healing." In *Perilous Memories: The Asia-Pacific War(s)*, ed. T. Fujitani, Geoffrey White, and Lisa Yoneyama. Durham, N.C.: Duke University Press, 395–410.

Choi, Susan. 2003. *American Woman*. New York: HarperCollins.

——. 1998. *The Foreign Student*. New York: HarperFlamingo.

Chu, Patricia P. 2000. *Assimilating Asians: Gendered Strategies of Authorship in Asian America*. Durham, N.C.: Duke University Press.

Chuh, Kandice. 2003. *Imagine Otherwise: On Asian Americanist Critique*. Durham, N.C.: Duke University Press.

Chuh, Kandice, and Karen Shimakawa, eds. 2001. *Orientations: Mapping Studies in the Asian Diaspora*. Durham, N.C.: Duke University Press.

Cochran, Johnnie (with David Fisher). 2002. *A Lawyer's Life*. New York: St. Martin's Press, Thomas Dunne Books.

Cumings, Bruce. 2004. *North Korea: Another Country*. New York: New Press.

——. 1997. *Korea's Place in the Sun: A Modern History*. New York: Norton.

Cvetkovich, Ann. 2003. *An Archive of Feeling: Trauma, Sexuality, and Lesbian Public Cultures*. Durham, N.C.: Duke University Press.

Davis, Mike. 2002. *Dead Cities and Other Tales*. New York: New Press.

——. 2001. *Late Victorian Holocaust: El Niño Famines and the Making of the Third World*. London: Verso.

——. 1998. *Ecology of Fear: Los Angeles and the Imagination of Disaster*. New York: Metropolitan.

——. 1993. "Uprising and Repression in L.A.: An Interview with Mike Davis by the

CovertAction Information Bulletin." In *Reading Rodney King, Reading Urban Uprising*, ed. Robert Gooding-Williams. New York: Routledge, 142–156.

———. 1992a. *L.A. Was Just the Beginning*. Westfield, N.J.: Open Magazine Pamphlet Series.

———. 1992b [1990]. *City of Quartz: Excavating the Future in Los Angeles*. New York: Random House, Vintage.

———. 1986. *Prisoners of the American Dream: Politics and Economy in the History of the U.S. Working Class*. London: Verso.

Dooner, P. W. 1978 [1879]. *Last Days of the Republic*. New York: Arno Press.

Dousset, Bénédicte, Pierre Flamen, and Robert Bernstein. 1993. "Los Angeles Fires Seen from Space." *Eos* 74:33, 37–38.

Duany, Andres, Elizabeth Plater-Zyberk, and Jeff Speck. 2000. *Suburban Nation: The Rise of Sprawl and the Decline of the American Dream*. New York: North Point Press.

Duggan, Lisa. 2003. *The Twilight of Equality? Neoliberalism, Cultural Politics, and the Attack on Democracy*. Boston: Beacon Press.

Dumm, Thomas. 1999. *A Politics of the Ordinary*. New York: New York University Press.

———. 1993. "The New Enclosures: Racism in the Normalized Community." In *Reading Rodney King, Reading Urban Uprising*, ed. Robert Gooding-Williams. New York: Routledge, 178–195.

Dyson, Michael. 2000. *I May Not Get There with You: The True Martin Luther King, Jr.* New York: Simon and Schuster, Touchstone.

Ehrenreich, Barbara. 2001. *Nickel and Dimed: On (Not) Getting By in America*. New York: Henry Holt.

Eng, David. 2001. *Racial Castration: Managing Masculinity in Asian America*. Durham, N.C.: Duke University Press.

Eng, David, and Alice Hom. 1998. *Q&A: Queer in Asian America*. Philadelphia: Temple University Press.

Eng, David, and Shinhee Han. 2000. "A Dialogue on Racial Melancholia." *Psychoanalytic Dialogues* 10:667–700.

Farrell, Kirby. 1998. *Post-traumatic Culture: Injury and Interpretation in the Nineties*. Baltimore: Johns Hopkins University Press.

Feffer, John. 2003. *North Korea/South Korea: U.S. Policy at a Time of Crisis*. New York: Seven Stories Press.

Fenkl, Heinz Insu. 1996. *Memories of My Ghost Brother*. New York: Plume.

Freud, Sigmund. 1917. "Mourning and Melancholia." *Standard Edition* 14:243–258.

Fulton, William. 1997. *The Reluctant Metropolis: The Politics of Urban Growth in Los Angeles*. Point Area, Calif.: Solano Press Books.

Garreau, Joel. 1991. *Edge City: Life on the New Frontier*. New York: Doubleday.

Gilmore, Ruth Wilson. 1998/1999. "Globalisation and U.S. Prison Growth: From Military Keynesianism to Post-Keynesian Militarism." *Race and Class* 40:171–188.

Gilroy, Paul. 2000. *Against Race: Imagining Political Culture beyond the Color Line.* Cambridge, Mass.: Harvard University Press.

Gitlin, Todd. 1995. *The Twilight of Common Dreams: Why America Is Wracked by Culture Wars.* New York: Henry Holt, Metropolitan.

Gladstone, David, and Susan Fainstein. 2003. "The New York and Los Angeles Economics." In *New York and Los Angeles: Politics, Society, and Culture, A Comparative View*, ed. David Halle. Chicago: University of Chicago Press, 79–98.

Glazer, Nathan. 1997. *We Are All Multiculturalists Now.* Cambridge, Mass.: Harvard University Press.

Glionna, John. 1998. "A Murder That Woke up L.A." *Los Angeles Times*, 30 January, A1+.

Goldberg, Jeffrey. 1995. "The Soul of the New Koreans." *New York Magazine*, 10 April, 43–51.

Gooding-Williams, Robert, ed. 1993. *Reading Rodney King, Reading Urban Uprising.* New York: Routledge.

Goodwin, Doris Kearns. 1991 [1976]. *Lyndon Johnson and the American Dream.* New York: St. Martin's Press.

Gordon, Avery. 1997. *Ghostly Matters: Haunting and the Sociological Imagination.* Minneapolis: University of Minnesota Press.

Gordon, Avery, and Christopher Newfield, eds. 1996. *Mapping Multiculturalism.* Minneapolis: University of Minnesota Press.

Gormley, Paul. 2003. "The Affective City: Urban Black Bodies and Milieu in *Menace II Society* and *Pulp Fiction*." In *Screening the City*, ed. Mark Shiel and Tony Fitzmaurice. London: Verso, 180–199.

Gotanda, Neil. 1996. "Multiculturalism and Racial Stratification." In *Mapping Multiculturalism*, ed. Avery Gordon and Christopher Newfield. Minneapolis: University of Minnesota Press, 238–252.

Gutiérrez-Jones, Carl. 2001. *Critical Race Narratives: A Study of Race, Rhetoric, and Injury.* New York: New York University Press.

Hagedorn, Jessica. 2003. *Dream Jungle.* New York: Viking.

Halle, David, ed. 2003. *New York and Los Angeles: Politics, Society, and Culture: A Comparative View.* Chicago: University of Chicago Press.

Halter, Marilyn. 2000. *Shopping for Identity: The Marketing of Ethnicity.* New York: Random House, Schocken.

Hamilton, Nora, and Norma Stoltz Chinchilla. 2001. *Seeking Community in a Global City: Guatemalans and Salvadoran in Los Angeles.* Philadelphia: Temple University Press.

Hardt, Michael, and Antonio Negri. 2000. *Empire.* Cambridge, Mass.: Harvard University Press.

Hartman, Saidiya. 1997. *Scenes of Subjection: Terror, Slavery, and Self-Making in Nineteenth-Century America*. New York: Oxford University Press.

Harvey, David. 1990. *The Condition of Postmodernity: An Enquiry into the Origins of Cultural Change*. Cambridge, Mass.: Blackwell.

Hattori, Tomo. 1999. "Model Minority Discourse and Asian American Jouis-Sense." *differences* 11:228–247.

Hazen, Dan, ed. 1992. *Inside the L.A. Riots: What Really Happened—and Why It Will Happen Again*. New York: Institute for Alternative Journalism.

Heidegger, Martin. 1962. *Being and Time*. Trans. John Macquarrie and Edward Robinson. San Francisco: HarperSanFrancisco.

Herbert, Steve. 1997. *Policing Space: Territoriality and the Los Angeles Police Department*. Minneapolis: University of Minnesota Press.

Herman, Judith. 1992. *Trauma and Recovery: The Aftermath of Violence—from Domestic Abuse to Political Terror*. New York: Basic Books.

Herrnstein, Richard, and Charles Murray. 1994. *The Bell Curve: Intelligence and Class Structure in American Life*. New York: Free Press.

Hing, Bill Ong. 1993. *Making and Remaking Asian America through Immigration Policy, 1850–1990*. Stanford, Calif.: Stanford University Press.

Hise, Greg. 1997. *Magnetic Los Angeles: Planning the Twentieth-Century Metropolis*. Baltimore: Johns Hopkins University Press.

Hollinger, David. 1995. *Postethnic America: Beyond Multiculturalism*. New York: Basic Books.

Honig, Bonnie. 2001. *Democracy and the Foreigner*. Princeton, N.J.: Princeton University Press.

Horne, Gerald. 1997. *Fire This Time: The Watts Uprising and the 1960s*. New York: Da Capo Press.

Howell, David. 2002. "Increasing Earning Inequality and Unemployment in Developed Countries: Markets, Institutions, and 'Unified Theory.'" Center for Economic Policy Analysis (CEPA) the New School for Social Research, Working Papers Series, January, revised. Web page visited 9 January 2005, printout on file with author.

Huntington, Samuel. 1996. *The Clash of Civilizations: Remaking of Word Order*. New York: Simon and Schuster, Touchstone.

Independent Commission on the Los Angeles Police Department. 1991. Report. 9 July.

Jameson, Fredric. 1991. *Postmodernism, or, the Cultural Logic of Late Capitalism*. Durham, N.C.: Duke University Press.

——. 1984. "Postmodernism, or the Cultural Logic of Late Capitalism." *New Left Review* 146:53–92.

Jamison, Kay Redfield. 1999. *Night Falls Fast: Understanding Suicide*. New York: Knopf.

Johnson, James, Walter Farrell, and Jennifer Stoloff. 2000. "African American Males in Decline: A Los Angeles Case Study." In *Prismatic Metropolis: Inequality in Los Angeles*, ed. Lawrence Bobo, Melvin Oliver, James Johnson, and Abel Valenzuela. New York: Sage, 315–337.

Jones, Jacqueline. 1992. *The Dispossessed: America's Underclasses from the Civil War to the Present*. New York: Basic Books.

Jones, Robert. 1999. "The Truth Squad of History." *Los Angeles Times*, 10 January, B1+.

Jurca, Catherine. 2001. *White Diaspora: The Suburbs and the Twentieth-Century American Novel*. Princeton, N.J.: Princeton University Press.

Kadohata, Cynthia. 1992. *In the Heart of the Valley of Love*. New York: Viking.

——. 1989. *The Floating World*. New York: Viking.

Kadoudaki, Despina. 2002. "Spectacles of History: Race Relations, Melodrama, and the Science Fiction / Disaster Film." *Camera Obscura* 17:109–152.

Kang, Younghill. 1997 [1937]. *East Goes West*. New York: Kaya.

——. 1931. *The Grass Roof*. New York: Scribner's.

Keisaburô, Toyonaga. 2001. "Colonialism and Atom Bombs about Survivors of Hiroshima Living in Korea." In *Perilous Memories: The Asia-Pacific War(s)*, ed. T. Fujitani, Geoffrey White, and Lisa Yoneyama. Durham, N.C.: Duke University Press, 378–394.

Keller, Nora Okja. 2002. *Fox Girl*. New York: Viking.

——. 1997. *Comfort Woman*. New York: Penguin.

Kelley, Robin. 2000. "'Slangin' Rocks . . . Palestinian Style': Dispatches from the Occupied Zones of North America." In *Police Brutality: An Anthology*, ed. Jill Nelson. New York: Norton, 21–59.

Kich, Martin. 2000. "Chang-rae Lee." In *Asian American Novelists*, ed. Emmanuel Nelson. Westport, Conn.: Greenwood Press, 175–179.

Kim, Claire Jean. 2000. *Bitter Fruit: The Politics of Black-Korean Conflict in New York City*. New Haven, Conn.: Yale University Press.

Kim, Elaine. 1997. "Korean American Literature." In *An Interethnic Companion to Asian American Literature*, ed. King-Kok Cheung. New York: Cambridge University Press, 156–191.

——. 1993. "Home Is Where the *Han* Is: A Korean-American Perspective on the Los Angeles Upheavals." In *Reading Rodney King, Reading Urban Uprising*, ed. Robert Gooding-Williams. New York: Routledge, 215–235.

Kim, Elaine, and Laura Hyun Yi Kang. 2003. *Echoes Upon Echoes: New Korean American Writings*. Philadelphia: Temple University Press-Asian American Writers Workshop.

Kim, Elaine, and Eui-Young Yu, eds. 1996. *East to America: Korean American Life Stories*. New York: New Press.

Kim, Kwang Chung, ed. 1999. *Koreans in the Hood: Conflict with African Americans*. Baltimore: Johns Hopkins University Press.

Kim, Kwang Chung, and Shin Kim. 1999. "The Multiracial Nature of the Los Angeles Unrest of 1992." In *Koreans in the Hood: Conflict with African Americans*, ed. Kwang Chung Kim. Baltimore: Johns Hopkins University Press, 17–38.

Kim, Min-Jung. 1997. "Moments of Danger in the (Dis)continuous Relation of Korean Nationalism and Korean American Nationalism." *positions: east asian cultures critique* 5:357–389.

Kim, Patti. 1998. *A Cab Called Reliable*. New York: St. Martin's Press.

Kim, Suki. 2003. *The Interpreter*. New York: Farrar, Strauss, Giroux.

Kingston, Maxine Hong. 2003. *The Fifth Book of Peace*. New York: Knopf.

——. 1989 [1975]. *The Woman Warrior: Memoirs of a Girlhood Among Ghosts*. New York: Vintage-Random House.

Klein, Norman. 1997. *The History of Forgetting: Los Angeles and the Erasure of Memory*. London: Verso.

Klinenberg, Eric. 2002. *Heat Wave: A Social Autopsy of Disaster in Chicago*. Chicago: University of Chicago Press.

Klinkenborg, Verlyn. 1995. "Witness to Strangeness, Espionage Is Only One of a Korean-American Hero's Secrets." *New Yorker*, 10 July, 76–77.

Kondo, Dorinne. 1996. "Shades of Twilight: Anna Deavere Smith and *Twilight: Los Angeles 1992*." In *Connected: Engagements with Media (Late Editions 3)*, ed. George Marcus. Chicago: University of Chicago Press, 313–346.

Koo, Hagan. 2001. *Korean Workers: The Culture and Politics of Class Formation*. Ithaca, N.Y.: Cornell University Press.

Kristeva, Julia. 1992. *Black Sun*. Trans. Leon S. Roudiez. New York: Columbia University Press.

——. 1991. *Strangers to Ourselves*. Trans. Leon S. Roudiez. New York: Columbia University Press.

——. 1982. *The Powers of Horror: An Essay on Abjection*. Trans. Leon S. Roudiez. New York: Columbia University Press.

Krugman, Paul. 2002. "For Richer." *New York Times*, 20 October, sec. 6, 62+.

Kübler-Ross, Elizabeth. 1969. *On Death and Dying: What the Dying Have to Teach Doctors, Nurses, Clergy, and Their Own Families*. New York: Touchstone Books.

LA 2000: A City for the Future. 1988. Final Report of the Los Angeles 2000 Committee. Los Angeles.

LaCapra, Dominick. 2001. *Writing History, Writing Trauma*. Baltimore: Johns Hopkins University Press.

La Ferla, Ruth. 2003. "Generation E.A.: Ethnically Ambiguous." *New York Times*, 28 December, 9.1+.

Lahiri, Jhumpa. 2003. *The Namesake*. New York: Houghton Mifflin.

Lanzmann, Claude. 1995. "The Obscenity of Understanding: An Evening with Claude Lanzmann." In *Trauma: Explorations in Memory*, ed. Cathy Caruth. Baltimore: Johns Hopkins University Press, 200–220.

Lawrence, Regina. 2000. *The Politics of Force: Media and the Construction of Police Brutality*. Berkeley: University of California Press.

Lee, Chang-rae. 2004. *Aloft*. New York: Penguin, Riverhead.

——. 1999. *A Gesture Life*. New York: Penguin, Riverhead.

——. 1995. *Native Speaker*. New York: Penguin, Riverhead.

Lee, Don. 2004. *Country of Origin*. New York: Norton.

——. 2001. *Yellow*. New York: Norton.

Lee, James Kyung-Jin. 2004. *Urban Triage: Race and the Fictions of Multiculturalism*. Minneapolis: University of Minnesota Press.

Lee, Jennifer. 2002. *Civility in the City: Blacks, Jews, and Koreans in Urban America*. Cambridge, Mass.: Harvard University Press.

Lee, Rachel. 1999. *The Americas of Asian American Literature*. Princeton, N.J.: Princeton University Press.

lê thi diem thúy. 2003. *The Gangster We Are All Looking For*. New York: Knopf.

Leys, Ruth. 2000. *Trauma: A Genealogy*. Chicago: University of Chicago Press.

Li, David Leiwei. 1998. *Imagining the Nation: Asian American Literature and Cultural Consent*. Stanford, Calif.: Stanford University Press.

Lipsitz, George. 2001. " 'To Tell the Truth and Not Get Trapped': Why Interethnic Antiracism Matters Now." In *Orientations: Mapping Studies in the Asian Diaspora*, ed. Kandice Chu and Karen Shimakawa. Durham, N.C.: Duke University Press, 296–310.

——. 1998. *The Possessive Investment in Whiteness: How White People Profit from Identity Politics*. Philadelphia: Temple University Press.

Liu, John, and Lucie Cheng. 1994. "Pacific Rim Development and the Duality of Post-1965 Asian Immigration to the United States." In *The New Asian Immigration in Los Angeles and Global Restructuring*, ed. Paul Ong, Edna Bonacich, and Lucie Cheng. Philadelphia: Temple University Press, 74–99.

López-Garza, Marta, and David Diaz, eds. 2001. *Asians and Latino Immigrants in a Restructuring Economy: The Metamorphosis of Southern California*. Stanford, Calif.: Stanford University Press.

Los Angeles Times. 1992. *Understanding the Riots: Los Angeles before and after the Rodney King Case*. Los Angeles: Los Angeles Times.

Lowe, Lisa. 1996. *Immigrant Acts: On Asian American Cultural Politics*. Durham, N.C.: Duke University Press.

Luibhéid, Ethne. 2002. *Entry Denied: Controlling Sexuality at the Border*. Minneapolis: University of Minnesota Press.

——. 1997. "The 1965 Immigration and Nationality Act: The 'End' of Exclusion?" *positions: east asian cultures critique* 5:501–522.

Mabhubati, Haki, ed. 1993. *Why L.A. Happened: Implications of the '92 Los Angeles Rebellion*. Chicago: Third World Press.

Marable, Manning. 1995. *Beyond Black and White: Transforming African-American Politics*. London: Verso.

Mbembe, Achille. 2003. "Necropolitics." *Public Culture* 15:11–40.

McWilliams, Carey. 1983 [1946]. *Southern California: An Island on the Land*. Salt Lake City: Peregrine Smith Books.

Min, Pyong Gap. 1996. *Caught in the Middle: Korean Merchants in America's Multi-ethnic Cities*. Berkeley: University of California Press.

Mishel, Lawrence, Jared Bernstein, and John Schmitt. 2001. *The State of Working America, 2001/2002*. Ithaca, N.Y.: Cornell University Press.

Modleski, Tania. 1997. "Doing Justice to the Subjects: Mimetic Art in a Multicultural Society. The Work of Anna Deavere Smith." In *Female Subjects in Black and White: Race, Psychoanalysis, Feminism*, ed. Elizabeth Abel, Barbara Christian, and Helen Moglen. Berkeley: University of California Press, 57–76.

Mosley, Walter. 1994. *Black Betty*. New York: Simon and Schuster, Pocket.

——. 1992. *White Butterfly*. New York: Simon and Schuster, Pocket.

——. 1991. *A Red Death*. New York: Simon and Schuster, Pocket.

——. 1990. *Devil in a Blue Dress*. New York: Simon and Schuster, Pocket.

Murray, Charles. 1994 [1984]. *Loosing Ground: American Social Policy, 1950–1980*. 2nd ed. New York: BasicBooks.

Nelson, Jill, ed. 2000. *Police Brutality: An Anthology*. New York: Norton.

Nguyen, Viet Thanh. 2002. *Race and Resistance: Literature and Politics in Asian America*. New York: Oxford University Press.

Noble, Marianne. 2000. *The Masochistic Pleasures of Sentimental Literature*. Princeton, N.J.: Princeton University Press.

Oberdorfer, Don. 1997. *The Two Koreas: A Contemporary History*. New York: Basic Books.

Oh, Seiwoong. 2003/2004. "*Hansu's Journey* by Philip Jaisohn: The First Fiction in English from Korean America." *Amerasia* 29:43–55.

Oliver, Melvin, and Thomas Shapiro. 1995. *Black Wealth / White Wealth*. New York: Routledge.

Omatsu, Glenn. 2000 [1993]. "The 'Four Prisons' and the Movements of Liberation: Asian American Activism from the 1960s." In *Asian American Studies: A Reader*, ed. Jean Wu and Min Song. New Brunswick, N.J.: Rutgers University Press, 164–198.

Omi, Michael, and Howard Winant. 1994. *Racial Formation in the United States: From the 1960 to the 1990s*. 2nd ed. New York: Routledge.

Pak, Gary. 1998. *A Ricepaper Airplane*. Honolulu: University of Hawai'i Press.

Park, Edward. 2001a. "Community Divided: Korean American Politics in Post-civil Unrest Los Angeles." In *Asians and Latino Immigrants in a Restructuring Economy: The Metamorphosis of Southern California*, ed. Marta López-Garza and David Diaz. Stanford, Calif.: Stanford University Press, 273–288.

——. 2001b. "The Impact of Mainstream Political Mobilization on Asian American Communities: The Case of Korean Americans in Los Angeles, 1992–1998." In

Asian Americans and Politics: Perspectives, Experiences, Prospects, ed. Gordon
  Chang. Washington, D.C.: Woodrow Wilson Press, 285–310.

Park, Frances. 2000. *When My Sister Was Cleopatra Moon*. New York: Hyperion.

Park, Kyeyoung. 1999. "Use and Abuse of Race and Culture: Black-Korean Tension in
  America." In *Koreans in the Hood: Conflict with African Americans*, ed. Kwang
  Chung Kim. Baltimore: Johns Hopkins University Press, 60–74.

———. 1997. *The Korean American Dream: Immigrants and Small Business in New York
  City*. Ithaca, N.Y.: Cornell University Press.

Park, You-me, and Gayle Wald. 1998. "Native Daughters in the Promised Land: Gender, Race, and the Question of Separate Spheres." *American Literature* 70:607–635.

Pastor, Manuel. 2001. "Economics and Ethnicity: Poverty, Race, and Immigration in
  Los Angeles County." In *Asians and Latino Immigrants in a Restructuring Econ-
  omy: The Metamorphosis of Southern California*, ed. Marta López-Garza and
  David Diaz. Stanford, Calif.: Stanford University Press, 102–138.

Pavey, Ruth. 1995. "Scabrous Mouthfuls." *The New Statesman and Society*, 25 August,
  32.

Phelan, Peggy. 1997. *Mourning Sex: Performing Public Memories*. London: Routledge.

Phillips, Gary. 1994. *Violent Spring*. Portland, Ore.: West Coast Crime.

Portman, Jamie. 1995. "Strange Days for a Female Director under Attack for Her
  Style: Kathryn Bigelow Comes under Fire for Her Gruesome Use of Film Violence." *Vancouver Sun*, 25 October, C5.

Prashad, Viajay. 2002. *Everybody Was Kung Fu Fighting: Afro-Asian Connections and
  the Myth of Cultural Purity*. Boston: Beacon.

———. 2000. *The Karma of Brown Folk*. Minneapolis: University of Minnesota Press.

Putnam, Robert. 2000. *Bowling Alone: The Collapse and Revival of American Community*. New York: Simon and Schuster.

Reimers, David. 1992 [1985]. *Still the Gold Door: The Third World Comes to America*.
  2nd ed. New York: Columbia University Press.

Rieff, David. 1991. *Los Angeles: Capitol of the Third World*. New York: Simon and
  Schuster.

Robbins, Bruce. 1999. *Feeling Global: Internationalism in Distress*. New York: New
  York University Press.

Rodriguez, Luis. 1993. *Always Running, La Vida Loca: Gang Days in L.A.* New York:
  Touchstone.

Roediger, David. 1991. *The Wages of Whiteness: Race and the Making of the American
  Working Class*. London: Verso.

Rogin, Michael. 1998. *Independence Day, or How I Learned to Stop Worrying and Love
  the Enola Gay*. London: British Film Institute.

Rohrlich, Ted. 1999. "Seer of L.A., or Blinded by Its Light? Can *Ecology of Fear* Author
  Mike Davis, with His Taste for Hyperbole, Be Believed? The Answer is Maybe as a
  Polemicist, but Not as a Historian." *Los Angeles Times*, 13 April, A1.

Rorty, Richard. 1998. *Achieving Our Country: Leftist Thought in Twentieth-Century America*. Cambridge, Mass.: Harvard University Press.

Rosaldo, Renato. 1993 [1989]. *Culture and Truth: The Remaking of Social Analysis*. Boston: Beacon Press.

Sánchez, George. 2000. "Creating the Multicultural Nation: Adventures in Post-nationalist American Studies in the 1990s." In *Post-nationalist American Studies*, ed. John Carlos Ransom. Berkeley: University of California Press, 40–58.

Sanders, Catherine. 1999. *Grief, The Mourning After: Dealing with Adult Bereavement*. 2nd ed. New York: John Wiley and Sons.

Sanz, Cynthia. 1999. "Riot Victim Denny Bears Scars but No Bitterness." *People*, 15 March, 233.

Sassen, Saskia. 2000. *The Global City: New York, London, Tokyo*. 2nd ed. Princeton, N.J.: Princeton University Press.

Scarry, Elaine. 1985. *The Body in Pain: The Making and Unmaking of the World*. New York: Oxford University Press.

Schiesl, Martin. 1991. "Designing the Model Community: The Irvine Company and Suburban Development, 1950–88." In *Postsuburban California: The Transformation of Orange County since World War II*, ed. Rob Klin, Spencer Olin, and Mark Poster. Berkeley: University of California Press, 55–91.

Schlesinger, Arthur, Jr. 1992. *The Disuniting of America*. New York: Norton.

Scott, Allen J. 1996. "The Manufacturing Economy: Ethnic and Gender Divisions of Labor." In *Ethnic Los Angeles*, ed. Roger Waldinger and Mehdi Bozorghmehr. New York: Sage, 215–244.

Scott, Allen J., and Edward W. Soja, eds. 1996. *The City: Los Angeles and Urban Theory at the End of the Twentieth Century*. Berkeley: University of California Press.

Seltzer, Mark. 1998. *Serial Killers: Death and Life in America's Wound Culture*. New York: Routledge.

Sen, Amartya. 1999. *Development as Freedom*. New York: Random House, Anchor.

Shah, Nayan. 2001. *Contagious Divides: Epidemics and Race in San Francisco's Chinatown*. Berkeley: University of California Press.

Shankar, Lavina Dhangra, and Rajini Srikanth, ed. 1998. *A Part, Yet Apart: South Asians in Asian America*. Philadelphia: Temple University Press.

Shiel, Mark, and Tony Fitzmaurice, eds. 2003. *Screening the City*. London: Verso.

Shimakawa, Karen. 2002. *National Abjection: The Asian American Body Onstage*. Durham, N.C.: Duke University Press.

Shipler, David. 2004. *The Working Poor: Invisible in America*. New York: Knopf.

Silko, Leslie Marmon. 1991. *Almanac of the Dead*. New York: Penguin.

Silverman, Kaja. 2000. *World Spectators*. Stanford, Calif.: Stanford University Press.

——. 1996. *The Threshold of the Visible World*. New York: Routledge.

——. 1992. *Male Subjectivity at the Margins*. New York: Routledge.

Skerry, Peter. 1993. *Mexican Americans: The Ambivalent Minority*. New York: Free Press.

Smith, Anna Deavere. 2000. *Talk to Me: Travels in Media and Politics*. New York: Anchor.

——. 1994. *Twilight: Los Angeles, 1992*. New York: Anchor.

——. 1993. *Fires in the Mirror: Crown Heights, Brooklyn and Other Identities*. New York: Anchor.

Smith, Paul. 1997. *Millennial Dreams: Contemporary Culture and Capital in the North*. London: Verso.

Song, Min Hyoung. 2004. "*Sa-I-Gu* Revisited: An Interview with Elaine Kim." *Amerasia* 30:229–42.

Stephenson, Neal. 1992. *Snow Crash*. New York: Bantam.

Stewart, Susan. 1993. *On Longing: Narratives of the Miniature, the Gigantic, the Souvenir, the Collection*. Durham, N.C.: Duke University Press.

Stout, Mira. 1998. *One Thousand Chestnut Trees: A Novel of Korea*. New York: Riverhead.

Su, Julie, and Chanchanit Martorell. 2001. "Exploitation and Abuse in the Garment Industry: The Case of the Thai Slave-Labor Compound in El Monte." In *Asians and Latino Immigrants in a Restructuring Economy: The Metamorphosis of Southern California*, ed. Marta López-Garza and David Diaz. Stanford, Calif.: Stanford University Press, 21–45.

Sugrue, Thomas. 1996. *The Origins of the Urban Crisis: Race and Inequality in Postwar Detroit*. Princeton, N.J.: Princeton University Press.

Tal, Kalí. 1996. *Worlds of Hurt: Reading the Literature of Trauma*. New York: Cambridge University Press.

Tölölyan, Khachig. 1996. "Rethinking Diaspora(s): Stateless Power in the Transnational Moment." *Diaspora* 5:3–37.

Totten, George O., and H. Eric Schockman, eds. 1994. *Community in Crisis: The Korean American Community after the Los Angeles Civil Unrest of April 1992*. Los Angeles: Center for Multiethnic and Transnational Studies, University of Southern California.

Truong, Monique. 2003. *The Book of Salt*. New York: Houghton Mifflin.

Valle, Victor, and Rodolfo Torres. 2000. *Latino Metropolis*. Minneapolis: University of Minnesota Press.

van der Kolk, Bessel, and Otto van der Hart. 1995. "The Intrusive Past: The Flexibility of Memory and the Engraving of Trauma." In *Trauma: Explorations in Memory*, ed. Cathy Caruth. Baltimore: Johns Hopkins University Press, 158–182.

Wallerstein, Immanuel. 2003. *The Decline of American Power*. New York: New Press.

Weinstein, Richard S. 1996. "The First American City." In *The City: Los Angeles and*

Urban Theory at the End of the Twentieth Century, ed. Allen J. Scott and Edward W. Soja. Berkeley: University of California Press, 22–46.

Williams, Raymond. 1961. *The Long Revolution*. New York: Columbia University Press.

Williams, Rhonda. 1993. "Accumulation as Evisceration: Urban Rebellion and the New Growth Dynamics." In *Reading Rodney King, Reading Urban Uprising*, ed. Robert Gooding-Williams. New York: Routledge, 82–96.

Wilson, William Julius. 1996. *When Work Disappears: The World of the New Urban Poor*. New York: Vintage-Random House.

Winant, Howard. 1994. *Racial Conditions: Politics, Theory, Comparisons*. Minneapolis: University of Minnesota Press.

Wingrove, David. 1990. *Chung Kuo: The Middle Kingdom*. New York: Dell.

Wolfe, Alan. 2003. *An Intellectual in Public*. Ann Arbor: University of Michigan Press.

Woods, Paula. 1999. *Inner City Blues*. New York: Ballantine, One World.

Woolf, Virginia. 1978 [1950]. *The Captain's Death Bed and Other Essays*. New York: Harcourt, Brace, Jovanovich; Harvest.

Yamashita, Karen Tei. 1997. *Tropic of Orange*. Minneapolis: Coffee House Press.

——. 1990. *Through the Arc of the Rain Forest*. Minneapolis: Coffee House Press.

Yates, Michael. 2003. *Naming the System: Inequality and Work in the Global Economy*. New York: Monthly Review Press.

Young, Allan. 1995. *The Harmony of Illusions: Inventing Post-traumatic Stress Disorder*. Princeton, N.J.: Princeton University Press.

Yu, Eui-Young, ed. 1994. *Black-Korean Encounter: Toward Understanding and Alliance. Dialogue between Black and Korean Americans in the Aftermath of the 1992 Los Angeles Riots. A Two-Day Symposium, May 22–23, 1992*. Los Angeles: Institute for Asian Pacific American Studies, California State University.

Yu, Eui-Young, and Peter Choe. 2003/2004. "Korean Population in the United States as Reflected in the Year 2000 U.S. Census." *Amerasia* 29:2–22.

Yun, Mia. 1998. *House of the Winds*. New York: Penguin.

Filmography

2001: A Space Odyssey. 1968, Stanley Kubrick. 139 minutes.

Another America. 1996, Michael Cho. 56 minutes.

Bad Lieutenant. 1992, Abel Ferrera. 96 minutes.

Blade Runner. 1982, Ridley Scott. 118 minutes. Based on the novel, *Do Androids Dream of Electric Sheep?* by Philip K. Dick.

Blue Steel. 1990, Kathryn Bigelow. 102 minutes.

Boyz N the Hood. 1991, John Singleton. 107 minutes.

Colors. 1988, Dennis Hopper. 120 minutes.

Dark Blue. 2002, Ron Shelton. 118 minutes.

Deep Impact. 1998, Mimi Leder. 120 minutes.

The Exorcist. 1973, William Freidkin. 122 minutes.

Falling Down. 1993, Joel Schumacher. 113 minutes.

The Game of Their Lives. 2003, Dan Gordon. Unknown minutes.

Homes Apart. 1991, J. T. Takagi. 55 minutes.

Independence Day. 1996, Roland Emmerich. 145 minutes.

Invasion of the Body Snatchers. 1956, Don Siegal. 80 minutes.

K-19: The Widow Maker. 2002, Kathryn Bigelow. 138 minutes.

Kids. 1995, Larry Clark. 91 minutes.

The Matrix. 1999, Andy and Larry Wachowski. 136 minutes.

The Matrix Reloaded. 2003, Andy and Larry Wachowski. 138 minutes.

The Matrix Revolutions. 2003, Andy and Larry Wachowski. 129 minutes.

Menace II Society. 1993, Allen and Albert Hughes. 104 minutes.

Near Dark. 1987, Kathryn Bigelow. 95 minutes.

The Peacemaker. 1997, Mimi Leder. 124 minutes.

Point Break. 1991, Kathryn Bigelow. 122 minutes.

Rashomon. 1950, Akira Kurosawa. 88 minutes. Japanese with subtitles.

Safe. 1995, Todd Haynes. 119 minutes.

Sa-I-Gu: From Korean Women's Perspective. 1993, Dai Sil Kim-Gibson. 36 minutes.

The Sixth Sense. 1999, M. Night Shyamalan. 107 minutes.

Twilight: Los Angeles. 2001, Marc Levin. 76 minutes.

Shoah. 1985, Claude Lanzmann. 544 minutes.

Strange Days. 1995, Kathryn Bigelow. 145 minutes.

Volcano. 1997, Mick Jackson. 104 minutes.

The Weight of Water. 2000, Kathryn Bigelow. 113 minutes.

Wet Sand: Voices from L.A. Ten Years Later. 2003, Dai Sil Kim-Gibson. 60 minutes.

Index

scholarly works, 2–3, 197–98. *See also* trauma culture

Cumings, Bruce, 246 n.13, 247 n.2, 256 n.6

Cvetkovich, Ann, 135–36

Dark Blue (film), 2

Davis, Mike, 2, 67, 216 n.3, 229 n.15; funeral decade, 45; pessimism for the future, 30–33, 39, 224–26 nn.2–5; *Twilight: Los Angeles* interview, 133, 224 n.2

Delany, Samuel, 37

Denny, Reginald, 76, 99, 200; daily encounters with Others, 107–8, 237 n.5; experiences of love and compassion, 113–14; intrusion into neighborhood space, 106–9; lawsuit against the LAPD, 114; naïveté, 103–14, 238 n.7; parallels with Rodney King beating, 113; physical wounds, 109–12; sympathy, 104–6, 113

Diallo, Amado, 232 n.4

diaspora experiences, 185–92; the American dream, 185–89; breakdown of the nation-state, 180; definition, 180–83, 197; historical trauma, 176–80, 251–52 n.13

Dinkins, David, 246 n.14

The Disuniting of America (Schlesinger), 1, 3, 215 n.1, 216 n.4

Dooner, P. W., 35

Douglass, Frederick, 72

Dr. Luzan (*Native Speaker* character), 174–75

Dream Jungle (Hagedorn), 196–97

drug use, 58–59

Du, Soon Ja, 183–84, 200

Duany, Andres, 228 n.10

Duggan, Lisa, 63, 216–17 n.4

Duke, Charles, 130–31, 240 n.13

Dumm, Thomas, 153, 229–30 n.15

Dyson, Michael, 255 n.4

East Goes West (Kang), 249 n.7

East to America: Korean American Life Stories (Kim and Yu), 3

Ecology of Fear: Los Angeles and the Imagination of Disaster (Davis), 30–33, 39, 45, 224–26 nn.2–3

economic factors: entrepreneurship, 210–12; foreign investment, 54, 59–60, 66; free-market ideology, 209–11; Keynesianism, 7, 218–19 n.7; manufacturing in L.A., 56–57, 219–20 nn.8–9; middle class rise and fall, 6–8, 19, 57–58, 210–12, 218–19 nn.7–8; neoliberal views, 180, 205, 213, 216–17 n.4, 218–19 n.7; opportunism, 4; poverty levels, 56; recession of the 1990s, 56–67; suburban development, 6–7, 218–19 n.7; wealth inequality, 57–58, 62–67, 219–20 nn.8–9

educational factors: depression in Asian American students, 147–49; ethnic studies programs, 148–49, 244 n.8; Korean American experiences, 167–68, 247–48 n.3; literacy, 58; middle-class expectations, 62–63; race studies programs, ix; school achievement stereotypes, 167, 197, 248 n.4

Ehrenreich, Barbara, 219 n.8

Eisenhower, Dwight D., 43–44, 256 n.6

empathy, 87–97, 235–36 n.11

Eng, David, 147–49, 159, 233 n.7, 243–44 n.7, 245–46 n.12

English language-learning, 192–96

ethnicity. *See* racial factors

The Exorcist, 199–201

Falling Down (film), 2, 235 n.10

Farrell, Kirby, 243 n.7

dividuality, 169–74; role of commu-
nity connectedness, 168–69, 185–92;
teaching acculturation, 192–94
Herbert, Steve, 80–81
Herman, Judith, 243 n.7
Hing, Bill Ong, 248 n.4
Hise, Greg, 39–41
Hispanics. *See* Latinos
historical overdetermination, 12–13
historical trauma, 176–80, 183–85, 190,
250–51 n.11, 251–52 n.13
Holliday video, 91, 202; iconography of,
68–70, 230 n.1
Hollinger, David, 254–55 n.2
Hom, Alice, 233 n.7
Honig, Bonnie, 137–38, 243 n.6, 249–50
n.8
House of the Winds (Yun), 168
Howell, David, 219 n.8
Huang, Yong Xin, 232 n.4
Huntington, Samuel, 222–23 n.16
Huntington Beach Fire Department, 131

identity issues: absolute identity of law-
breakers, 81–84; bigotry, 114–23;
group consciousness among Korean
Americans, 179–80, 184–92; historical
trauma, 176–80, 250–51 n.11; "ressentiment," 122–23; in *Twilight: Los Angeles*, 103, 114–23, 239–40 nn.9–10;
white national identity, 12, 74–75, 89–
90, 94, 158, 173, 206–7, 232 n.5, 233–34
n.8, 236–37 n.13
immigration, 6, 10–12, 221–22 nn.13–14;
abandonment of American dream,
154–56, 158–59; acculturation activities, 192–97; American exceptionalism, 137–40; assimilation goals,
8–9, 135–40, 206–7; beliefs in the
American dream, 197–98; bilingual
education, 57; children and the future,

157; citizenship, 172–73, 249–50 n.8;
deportations, 211; diaspora experiences, 180–83; employment options,
56–59; Hart-Celler Immigration and
Nationality Act, 9, 166–67; language-
learning challenges, 194–96, 220–21
n.11; post–civil-rights era, 208–9;
Proposition 187, 12, 57, 222–23 n.16.
See also Korean Americans
Immigration and Naturalization Service
(INS), 152–53, 211
incarceration as social control, 30, 60–
61, 209, 229–30 n.15
Independence Day (film), 2
Independent Commission on the Los
Angeles Police Department, 217–18
n.6
injury metaphor, 21–25, 23*f*, 103, 114–23;
bigotry, 117–22; hatred of police, 115–
16
Inner City Blues (Woods), 2
interpellated term, 8, 220–21 n.11
The Interpreter (Kim), 196, 248–49 n.5
interstate highways, 6–7, 30–41, 218–19
n.7
In the Heart of the Valley of Love (Kadohata), 29–30, 59–67
Iris (*Strange Days* character), 84–86, 91–
99
Irvine, California, 41, 228 n.10

Jackson, Jesse, 104, 106
Jameson, Fredric, 223 n.17
Jamison, Kay Redfield, 243 n.7
Japanese American internment, 44
Japanese investment in Southern Cal-
ifornia, 54, 59–60, 66
Jeriko One (*Strange Days* character), 83–
89, 91–93
John Kwang (*Native Speaker* character),
176–80, 183, 198; belief in community

rest, 54–62; official multiculturalism, 205–7, 212; optimistic fictions, 32, 204–13, 256 n.6; origins, 215 n.1, 216–17 n.4; post–civil-rights era, 205

neoliberal economics, 180, 205, 213, 216–17 n.4, 218–19 n.7

Newfield, Christopher, 255 n.3

Nguyen, Viet Thanh, 63, 250 n.9

Nietzsche, Friedrich, 122

Noble, Marianne, 87–88

"No justice, no peace" slogan, 204

North Korea, 165, 247 n.2

nostalgia and imagined futures, 30–41, 226 n.4; in Bradbury's science fiction, 36–45; funeral decade, 45; racial factors, 35–36; in *Strange Days* (film), 89–90

Oberdorfer, Don, 247 n.2

official multiculturalism, 205–7, 255 n.3

Oh, Angela, 167

Oliver, Melvin, 219 n.8

Omatsu, Glenn, 250 n.9

Omi, Michael, 216–17 n.4

One Thousand Chestnut Trees: A Novel of Korea (Stout), 168

Operation Hammer, 60–61, 229–30 n.15

orthodoxy definition, 29, 223–24 n.1

Otis, Harrison Gray, 125

overdetermination, 12–17

Page Law of 1875, 157

pain metaphor, 19–25, 23*f*

Pak, Gary, 248–49 n.5

Parable of the Sower (Butler), 203–5

Park, Edward, 3, 222 n.15, 242–43 n.4

Park, Frances, 248–49 n.5

Park, Hyungji, 176, 250 n.10

Park, Kyeyoung, 3

Park, You-me, 171, 192

Park Chung Hee, 165

Parker, Paul, 113, 117–18, 121–22, 239–40 n.10

PBS broadcast of *Sa-I-Gu,* 241–42 n.3

pessimism, 1–5, 202–13, 215 n.1; causes, 5–12; cultural responses, 24–26; Davis's, for the future, 30–33, 39, 224–26 nn.2–5; trauma metaphor, 155–56; wound culture, 109–10, 237–38 n.6

Petty, Celia, 243 n.7

Phelan, Peggy, 145

Phillips, Gary, 2, 221 n.12

Plater-Zyberk, Elizabeth, 228 n.10

police, 54–62; authority role in *Strange Days* (film), 90–97; as gang, 51–52, 91; ownership of public spaces, 80–83; racial violence, 51–52, 58–59, 69–71, 117, 199, 231–32 nn.3–4. *See also* Los Angeles Police Department (LAPD)

political bildungsroman form, 173–85

political perspectives. *See* government actions; nation-states

Portman, Jamie, 230–31 n.2

post–civil-rights era, 205, 207–9, 211, 255–56 n.4

postmodernism, 17, 223 n.17

post-traumatic stress disorder, 250–51 n.11

Powell, Laurence, 130–31

power production, 124, 240 n.11

Prashad, Vijay, 153, 183, 249–50 n.8, 255 n.3, 255 n.3

prison. *See* criminality

professionalism, 123–32; elected officials, 127–29; media personnel, 124–27, 240 n.12; public officials, 129–32, 240–41 n.13

Proposition 13, 56–57

Proposition 187, 12, 57, 222–23 n.16

Proposition 207, 57

Proposition 209, 208–9, 256 n.5

Proposition 227, 57

Proposition F, 129–30

psychoanalytic views, 146–50, 245–46 n.12

Putnam, Robert, 217 n.5

Race and Resistance: Literature and Politics in Asian America (V. T. Nguyen), 63

race studies, ix

racial factors, 39–40; abjection, 114, 238–39 n.8; absolute identity of law-breakers, 81–84; affirmative action, 57, 256 n.5; black body in pain, 70–77, 96–99, 234–35 n.9; black-white dichotomy, 72–77; colorblind policies, 63, 149, 153–55; discrimination experiences, 175–76, 204–5; grief, 143–50; Hart-Celler Immigration and Nationality Act, 9, 166–67; iconography of Holliday video, 68–70, 230 n.1; identity politics and bigotry, 114–23, 239–40 nn.9–10; immigration, 10–12, 206–7, 221–22 nn.13–14; incarceration, 30, 60–61, 209, 229–30 n.15; intermarriage, 254–55 n.2; intra-minority racism, 11–12, 116–17; media representations of white culture, 94, 236–37 n.13; national identity, 12; official multiculturalism, 205–7, 255 n.3; Pacific Wars and racism, 43–44; perspectives of mainstream culture, 93–94; planned suburban communities, 29–30, 39–41; police violence, 49–54, 69, 71, 117–18, 199, 231–32 nn.3–4; post–civil-rights era, 205, 207–9, 255–56 n.4; poverty levels, 56; property, 49–54; Proposition 187, 12, 57, 222–23 n.16; psychoanalytic views, 146–50, 245–46 n.12; racial categories, 72–83, 232–34 nn.6–8; racial melancholia, 146–50, 156–63, 244–45 nn.9–10; racial profiling, 84, 117, 128–29; racial

scapegoating, 137–40, 159–61, 243 n.5; Rodney King beating, 68–69, 71–72; scientific racism, 35–36, 226–27 nn.6–7; segregation, 45–48, 51–54; sports, 71; sympathy/empathy dichotomy, 87–90; trauma, 150–57; Vietnam War, 53; violence, 49–54, 72, 74–77; wealth inequality, 219–20 nn.8–9; whites as normative, 74–75, 89–90, 94, 158, 173, 206–7, 232 n.5, 233–34 n.8, 236–37 n.13. *See also* Asian Americans; blacks; Korean Americans; Latinos; white culture

racial geography, 27–67; Asian Americans' ambiguous place, 63–64, 66; Bradbury's Martian landscape, 37–38, 43–45; control of social unrest, 54–67; edge cities, 40–41, 227–28 n.9; end of whiteness, 59–67; funeral decade, 45; gang affiliations, 45–54, 77; historical Southern California, 45; imprisonment as social control, 30, 60–61, 229–30 n.15; negative spaces, 27–30, 45–54, 67; ownership of public spaces, 50–51, 53, 78–81; police, 51–52; postracial world, 66–67; suburban development, 38–41

Ramirez, Chente, 52–54

Reagan, Ronald, 18, 256 n.6

reflective nostalgia, 31–33, 226 n.4

Reimers, David, 221–22 n.13

"ressentiment," 122–23, 127

restorative nostalgia, 31–33, 226 n.4

Rhee, Syngman, 165

riot term, 14–15

Robbins, Bruce, 232–33 n.6

Rodriguez, Luis, 25, 29–30, 45–54, 67

Roediger, David, 250 n.10

Rohn (character, *In the Heart . . .*), 60

Rorty, Richard, 156, 215–16 n.2, 232–33 n.6

Rosaldo, Renato, 145–46, 243–44 n.7

Valle, Victor, 76

Vietnam War, 43–44, 53

Violent Spring (Phillips), 2, 221 n.12

virtue, 88–89

vocabulary, 19–24

Volcano (film), 2

Wald, Gayle, 171, 192

Wallerstein, Immanuel, 215 n.1

Waters, Maxine, 128–29

Watts Uprising of 1965, 9, 14, 217–18 n.6

wealth inequality, 57–58, 62–67, 219–20 nn.8–9

Weinstein, Richard, 228 n.11

West, Cornel, 133

Wet Sand: Voices from L.A. Ten Years Later (Kim-Gibson), 3, 245 n.11

The White Boy Shuffle (Beatty), 2, 206–7, 253–54 n.1

white culture, 9; in Bradbury's works, 34, 36, 38–41, 44–45; colorblindness, 153–55; concerns about immigration, 10, 222 n.14; exodus from L.A. neighborhoods, 10; fear of violence, 30, 60–61, 229–30 n.15; future minority status, 9, 59–67, 230 n.16; normative status, 74–75, 89–90, 94, 158, 173, 206–7, 232 n.5, 233–34 n.8, 236–37 n.13; perspectives of mainstream culture, 93–94; public spaces, 50–51, 53, 78–81; response to Rodney King beating, 71–72, 87, 235–36 n.11; scientific racism, 35–36, 226–27 nn.6–7; status of home, 38, 227 n.8; suburban development, 6–7, 38–41, 218–19 n.7; sympathy for Reginald Denny, 104–6, 113; television and film representations, 94, 236–37 n.13

Williams, Raymond, 148–49

Williams, Rhonda, 219–20 n.9

Wilson, William Julius, 218–19 n.7

Winant, Howard, 216–17 n.4

Wingrove, David, 35, 226 n.6

Wolfe, Alan, 249–50 n.8

Woods, Paula, 2

Woolf, Virginia, 67, 230 n.17

World War II, 43–44, 165, 246–47 n.1

wounding metaphor, 20–25, 23f, 102–33; double meaning, 109–11, 124; limits of speech, 131–32; Reginald Denny's naïveté, 106; social isolation, 102–3; wound culture, 109–10, 237–38 n.6

Wovoka ghost dance, 22

Yamashita, Karen Tei, 2, 215–16 n.2

Yates, Michael, 218–19 n.7

Young, Allan, 243 n.7

Yu, Eui-Young, 3, 251–52 n.13

Yun, Mia, 168, 249 n.6

Zarraga, Daniel García, 232 n.4

Zoot Suit Riots of 1942, 44, 115–16

Min Hyoung Song is an Associate Professor
of English at Boston College.

Library of Congress Cataloging-in-Publication Data

Song, Min.

Strange future : pessimism and the 1992 Los Angeles riots /

Min Hyoung Song.

p. cm.

Includes bibliographical references and index.

ISBN 0-8223-3579-4 (cloth: alk. paper)

ISBN 0-8223-3592-1 (pbk. : alk. paper)

1. Los Angeles (Calif.)—Race relations. 2. Race riots—California—

Los Angeles—History—20th century. 3. Korean Americans—California—

Los Angeles—Social conditions. 4. African Americans—California—Los Angeles—

Social conditions. 5. Urban poor—California—Los Angeles—Social conditions.

6. Race relations in literature. 7. Ethnicity in literature. 8. American literature—

Korean American authors—History and criticism. 9. United States—Race relations—

Psychological aspects. 10. Pessimism—

Social aspects—United States. I. Title.

F869.L89A27 2005

305.8′009794′94—dc22

2005006511